THE FEDERAL MACHINE

THE
FEDERAL
MACHINE

Beginnings of Bureaucracy
in Jacksonian America

MATTHEW A. CRENSON

THE JOHNS HOPKINS UNIVERSITY PRESS
Baltimore and London

This book has been brought to publication with
the generous assistance of the Andrew W. Mellon
Foundation.

Manufactured in the United States of America

The Johns Hopkins University Press, Baltimore, Maryland 21218
The Johns Hopkins University Press Ltd., London

Library of Congress Catalog Card Number 74-6818
ISBN 0-8018-1586-X

To Ethan and Matthew

CONTENTS

PREFACE

Hostility toward "bureaucracy" has been a durable feature of American political life for generations. Until recently, however, this animosity was usually concentrated among political conservatives, who regarded bureaucracy as a manifestation of big government and an instrument for governmental interference in the operations of private enterprise. But today, as James Q. Wilson has pointed out, the distaste for bureaucracy has come to be shared by other Americans of sharply differing political persuasions.[1] Indeed, the disenchantment with big, bureaucratic government has become so widespread that some observers are both predicting and recommending the abandonment of the bureaucratic form of organization itself. In this view, decisions now made by public agencies would be turned over to collegial groups of citizen-administrators, to private consumers purchasing services in a marketplace, or to temporary organizations that would disband once their missions were completed.

Since animosity toward bureaucracy has been so persistent in the United States and since proposals for the abandonment of public bureaucracy have recently become so widespread, it seems reasonable to inquire just what conditions once led us to abandon *non*bureaucratic forms of government administration. This book attempts to provide at least a partial answer to that question. Its purpose is to determine when, how, and why bureaucratic forms of organization were superimposed upon the business of the national government.

There may have been some respects, of course, in which the

1. James Q. Wilson, "The Bureaucracy Problem," *The Public Interest,* no. 6 (Winter 1967), p. 3.

national government was always bureaucratic. In fact, the Constitution itself may be said to have embodied certain bureaucratic elements. The ideal of a government of laws and not of men seems to have anticipated the organizational impersonality—the formal rules and regulations—of a bureaucratic order. But these organizational possibilities were not realized in the conduct of everyday government business for more than a generation. Under George Washington, for example, the principal reliance of government administration seems to have been, not formal rules and regulations, but the personal virtue and reputation of the administrator, his "fitness of character." Insofar as administration was concerned, government remained a government of men.

Major departures from this prebureaucratic condition occurred during the presidency of Andrew Jackson. The present study attempts to examine and explain those changes. Its scope, therefore, is not so broad as that of Leonard White's comprehensive survey of Jacksonian administration. It does not review the conduct of business in every government agency nor the entire business of any particular agency. It concentrates instead upon important episodes of organizational change and the factors which appear to have triggered them. Much of its attention is devoted to those efforts at formal administrative reorganization that were launched by Jacksonian executives. These deliberate attempts to transform public agencies marked a significant turning point in the history of the executive branch not only because reorganization plans could be vehicles for administrative change but because the attempt at deliberate reorganization was itself relatively new.

Until the Jacksonians captured the White House, reorganizations of executive departments had rarely occurred, and those that did may reasonably be regarded as administrative aberrations. The most important of them were responses to the heavy administrative burdens imposed upon some federal agencies by the War of 1812—burdens that were both extraordinary and temporary. The Jacksonian reorganizations, by contrast, were not brought on by foreign invasion and its aftermath, but by conditions endemic to American society and politics. Moreover, the Jacksonians did not confine their reorganization efforts to one or two subdivisions of the executive branch. Hardly an agency escaped their attention, and the available evidence indicates that there were important points of similarity between the various reorganization plans that were proposed for different agencies.

Some of these plans fell victim to congressional disapproval or inaction. Two plans that survived the legislative test were the reorganization proposals for the Post Office Department and the General Land Office; these will receive special attention not only because they ran the full course from inception to enactment but because the agencies themselves were particularly important. The Post Office and the Land Office were among the largest subdivisions of the federal government. Together, they easily accounted for more than three-quarters of the civilian manpower employed by the executive branch. They were also agencies whose business required them to deal regularly and directly with the general public. For this reason, they functioned not only as providers of services but as important points of contact between national political authorities and the people of the country—between the condition of the government and the condition of society.

The condition of society was a factor of decisive importance for the bureaucratization of the federal government. The Jacksonian era was a period of transformation for American social institutions, and some of the social changes that were occurring seem to have reverberated throughout the administrative apparatus of the national government. There is certainly no attempt in the present study to provide a detailed social history of the Jackson years but merely to survey what is already known about Jacksonian society, from the work of historians and the testimony of Jackson's contemporaries, in order to identify those dimensions of social change that may have affected the conduct of government business. The existing evidence, together with some newly collected evidence about the operations of public agencies under Andrew Jackson, provide the beginnings, at least, of an explanation for the bureaucratization of the federal government.

The research effort that led me to this explanation began some years ago in a brief study of the career of Amos Kendall, one of Andrew Jackson's most illustrious administrators. The story of Kendall's career aroused my curiosity about other Jacksonian administrators, and, as a graduate student at the University of Chicago, I was encouraged to pursue this interest by the late Morton Grodzins. I owe him a debt both for his encouragement and for his guidance, which helped to give shape to some rather ill-formed research interests. Subsequently, Grant McConnell and Herbert Storing supplied much valuable advice, which served to sharpen my analysis of the historical evidence and my interest in Jacksonian bureaucracy. Later still, Herbert Kaufman, Francis Rourke, and Alfred Chandler, Jr. read some preliminary versions of this book and suggested several improvements. And David Donald provided both advice and moral support at a critical stage in the study—getting it finished. His assistance has been invaluable.

Over the years, I have incurred debts to many other people—among them, the students and colleagues who have listened patiently, for the most part, while I discussed such things as the postal reorganization of 1836. My wife, Alene, has not only listened longer and more patiently than anyone, but she has typed and retyped drafts and revised drafts of this study and its predecessors and tactfully suggested improvements in my prose.

INTRODUCTION

On inauguration day, 1829, Andrew Jackson, dressed in a plain black suit, walked down the front steps of Gadsby's Hotel and greeted fifteen Revolutionary War veterans who awaited him in the street. Followed by a large crowd, the sixteen old soldiers marched toward the Capitol, where Jackson pronounced the presidential oath of office and delivered a brief address.[1]

In majesty, the morning's ceremonies could not equal those of four years earlier, when President-Elect John Quincy Adams had arrived at the Capitol in a fine carriage, escorted by several companies of uniformed militia.[2] In eloquence, Old Hickory's speech was no match for the one that Adams had delivered, and it was only half as long. In substance too, Jackson's oration differed from that of his predecessor. Adams had mounted the Capitol steps for the purpose, he said, of "unfolding to my countrymen the principles by which I shall be governed." But Jackson prefaced his recitation of principles with an expression of gratitude to his people and a "zealous dedication of [his] humble abilities to their service and their good."[3]

In the eight years that followed his swearing in, Jackson would multiply and magnify the distinctions between himself and John Quincy Adams. To the trifling ceremonial and oratorical differences, Old Hickory would add momentous actions that would set him apart

1. *United States Telegraph* (Washington), 5 March 1829.
2. *The Diary of John Quincy Adams, 1794–1845: American Political, Social, and Intellectual Life from Washington to Polk,* ed. Allan Nevins (New York: Longmans, Green, & Co., 1928), p. 343.
3. James D. Richardson, ed., *A Compilation of the Messages and Papers of the Presidents,* 10 vols. (Washington: Government Printing Office, 1899), 2:294, 442.

not only from his immediate predecessor but from all the presidents who had gone before him. As early as 1829, there were men who sensed that important changes were in the offing. In many places, an unsettling apprehensiveness clouded the anticipation of Andrew Jackson's regime. "When he comes," wrote Daniel Webster, "he will bring a breeze with him. Which way it will blow I cannot tell . . . [but] my *fear* is greater than my *hope*."[4]

The Jacksonian breeze wafted an old order into retirement. This, at least, has been the retrospective assessment of most American historians. A shift of power and belief had, according to this view, raised a new breed of men to prominence and transformed the political life of the republic. The Congressional Caucus crumbled before the powerful new party organizations. Old aristocrats from the first families of the nation retreated testily to their New England or plantation fastnesses. And on every side, old privilege, old authority, and old principle buckled. Recent investigators of Old Hickory's era—Lee Benson, Bray Hammond, and others[5]—have done much to mute the clamor of political upheaval that attaches to the name Andrew Jackson. Still, though they minimize the revolutionary character of Jacksonism, these writers continue to assert that its appearance marked an important breaking point in the political history of the nation.

Yet some prominent sectors of the republic's political life have been exempted from the weighty impact of Jacksonism. The governmental offices through which the Jackson men conducted the public business were, according to Leonard White, relatively undisturbed by the political turmoils of the era. In these conspicuous enclaves, under the very noses of the agents of change, the old order was able to maintain a foothold. True, the notorious spoils system peopled the federal offices with new administrators; but, says White, governmental administration "did not depart from the original foundations on which it had been set." The Jacksonians might alter the "spirit" of the federal bureaucracy, but its essential "form" remained intact.[6]

White's definitive study of Jacksonian administration correctly

4. *The Letters of Daniel Webster, from Documents Owned Principally by the New Hampshire Historical Society,* ed. Claude H. Van Tyne (New York: McClure, Phillips, & Co., 1902), pp. 142–43.

5. Lee Benson, *The Concept of Jacksonian Democracy: New York as a Test Case* (Princeton: Princeton University Press, 1961); Bray Hammond, *Banks and Politics in America* (Princeton: Princeton University Press, 1959).

6. Leonard White, *The Jacksonians: A Study in Administrative History, 1829–1861* (New York: Macmillan Co., 1954), p. 552.

calls attention to the many legal and organizational continuities that linked the Jacksonian executive branch to the past. Indeed, as White points out, there "were no constitutional amendments; the body of administrative law was substantially untouched; the courts continued to mark the legal limits of administrative action. . . . The primacy of the Chief Executive in matters of administration stood intact," and "the concentration of authority in the respective Secretaries was denied by no one."[7] In these and many other respects, the federal establishment remained firmly attached to its "original foundations" in spite of the political upheavals of the era. Even the controversial spoils system had its Federalist and Jeffersonian antecedents.[8] But there are some features of Jacksonian administration which suggest the occurrence of major discontinuities not only in the "spirit" but also in the "form" of the federal establishment.

Consider, in particular, the frequency of formal administrative reorganizations in the executive branch. During the forty years following the ratification of the Constitution, there were only two formal reorganizations worthy of notice. The accounting procedures of the Treasury Department were revised, and the Navy Department was reorganized.[9] But during the eight years of Andrew Jackson's administration, almost every federal department was overhauled at least once. The Post Office and the General Land Office experienced sweeping change. Partial reorganizations occurred twice in the War Department and three times in the State Department. Some minor changes were suggested for the attorney general's office. Comprehensive reorganization plans were proposed for the Treasury Department and the Navy Department but never enacted by Congress. Furthermore, most of the administrative renovations were proposed during the second half of the Jackson administration.

The reorganization plans themselves are of little lasting importance. Their significance lies instead in what they suggest about the state of administration. The capacity to reorganize implies an ability to deal with administrative operations in formal and abstract terms. Existing administrative arrangements have to be made explicit before they can be deliberately changed. Administrative functions have to be abstracted from the people who perform them before they can be

7. Ibid., pp. 553–54.

8. Carl Russell Fish, *The Civil Service and the Patronage* (New York: Longmans, Green & Co., 1905), pp. 9, 14, 42; Paul P. Van Riper, *History of the United States Civil Service* (Evanston, Ill.: Row, Peterson, & Co., 1958), p. 22.

9. Leonard White, *The Jeffersonians: A Study in Administrative History, 1801–1829* (New York: Macmillan Co., 1951), pp. 171–77, 272–80.

divided, combined, or redistributed. It appears that the use of these conceptual abilities, if not their extent, increased sharply during the Jackson administration, and the result was that government administration became considerably more formal and impersonal. Stated briefly, the chief administrative legacy of the Jacksonians was bureaucracy.

Within a relatively short time, the supposed representatives of frontier rusticity took most of the essential steps to convert the executive branch into a bureaucratic institution. At least one historian has seen the seeds of this development in the Jacksonian spoils system,[10] but the features of Jacksonian bureaucracy did not become manifest until after the spoils system had done its work and the Jackson men began to change administrative structure rather than administrative personnel. The effect of these structural modifications was either to introduce or to enhance the bureaucratic characteristics of federal administration.[11]

What was informal became formal. Administrative jurisdictions and responsibilities were explicitly defined (in many cases, for the first time), and the official duties of administrators were carefully separated from their private activities. In the process, administrative agencies were converted into organizational abstractions with an existence independent of the particular human beings who worked for them.

Generalists became specialists. Under several of the Jacksonian reorganization plans, the various functions of government agencies were sifted out from one another and assigned to different internal divisions or offices.

As a result, administrative hierarchies became both more formal and more elaborate. The division of agencies into specialized bureaus and offices created additional layers of authority within the government, and the exercise of this authority became increasingly impersonal. In several agencies, bureaucratic executives no longer attempted to exercise control over their subordinates simply through personal supervision; they relied instead on complicated accounting and information systems in order to assure the honesty and diligence of their employees.

10. Lynn Marshall, "The Strange Stillbirth of the Whig Party," *American Historical Review* 72 (January 1967): 455.
11. For a standard description of bureaucratic organization, see Hans Gerth and C. Wright Mills, eds., *From Max Weber: Essays in Sociology* (New York: Oxford University Press, 1958), pp. 196–98.

It cannot be said that the Jackson men revolutionized administrative science. They undertook their overhaul of the executive branch without much attention to general principles of management or theories of administration. As Leonard White points out, their discourses on the "art of administration" seldom extended beyond the current problems of particular government agencies. The Jacksonians were practical men who depended on common sense and experience.[12] Their failure to make any important contributions to the general administrative art probably weighed heavily in White's judgment that the Jacksonian era did not dislodge the federal establishment from its original foundations. White's historical studies of the executive branch are organized around the development of this administrative art, and he searches the history of the federal establishment for successive additions to the body of general management techniques. The Jacksonians were not self-conscious enough about their administrative innovations to make any significant contribution to this body of general principles, and it is therefore not surprising that White should emphasize the continuity between Old Hickory's administrative regime and its predecessors.

With respect to the technology of management, the Jacksonian period was prehistoric. It is doubtful whether Old Hickory's contemporaries recognized the existence of any "technique of management" separate from the commands of the law, the rules of accounting, and ordinary common sense. The quest for technical proficiency had always been submerged beneath nontechnical considerations. In the semiaristocratic society of pre-Jacksonian days, the federal establishment was fashioned to the tastes of men who had been born to rule. Management was a mystery, not reducible to rational and explicit techniques, a fitting vocation for men who were supposed to carry the knack for governance in their blood and breeding. The operations of federal offices during this period tended to be idiosyncratic, reflecting the personal tastes and intuitions of highborn administrative chieftains.

Like many of the age's institutions, this old administrative regime did not survive the rise of Jacksonism. The "foundations on which it had been set" were not the techniques of aristocratic management, but the elements of an aristocratic political and social order, and when that order was undermined, its administrative apparatus was transformed. It was political and social change, not the dynamics of

12. White, *The Jacksonians*, p. 551.

technological progress, which produced the bureaucratic characteristics of Jacksonian administration.

The federal establishment was itself an organ of the political order,
as much a part of the political struggle as were the party organizations. In fact, there is a sense in which the federal establishment may
be said to have resembled a political party. It was not simply that the
executive branch was staffed with party workers but, more important, that the administrative apparatus provided a link between the
nation's political authorities and its citizens. In this capacity, administrative agencies performed functions very much like those of the
modern political party—they helped to organize support for the
republic's political regime. And perhaps it is no coincidence that the
bureaucratization of the Jacksonian executive branch occurred at the
same time that the organizational apparatus of American political
parties was being extended and formalized.[13]

The ways in which federal administration might attach the people
to their government were not always the same as those used by party
organizations. The bureaucracy, like the party, might secure the
cooperation of an influential group by giving it a role in organizational decision making. But the federal establishment needed more
than mere cooperation. Somewhere it had to find men who would
give the government not just their assent and occasional active
assistance but year-round labor. And if these men were to be effective in the performance of their administrative duties, the organizational arrangements of the government would have to be adapted to
the habits, strengths, and even the weaknesses of these prospective
civil servants. The political party attempted to make citizens into
loyal voters; the federal bureaucracy had to convert them into
useable manpower.

Both party and bureaucracy attempted to gather the most influential sorts of men to their respective bosoms. In the case of the party,
the advantages of this policy were obvious. For bureaucracy, the
benefits were less obvious, but nevertheless widely recognized. Even
the administratively unselfconscious Jacksonians perceived that a
cardinal duty of the republic's administrative representatives was "to
win the good will and affections of the people to the Government."[14] It was not an administrative responsibility that could easily

13. On the development of political party organizations during the Jacksonian period,
see Richard P. McCormick, *The Second American Party System: Party Formation in the
Jacksonian Era* (Chapel Hill: University of North Carolina Press, 1966).
14. *American State Papers: Public Lands*, 8 vols. (Washington: Gales & Seaton, 1832–
61), 7: 193.

be fulfilled by a man unable to command the respect of his friends and neighbors.

The federal establishment, then, required the services of influential groups and influential men. Just which groups and which men had influence was a matter of some importance to federal administration. Administrative arrangements would have to be fashioned so that the "right" groups would have easy access to points within the executive branch, and these arrangements would have to be modeled to fit the characteristics of suitably influential kinds of men. To a considerable extent, therefore, the configurations of national administration depended upon the distribution of power within American society. Changes in the distribution of power or in the characteristics of the men and groups who held power could be expected to work changes upon the government's administrative arrangements. In order to understand the administrative innovations of the Jackson men, it is important to know what kinds of political changes accompanied their ascent to power.

American historians have offered at least three distinct ways of characterizing the political alterations which occurred during the Jacksonian era. These varying lines of exposition are not necessarily incompatible with one another, and it is even conceivable that they may be joined together in a single account. The differences between them do not constitute logical contradictions, for the most part, but only variations in points of emphasis.

A longtime favorite of historians is the view advanced by Arthur Schlesinger, Jr.,[15] and by many scholars before him, that the Jacksonian era saw the rise to power of men of lowly origins. With the election of Old Hickory, the "mudsills of the republic were upheaved,"[16] and an old ruling class was swept from authority. Such dramatic changes in the social class backgrounds of government decision makers could very easily have affected the character of government administration. If they did, then we should be able to find evidence of these changes in the federal civil service. The backgrounds of Jacksonian administrators should have been humble.

15. Arthur M. Schlesinger, Jr., *The Age of Jackson* (Boston: Little, Brown & Co., 1945).
16. Gerald W. Johnson, *American Heroes and Hero Worship* (New York: Harper & Bros., 1943), p. 103.

Old Hickory's executive branch should be distinguishable from its predecessors by the class origins of Jacksonian civil servants.

A second interpretation of the Jacksonian phenomenon attributes its uniqueness to the new political beliefs which prevailed within Old Hickory's coalition. This view is frequently presented in tandem with the contention that the Jackson men rose up from the lower reaches of American society, but it deserves separate consideration. Political beliefs may change without any drastic redistribution of power among social classes. The meaning of a political principle may be altered even while a particular political elite remains in power, or an old ruling class may marshal its influence behind a new set of political attitudes. In any case, the distinctiveness of Jacksonian political beliefs may be related to the administrative innovations of the Jackson men, and this is a possibility which should be investigated.

A third description of the Jacksonian age discovers the distinctiveness of the era, not in new political beliefs or class upheaval, but in a new distribution of power within the groups that governed American society. Old institutions like the legal profession and the business community remained preeminent, according to this view, but they were bigger and less cohesive than they had formerly been. Their new internal disjointedness helped to account for the political uniqueness of the Jackson period,[17] and it may also help to account for the administrative innovations of the era.

Somewhere in the tumultuous political history of the Jacksonian age there may be a critical development which will help to explain why the federal government became a bureaucracy. If we are fortunate, an examination of the Jacksonian period will turn up some new feature in the political landscape that will provide an explanation for the unprecedented qualities of Jacksonian administration. A change in the social composition of the civil service, the political attitudes of civil servants, or the structure of powerful institutions would mark one of these areas as a possible promising source of bureaucratic transformation. It is unlikely, of course, that historical reality will be so kind as to provide such a simple basis for the interpretation of administrative change. Some variation probably occurred in all three areas. The ascent to power of men of lowly origins is likely to be accompanied by some change in prevalent political beliefs, and both of these factors may produce some alteration in the structure of

17. For an exposition of this view, see Stanley Elkins, *Slavery* (New York: Universal Library, 1963), pp. 27–37.

powerful institutions. It will be necessary to evaluate each of the various sources of administrative change in order to identify the particular kind of variation that was most pronounced and most critical for the configuration of the federal establishment. The test of this judgment will be the ability to make sensible connections between a particular source of administrative change and the changes themselves. The bureaucratic innovations of the Jackson era must therefore occupy the center of our attention. And the focus of this attention will be change of the most unambiguous sort—those formal plans for administrative reorganization that the Jackson men imposed upon the executive branch.

Here, it is necessary to reconsider the "technological" explanations of administrative change, for it may be argued that administrative machinery has its own internal dynamic that works changes upon organizational arrangements with or without the help of large political movements. Though the Jackson men were innocent of management science, they may nevertheless have been responding to technological imperatives that are explicitly set out in modern "principles of administration." The Jacksonian bureaucratization of the federal establishment, for example, may have been a simple, technical response to an increase in the size of public agencies and the volume of public business—matters of administrative expediency and nothing more. Administrative theorists have often maintained that bureaucracy and bigness go hand in hand. Organizational growth is regarded as an important stimulus to bureaucratization.[18] It makes little difference whether the bureaucrats are Jacksonians or Whigs, Federalists or Communists. Administration, as Leonard White has maintained, is a unified and universal craft, essentially the same wherever we find it.[19] It transcends time and place, operates according to its own laws, and dictates its own alterations.

The purpose of the present investigation is to examine and if possible explain the administrative changes that overtook the federal establishment during the tenure of Andrew Jackson. We know that these changes could not have proceeded from any coherent "theory of management" because the Jacksonians had none. And yet there is a remarkable consistency in the character of these administrative changes, from one federal agency to the next. Almost all of them

18. Gerth and Mills, *From Max Weber,* pp. 209–11.
19. Leonard White, *Introduction to the Study of Public Administration,* 4th ed. (New York: Macmillan Co., 1955), p. xvi.

contributed, in similar ways, to the bureaucratization of the federal government. Because they share this common character, it is at least reasonable to surmise that these changes can be traced to a common source. We will examine the political characteristics of the Jackson men and their age in an attempt to locate that source—some common tie that may have set the Jacksonians apart from their predecessors— and we will look for traces of this common tie in the administrative innovations of the Jackson era. Here, the investigation will concentrate on the affairs of two government agencies, the Post Office Department and the General Land Office. Both of these organizations experienced substantial administrative renovation. Finally, these bureaucratic changes will have to be reexamined in the light of administration's internal, technological dynamic. The political bonds of Jacksonism must be weighed against the unity of the "administrative art" in order to decide whether the one or the other provides a more satisfactory basis for the interpretation of the beginnings of bureaucracy in American government.

I

SOCIAL BACKGROUNDS AND POLITICAL BELIEFS

Andrew Jackson intoned the final sentences of his inaugural address, walked down the Capitol steps, and strode off in the direction of the White House. Behind him, there collected a large and remarkably mixed group of people. From "the highest and most polished, down to the most vulgar and gross in the nation," they all tramped after Jackson toward the executive mansion, where orange punch awaited them with "wine and ice creams" for the ladies. Once there, some of the marchers stood on damask upholstered chairs to catch a glimpse of the new president. The "most vulgar and gross" jostled the "highest and most polished" in their efforts to shoulder a path toward the refreshments or the chief executive. Pails of orange punch were upset, and the waiters were unable to reach the ladies with their wine and ice creams. Justice Story, for one, was "glad to escape the scene as soon as possible."[1]

This disgraceful inauguration day spectacle has been embalmed in the writings of American historians as an instructive display of the social origins of Jacksonism.[2] The Jackson men, according to the most popular accounts, had come out of the forests in coonskins and buckskins to take the reins of government into their rough hands. They were men who had risen from the poor and primeval sections of society, rustic and ill-bred representatives of the western wilderness and the toiling classes. But the crowd that followed Jackson

1. James Parton, *The Life of Andrew Jackson,* 3 vols. (New York: Mason Bros., 1860), 3: 170–71.
2. See, for example, Carl Russell Fish, *The Civil Service and the Patronage* (New York: Longmans, Green & Co., 1905), p. 110.

contained not only the most vulgar and gross, who ruined White House upholstery; the highest and most polished were there, too, and some of them stayed on as Old Hickory's administrators.

The bureaucrats who assembled under the Jackson banner were a mixed lot, and it is difficult to discover in their heterogeneous social origins some common bond which set them apart from their Federalist and Jeffersonian predecessors. This shared feature of social background, if it existed, may have bred among them a unity of thought and action quite independent of any well-conceived system of moral or political beliefs. Even without a consciously and commonly held creed, the officers of the federal establishment might have shaped governmental organization in a coherent fashion and set it moving toward a particular sort of policy. Common social backgrounds, education, and occupational experience might have bound bureaucrats together in a way which allowed them to think and act in concert, simply by the action of commonly held habits.[3] These socially rooted habits, if they were unique to Old Hickory's bureaucrats, might have left a uniquely Jacksonian imprint upon the federal establishment.

Some of the evidence about the social backgrounds of Jacksonian administrators appears in table 1, which presents a summary of information compiled by Sidney H. Aronson, concerning occupations, education, social status, and parentage of officers in the administrative elites of John Adams, Thomas Jefferson, and Andrew Jackson. Aronson's purpose in collecting these data was not merely to enumerate the characteristics of bureaucrats but to discover if there were any differences between the three administrations with respect to the social status of men recruited for the higher civil service. The items listed in the table were selected by Aronson because they were good indicators of social position for the periods that he was investigating. The differences he discovered were not large, and they did not set the Jacksonians apart from all their predecessors. They separated "the aristocratic Adams, on the one hand," from "the democratic Jefferson and Jackson on the other."[4] The greatest differences, then, were between Adams men and Jeffer-

3. Donald R. Matthews, *The Social Backgrounds of Political Decision Makers* (Garden City, N.Y.: Doubleday & Co., 1954), pp. 6–8.

4. Sidney H. Aronson, "Status and Kinship in the Higher Civil Service: The Administrations of John Adams, Thomas Jefferson, and Andrew Jackson" (Ph.D. dissertation, Columbia University, Department of Sociology, 1961), p. 2. (Published in abridged form as *Status and Kinship in the Higher Civil Service* [Cambridge: Harvard University Press, 1964]). All page references are to the dissertation.

Table 1

Backgrounds of Members of Administrative Elites[a]

(in percent)

Background Characteristics of Administrators	Under Adams (N = 96)	Under Jefferson (N = 100)	Under Jackson (N = 127)
Father had high-ranking occupation	70	60	53
Father held political office	52	43	44
Father attended college	17	13	12
Held high-ranking occupation	92	93	90
Held political office prior to appointment	91	93	90
Member of voluntary associations	50	41	39
Officer in the military	52	39	32
Family in America in seventeenth century	55	48	48
Attended college	63	52	52
Professional training	69	74	81

[a]Adapted from Sidney H. Aronson, "Status and Kinship in the Higher Civil Service: The Administrations of John Adams, Thomas Jefferson, and Andrew Jackson" (Ph.D. dissertation, Columbia University, Department of Sociology, 1961), p. 431.

son men—as we can see by reading across the rows in table 1—and they were not very sizeable. The ascent of the Jacksonians to offices in the executive branch did not signify any sharp alteration in the social composition of the administrative elite.

The data thus far presented show only that Old Hickory's bureaucrats did not rise from a social class which had never before been tapped for civil servants; they were not men of humble origins. But there are finer distinctions than those between the high and the low. Within the highest stratum of society, there are men whose wealth and prestige are based upon the ownership of land, others who rise to distinction as manufacturers, and still others who make their fortunes and reputations in commerce or the professions. The interests of these groups are likely to diverge from time to time, and each may produce a distinct view of society and its problems. It is therefore important to consider the possibility that the Jackson men differed from their predecessors because they came from a different sector of the upper crust. We might examine this possibility by looking at the positions that the Jacksonian bureaucrats held before they embarked on careers in the public service.

But the mere enumeration of occupations does not lend itself to a full treatment of social backgrounds. It may be important not only

Table 2

Primary Occupations of Bureaucrats and Their Fathers
by Administration[a]

(in percent)

Occupational Field of Administrators	Under Adams (N = 96)		Under Jefferson (N = 100)		Under Jackson (N = 127)	
	Fathers	Sons	Fathers	Sons	Fathers	Sons
Professional	26	75	18	74	16	87
Commerce	28	20	20	16	22	7
Agriculture	34	3	40	6	43	5
Manufacturing	5	0	7	0	6	1
Don't know	7	2	15	4	13	0
Total	100	100	100	100	100	100

[a]Adapted from Aronson, "Status and Kinship in the Higher Civil Service," pp. 160–61, 222–23.

that a man was a lawyer but that he came to the legal profession from a certain part of society, and his father's occupation is one fair indication of the social region in which he began his journey. Table 2, therefore, presents the distribution among different career fields not only of the bureaucrats themselves but of their fathers as well. While we cannot follow the paths of individual administrators from their fathers' households to their own law or business offices, it is possible to observe a certain movement of the aggregate away from the callings of their fathers—commerce, agriculture, manufacturing—and into the professions—the ministry, law, medicine, the military, and so on.

Three things are apparent in table 2. First, the fathers of the Jacksonian and Jeffersonian administrators were not markedly different from one another. Here, as before, the largest differences were those between the administrators of Adams and of Jefferson, and even these were not very great. Second, in each administration the bureaucrats, however diverse the careers of their fathers, were drawn primarily from the professions. And in each case "the professions" consisted, for the most part, of the legal profession. Sixty-five of the 75 professionals in the Adams administration were lawyers; 62 of 74 in the Jefferson administration; and 105 of 111 in the Jackson

Table 3
Geographic Origins of Bureaucrats[a]

(in percent)

Geographic Region of Administrators	Under Adams (N = 96)	Under Jefferson (N = 100)	Under Jackson (N = 127)
New England	23	12	8
Middle Atlantic	19	21	21
South Atlantic	45	39	29
Southwest	6	17	28
Northwest	5	10	14
Don't know	2	1	—
Total	100	100	100

[a]Adapted from Aronson, "Status and Kinship in the Higher Civil Service," p. 291.

administration. Third, the lawyers were somewhat more numerous in the Jacksonian bureaucracy than in either of the earlier administrations, and men of the commercial class—merchants and traders—make up a smaller proportion of the Jacksonian elite.

The gross indicators of social status and class connections reveal no great disjunction between the Jacksonians and their predecessors. There are, however, certain other respects in which the Jacksonian bureaucracy was distinctive. It may be significant, for example, that there were more westerners among the Jackson men than in the administrations of Jefferson or Adams—as is apparent in table 3. Much of this increase may be attributed to changes in the distribution of the American population. There were few men of the West in Adams' bureaucracy simply because few westerners were to be had. In 1800, only 7.8 percent of the population lived west of the Alleghenies. In 1830, almost one out of every three Americans lived in a state or territory of the West.[5] But whatever the explanation for the change in the geographic connections of administrators, it cannot be denied that their "westerness" may have affected their handling of the public business. The influence of the West, however, would not have been unique to the Jackson administration, for, as Aronson points out, the trend toward western appointments appears under

5. George Tucker, *Progress of the United States in Population and Wealth in Fifty Years as Exhibited by the Decennial Census* (New York: Press of Hunt's Merchants' Magazine, 1843), pp. 19, 41.

Jefferson as well.[6] Still, it would be wise to keep this factor in mind
as a possible source of the Jacksonians' uniqueness. It may be that
the westerners could change the nature of the bureaucracy only
when they became as numerous as they were in the administration of
Andrew Jackson.

But for the increased proportions of westerners and lawyers, the
Jacksonian higher civil service was little different from that of Adams
or Jefferson. As in these earlier administrations, a majority of the
public servants were recruited from the top lawyers of society, and
there is, in the case of each administration, substantial evidence of a
close connection between the federal bureaucracy and the legal
profession. Where there are differences between the Jacksonian civil
service and its predecessors, they are small, and they appear as
continuations of a long-standing and very gradual trend toward the
democratization of the administrative elite (see table 1). Such indicators of status as rank of father's occupation, father's college
attendance, and membership in voluntary associations show a small
but consistent trend away from the predominance of men from high
social stations. We find here no evidence for the hypothesis advanced
by many historians that Jackson and the spoils system made a clean
sweep of the civil service and transformed it from an elite body to
one that was substantially more representative of the American
population. The gentlemanly administrators of an old political order
were not replaced by sons of the laboring class.

Unfortunately, most of our information about the social backgrounds of these civil servants deals only with upper-level administrators. While the Jacksonians seem to have introduced no major
changes in the social composition of the higher civil service, it is at
least conceivable that they may have recruited lower-level administrators from previously untapped sectors of society. It is difficult to
unearth biographical information about these lower-level employees
precisely because they were lower-level administrators and therefore
rather obscure persons. Some scraps of information about these
lesser bureaucrats, however, are preserved in the letters of application
and recommendation written by various office seekers and their
political backers to the patronage-dispensing officials in Washington.
Examination of these documents in an effort to determine whether
customs collectors and district land officers appointed by Andrew
Jackson had different social origins from the proscripted officials of

6. Aronson, "Status and Kinship in the Higher Civil Service," p. 298.

the Adams administration whom they replaced unfortunately yielded such fragmentary information that no systematic comparison of social backgrounds is possible, and no conclusions are warranted.

The little evidence we have, however, does not suggest that the social standing of Jacksonian appointees was significantly lower than the standing of their predecessors. It was probably true that many of the Adams officials removed by Jackson were prestigious members of their communities. Noah Noble, for example, a public land officer in Indianapolis, was a colonel in the local militia. So was William Ewing, a land officer in Vandalia, Illinois. Both were Adams administrators, and both fell victim to the spoils system. But the beneficiaries of the spoils system about whom we do have information could often produce the same social credentials as the victims. John Decatur, a Jackson man who replaced an Adams incumbent as customs collector of Portsmouth, New Hampshire, was also a colonel in the local militia, as was Joseph Friends, who became a public official at Ouachita, Louisiana. And Willis Green, who replaced an Adams incumbent in the land office at Palmyra, Missouri, was described by his sponsors as a doctor.[7]

In general, it does not appear that the uniqueness of Jacksonian administration can reasonably be attributed to the fact that Jacksonian bureaucrats came from sections of society which had previously been denied representation in the civil service. Certainly the highly placed Jacksonian administrators bore all the upper-class insignia of an earlier generation's civil servants. They and their Federalist and Jeffersonian predecessors shared a familiarity with comfortable origins, good educations, and prestigious careers. But there was one thing the Jackson men did not hold in common with earlier bureaucrats, and that was their Jacksonism. The political beliefs of Old Hickory's administrators may have set them apart from previous civil servants.

"Jacksonian Democracy" is not a term that appears in the writings of Old Hickory's contemporaries. The political creed that hallows the

---

7. M. C. Eggleston to John Quincy Adams, 7 January 1825, Department of State, Letters of Application and Recommendation During the Administration of James Monroe, National Archives, Washington. Edward Coles to Henry Clay, 22 February 1828, Department of State, Letters of Application and Recommendation During the Administration of John Quincy Adams, National Archives, Washington. Samuel Cushman to Henry Lee, 13

name of the Old Hero was unknown even to the most perceptive
observers of Jackson's rise to power. "His friends," wrote Daniel
Webster, "have no common principle—they are held together by no
common tie."[8] And, as late as 1897, the era dominated by Old
Hickory and his followers was still simply the "Middle Period" of
American history—an amorphous epoch that stretched from 1817 to
1852.[9] Nineteenth-century historians of the Jacksonian era hardly
knew what to make of the political attitudes that were characteristic
of the age. James Parton, who published his biography of Jackson in
1860, could only point out that the Jackson party's constitutional
doctrines identified it as the proponent of strict construction. But
this sketchy political denomination was not enough, as Parton himself recognized. Members of the coalition, including Jackson, could
and did depart from the party's constitutional interpretations.[10]

Almost twenty-five years after the publication of Parton's book,
William Graham Sumner was still mystified by the political beliefs of
the Jackson men, for they were "very incoherent in their political
creeds and their political codes." If there was any unity in this loose
collection of ideas, it was only of a negative sort. The "Era of Good
Feeling," thought Sumner,

had brought into politics a large number of men, products of continually
advancing political activity amongst the less educated classes, who were eager for
notoriety and spoils, for genteel living without work, and for public position.
These men were ready to be the janizaries of any party which would pay well.
They all joined the opposition [to John Quincy Adams], because they had
nothing to expect from the administration.[11]

The coalition, in this view, was not *for* anything, but responded to
the policies and programs of Adams by opposing everything that the
president favored and by supporting everything that he rejected. It
took a Frederick Jackson Turner to find some positive meaning—a
genuine common tie—in the rhetoric and bombast of the Jackson
period. It was clear to Turner that Jacksonism had something to do
with democracy and, of course, with the frontier. He fit the two
things together like this:

March 1829; J. H. Orenton and others to Andrew Jackson, 5 December 1835; John Miller to
Martin Van Buren, 27 December 1829, Department of State, Letters of Application and
Recommendation During the Administration of Andrew Jackson, National Archives, Wash-
ington.

    8. Quoted in Arthur Schlesinger, Jr., *The Age of Jackson* (Boston: Little, Brown & Co.,
1945), p. 4.

    9. John Burgess, *The Middle Period* (New York: C. Scribner's Sons, 1897).

    10. Parton, *The Life of Andrew Jackson,* 3:171.

    11. William Graham Sumner, *Andrew Jackson as a Public Man* (Boston: Houghton
Mifflin Co., 1883), p. 130.

Out of this frontier society where the freedom and abundance of land in the Great [Mississippi] Valley opened a refuge to the oppressed of all regions, came the Jacksonian democracy which governed the nation after the downfall of the party of John Quincy Adams.

Andrew Jackson himself "became the idol and mouthpiece of the popular will" because he personified the "essential western traits" of frontier democracy.[12]

With Turner, there came a reevaluation of the puzzling Middle Period and the discovery that Jacksonism had advanced the cause of the oppressed people who inhabited the region west of the Alleghenies. Subsequent writers added some embroidery to the idea of Jacksonian Democracy, but in all essential points the issue had been settled: Jacksonism was a democratic creed.[13]

But the subject of Jacksonian Democracy was moved to new ground and the question reopened. The modern controversy seems to have begun in 1945 with the publication of *The Age of Jackson* by Arthur Schlesinger, Jr. Schlesinger argued that the conflicts of the Jackson era were not sectional battles as they had been portrayed by scholars like Turner, but that they pitted class against class. And in these confrontations could be discovered the pith of Jacksonism. Schlesinger's Jacksonian Democracy was a movement "to control the power of capitalist groups, mainly Eastern, for the benefit of non-capitalist groups, farmers and laboring men, East, West, and South."[14] Jacksonian Democracy, therefore, was the ideological donation of the working class to American thought. It was a concept, according to Schlesinger, hammered out primarily in the workshops and factories of eastern cities, refined and articulated by the leaders of an infant labor movement, and shipped out to the nation.

Immediately, Schlesinger's interpretation came up against the criticism of Bray Hammond, a scholarly staff member of the Federal Reserve Board. Professor Schlesinger, wrote Hammond, properly emphasized

the fact that Jacksonian democracy reflected eastern as well as frontier influences, but he ... err[ed] in associating the eastern influence with labor alone and not with business enterprise. There was no more important factor in the Jacksonian movement than the democratization of business, which ceased thenceforth to be the *metier* of a predominantly mercantile, exclusive group, or

12. Frederick Jackson Turner, *The Frontier in American History* (New York: Henry Holt & Co., 1920), pp. 192, 254.
13. See, for example, Claude Bowers, *Party Battles of the Jackson Period* (New York: Houghton Mifflin Co., 1922), p. 31.
14. Schlesinger, *The Age of Jackson*, p. 307.

commercial aristocracy, as it was in the days of Hamilton, and became an interest of the common man.[15]

Under the hand of Hammond, Jacksonian Democracy became something quite different from the ideological signature of a democratic upheaval and more akin to the unprincipled scramble for power described by William Sumner. The Jackson men, thought Hammond, had concealed their true intent in the jargon of frontier democracy. "Though their cause was a sophisticated one of enterpriser against capitalist, of banker against regulation, and of Wall Street against Chestnut, the language was the same as if they were all back on the farm."[16] And American historians had been deceived by this pastoral rhetoric. They had perceived an uprising of the oppressed against eastern wealth and aristocratic culture. In reality, some of the Jacksonian warriors were wealthier than the effete aristocrats whom they claimed to have displaced. These rising entrepreneurs were no more democratic, no less greedy, and certainly no more virtuous than the supporters of the United States Bank or of federally financed internal improvements. The credo of the Jackson men, added Richard Hofstadter, was

not the philosophy of a radical leveling movement that proposes to uproot property or to reconstruct society along drastically different lines. It proceeds upon no Utopian premises—full equality is impossible, "distinctions will always exist," and the reward should rightly go to "superior industry, economy, and virtue." What is demanded is only the classic bourgeois ideal, equality before the law, the restriction of government to equal protection of its citizens. This is the philosophy of a rising middle class; its aim is not to throttle but to liberate business, to open every possible pathway for the creative enterprise of the people.[17]

The class-interest approaches of Schlesinger, Hammond, Hofstadter, and others have provoked still another scholarly reaction: delineation of the social differences which underlay Jacksonian political alignments has invested the concept of Jacksonian Democracy with a clarity and a coherence which it did not possess. In fact, writes Marvin Meyers, "social differences were subtly shaded and unstable; party policies were ambiguous in their probable effects

15. Bray Hammond, "Public Policy and National Banks," *Journal of Economic History* 6 (May 1946): 82.
16. Bray Hammond, *Banks and Politics in America*, (Princeton: Princeton University Press, 1959) pp. 328–29.
17. Richard Hofstadter, *The American Political Tradition* (New York: Vintage Books, 1954), p. 62.

upon group interests; and so no general and simple class difference appears in party preference."[18]

The substance of Jacksonian political belief, according to historians like Meyers and John Ward, was no simple extrapolation from narrow economic or social interests. General Jackson did not win his large and devoted following because he advanced the cause of the poor, the farmers, or the small businessmen, but because he, better than any man, embodied and expressed the moral feelings of the age.[19] It was not in their calculating brains or their principled intellects that the voters received Old Hickory's appeals; it was in their hearts that they knew him to be right.

The same appeals which attracted the support of American voters during the age of Jackson may well have excited the scholarly imaginations of American historians. The Jacksonian propagandists assaulted the sentiments of the public from many directions at once, using diverse policies and ideas to captivate popular attention. The scholars seem to have been captivated as well, for each seems to have shaped his concept of Jacksonian democracy after a part of the Jackson men's own propaganda, clarifying these appeals by linking them to stark group interests. And, as we have already seen, Andrew Jackson soon became all things to all historians. Meyers discovered in the pronouncements of the Jacksonians

distinct traces of every theme used by historians to explain the nature and import of Jacksonian Democracy. Jacksonian spokesmen drew upon an extensive repertory of moral plots which might engage the political attention of nineteenth century Americans: equality against privilege; liberty against domination; honest work against idle exploit; natural dignity against factitious superiority; patriotic conservatism against alien innovation; progress against dead precedent. A first ungraded inventory shows only a troubled mind groping for names to fit its discontent.[20]

But there was, argued Meyers, a recurrent theme in these apparently incoherent rantings. The Jacksonians were intent on recalling "agrarian republican innocence to a society drawn fatally . . . to the revolutionizing ways of acquisition, emulative consumption, promotion, and speculation. . . ."[21] They appealed to inchoate prejudices, not principles or interests, in order to rescue the nation from the

18. Marvin Meyers, *The Jacksonian Persuasion: Politics and Belief* (Stanford: Stanford University Press, 1957), p. 5.

19. See John Ward, *Andrew Jackson: Symbol for an Age* (New York: Oxford University Press, 1955), introduction.

20. Meyers, *The Jacksonian Persuasion*, p. 6.

21. Ibid., p. 10.

moral decay which lurked close behind flashy prosperity and the excesses of entrepreneurial ingenuity.

What we know about the social backgrounds of Jacksonian administrators warns us to be wary of any rendition of Jacksonian Democracy in which class interests or class origins play a leading role. Old Hickory's bureaucrats were barely distinguishable in social status from their Federalist and Jeffersonian predecessors, and it would probably be unwise to distinguish the political beliefs of the Jackson men in these terms. It may be argued, of course, that the Jacksonian administrators were not representative of the whole Jacksonian coalition, that somewhere near the grass roots, the class-based nature of Jacksonism became evident. Yet what we know of Jacksonism's grass roots indicates that Old Hickory's support was not unique for its class composition. Studies of Jacksonian leaders and activists in state and local politics reveal at most only very small differences between the wealth, occupations, and social status of the Jacksonian Democrats and their Whig opponents, and the nature of these minor differences varied from one state to the next. Investigations of voting behavior during the period show that rank-and-file supporters of Andrew Jackson were not noticeably poorer than rank-and-file Whigs. Such differences as there were between the adherents of the two parties suggest that religion, ethnicity, and perhaps "cultural" distinctions were more powerful determinants of allegiance to Old Hickory than were wealth, occupation, or status.[22]

The party of the "common man" had no monopoly on common men; indeed, it attracted some remarkably uncommon ones. The dying Federalist party—that malignant, antidemocratic force from which, it was charged, the Whigs were descended—was in fact an important source of Jacksonian manpower. Many old Federalists apparently discovered that their principles allowed them to lend political assistance to the Old Hero, and he rewarded them with important posts in his administration. Jackson placed more Federalists in government offices than did all of his Republican predecessors combined. In his own cabinet, John Berrien, Louis McLane, and even

22. Edward Pessen, *Jacksonian America: Society, Personality, and Politics* (Homewood, Ill.: Dorsey Press, 1969).

the Jacksonian stalwart Roger B. Taney were all recent converts from the ranks of the Federalists.[23]

As for the country at large, it has been estimated that what remained of the Federalist party in 1828 divided about evenly between the Jacksonians and the Whigs, and the Jacksonians may even have received a slightly larger share of Federalists than did their opponents.[24] The behavior of the Federalists, at least, suggests that the new political alignments of the Jackson era had very little to do with the old ideological division between elitists and democrats, the aristocracy and the common man.

In short, there is plentiful evidence that casts serious doubt upon the proposition that the Jacksonian creed was chiefly an expression of class interests—upper, lower, or middle. In the light of this evidence, the interpretations presented by Sumner, Hofstadter, Schlesinger, Hammond, and perhaps even Turner offer questionable approaches to understanding the main elements of Jacksonian ideology. We are left, then, with the work of historians like Marvin Meyers, John Ward, and James Parton. These commentators are not merely what remains after all the class interest historians have been eliminated; they share a certain unity of perspective.

In effect historians like Meyers and Ward have taken up again where James Parton left off. Like Parton, these twentieth-century scholars construct their accounts of the Jacksonian era almost entirely from the opinions of its citizens. They present Jacksonian Democracy from a Jacksonian perspective, and this is as we would wish it to be. Our purpose here is to isolate the intellectual component of Jacksonian actions—to examine it as an independent cause of bureaucratic behavior. It is essential, therefore, that we do not incorporate into the thoughts of Jackson men those objective social and economic conditions which no Jacksonian perceived. Jacksonism, for example, should not be identified as "the classic bourgeois ideal" if this estimation is based upon an analysis of social and economic ties which were not evident to the Jackson men themselves. Such a formulation might be a perfectly reasonable, shorthand description of everything Jacksonian, but it would fail to isolate the ideological and the intellectual from other sources of behavior.

The works of Parton, Meyers, and Ward, then, are not only

23. Shaw Livermore, *The Twilight of Federalism: The Disintegration of the Federalist Party, 1815–1830* (Princeton: Princeton University Press, 1962), pp. 140, 156.
24. Pessen, *Jacksonian America*, pp. 249–50.

exempt from some of the faults of the class interest approach; they possess a certain positive merit which makes them well suited to our present purposes. All three authors have examined the Jacksonian credo as it was known to the Jackson men and their contemporaries, and each has uncovered an emotional core in Jacksonism that was identified with no particular class or condition: a nostalgic desire to return to the old republican virtues. Parton, for example, in one of his many Jacksonian vignettes, recites Old Hickory's tirade against an American diplomat whose taste for continental luxury had overcome his republican sensibilities:

Tell this gentleman from me, that Benjamin Franklin in his woolen stockings was no disgrace to his country. This government will never sanction what these gentlemen wish. The same habits brought reflections upon the last administration—those beautiful portfolios, those treaty boxes, and other things of that kind. It shall not be done, sir. I say again, sir, and I wish those gentlemen to know it, that no man ever did such honor to his country abroad as old Ben Franklin, who wore his homespun blue woolen stockings, and all Paris loved him for it. . . . Have these things done—not meanly—but plain and simple, conformable to our republican principles.[25]

The restoration of republican virtue meant more, of course, than blue woolen stockings and plainness in diplomacy. It meant that the nation would abandon those public projects which tended to undermine the natural goodness of Americans. The narrow paths of government policy led away from the corruption of high finance and speculative scrambles, away from government-supported bank monopoly, federal participation in local improvement programs, excessive tariffs, public debt, and the use of public lands to generate a revenue for federal spending. Such things as internal improvements and the banking monopoly could be useful conveniences, as Jackson himself conceded, but he thought that the moral impediments of these conveniences outweighed their public utility. Internal improvements would inflame petty, parochial jealousies and might be "resorted to as artful expedients to shift upon the Government the losses of unsuccessful private speculation, and thus, by ministering to personal ambition and self-aggrandizement, tend to sap the foundations of public virtue."[26] But a close-hauled federal economic policy would "counteract that tendency to public and private profligacy

    25. Parton, *The Life of Andrew Jackson,* 3: 251.
    26. James D. Richardson, *A Compilation of the Messages and Papers of the Presidents,* 10 vols. (Washington: Government Printing Office, 1899), 2: 490.

which a profuse expenditure of money by the Government is but too apt to engender."[27]

In the Jacksonian scheme of things, government was not primarily a provider of peace and prosperity—although these things were certainly important. It was a guarantor of human goodness. The guiding purpose of public policy should be to "preserve the morals of the people," to "revive and perpetuate those habits of economy and simplicity which are so congenial to the characters of republicans. . . ."[28] And the best defense of virtue was the assurance that vice would not be rewarded. Honest toil, thought the Jackson men, should be the only road to happiness and material success. It was morally unhealthy for Americans to "see wealth passing continually out of the hands of those whose labor produced it, or whose economy saved it, into the hands of those who neither work nor save."[29] The financial windfalls that resulted from the monetary machinations of the Monster Bank or from the artful maneuvers of currency speculators made a mockery of simple virtue, thrift, and industry. Hence, the bank would have to be curbed, and the currency speculators deprived of opportunities for unearned riches, by a limitation on the use of paper banknotes as a medium of exchange and a return to hard coin. The grant of special privileges by the government was another path to instant riches which the Jacksonians sought to close. If a man could become wealthy by wheedling special favors from the government, then skill at political intrigue might come to replace honest labor as the means to material success. Government would therefore have to distribute its favors sparingly. There could be no grants of monopoly to private interests; internal improvements might be publicly financed only under special circumstances; government expenditures in general must be kept at a minimum.

The Jacksonian moral revival did not call on Americans to rise above the concern for their material well-being. It merely demanded that the material rewards should go to those who merited them by reason of hard work and personal virtue. Its ideal was to establish an equivalence between moral and material worth. Those whose honest

27. Ibid., p. 436.
28. Ibid., 3: 19, 166.
29. William Gouge, "The Artificial Inequality of Wealth," in Edwin C. Rozwenc, ed., *Ideology and Power in the Age of Jackson* (Garden City, N.Y.: Anchor Books, 1964), p. 115.

labor made a tangible addition to the goods of this world should enjoy the rewards of this world, not those who gathered in the money that was thrown off by the periodic shakes and shudders of the economic system. The goal, in short, was to assure that the financial incentives for industry and moral goodness were greater than those for idleness and vice. The function of government was primarily the negative one of refusing to provide access to the wages of sin, of assuring that public policy give no encouragement to immorality.

Democracy itself was a project of personal moral uplift. It was, in the words of one Jacksonian bureaucrat,

justice between man and man, between nation and nation. It is morality. It is "giving every man his due." It is "doing unto others as we would have them do unto us." It advocates the banishment of falsehood, fraud, and violence from the affairs of men. It is the moral code of all true philosophy; it is a fundamental doctrine of "Him who spake as never man spake;" it is the perfection of reason and the law of God.[30]

The first fruits of democracy were not peace, order, or wealth, but virtuous human beings, and the model of moral uprightness was Andrew Jackson himself.

The Old Hero's military exploit at New Orleans provided the speechmakers and songwriters of the day with a ready-made allegory of republican goodness. This epic of moral restoration, says John Ward, embodied the three essential components of Jacksonism. The first was nature. Old Hickory and his hardy Hunters of Kentucky had acquired the skill to defeat the British, not from elaborate professional training, but through their skins from nature herself. Nor had victory on the plains of Chalmette been bought by superior numbers or equipment; in both of these respects, Jackson's forces had been deficient. But Old Hickory made up for these superficial shortcomings with his own iron will and determination. It was this which had contributed to his triumph, and it was the unaided human will, says John Ward, that the Jacksonian orators and lyricists exalted. But there was more here than nature and human will. Jackson had, it was true, committed military errors at New Orleans, but these small mistakes had led him to a great victory. Here, clearly, was the hand of Providence. The Creator was obviously telling mankind that democracy was His chosen form of government, that He would protect

30. *Autobiography of Amos Kendall,* ed. William Stickney (Boston: Lee & Shepard, 1872), p. 437.

it, and that the fulfillment of democratic ideals was the fulfillment of God's will.[31]

The restoration of republican virtue, then, required a return to fields, forests, and hard work by which men might learn the true wisdom taught by nature; a retreat from synthetic social distinctions and artificial fortunes based on financial manipulation to the intrinsic power of the human will; and a return to the democratic path destined by God. In the Jacksonian moral world, there was little room at all for government. If the human will were to operate freely, government could impose few restraints upon its people. Its leading function was to keep temptation from falling across the paths of its citizens, so that they might realize their own natural moral discipline.[32]

The elements of the Jacksonian creed were not locked together by logic. If they possessed any unity at all, it was only that they all seemed to be embedded in the person of Andrew Jackson. Old Hickory's contemporaries recognized him as a symbolic representation of their own feelings. In him was "concentrated the spirit . . . that burned in their own bosoms,"[33] and his assaults upon the enemies of republican virtue provided a dramatic focus for their own resentments and aspirations. "Many a plain farmer or mechanic," wrote one of the Jacksonian partisans,

reflecting amid his solitary labors, on the "Great American System," the Bank, and other deeply contrived measures of public policy . . . has been astonished to find a veto message or proclamation, from the chief magistrate of the nation, suddenly lighting up his mind, unlocking as it were his own secret thoughts, coinciding with his own internal convictions, but displaying them with such clearness and strength as to leave him no longer in doubt.[34]

The Jacksonian diatribes against the speculators and jobbers and against the financial intriguers and their windfall fortunes seem to have touched a nerve in the hardworking farmers and mechanics who were likely to suffer when "fluctuations in the standard of value render uncertain the rewards of labor."[35] But the Jacksonian message seems also to have found a receptive audience beyond the

31. Ward, *Andrew Jackson*, pp. 24, 154, 108.
32. See Meyers, *The Jacksonian Persuasion*, p. 23.
33. Quoted in Ward, *Andrew Jackson*, p. 1.
34. William M. Holland, *The Life and Political Opinions of Martin Van Buren* (Hartford, Conn.: Belknap & Hammerslea, 1835), p. 360, and in Rozwenc, ed., *Ideology and Power in the Age of Jackson*, pp. 254–55.
35. Quoted in Meyers, *The Jacksonian Persuasion*, p. 27.

farmers and mechanics: bankers who were resentful of the privileges
and power enjoyed by Biddle's Bank of the United States, merchants
who were troubled by a flimsy and uncertain medium of exchange,
perhaps even some gentlemen of the "better sort" who were disturbed at the prospect of men of shoddy character and no personal
worth acquiring wealth on an aristocratic scale through guile and low
cunning. Men of many different social stations could find something
to respond to in Andrew Jackson.

Yet the personality of Andrew Jackson himself does not seem to
provide a coherent portrait of the Jacksonian creed. His character
was just as jumbled as his message. "He was," says James Parton,

a patriot and a traitor. He was one of the greatest generals and wholly ignorant
of the art of war. A writer brilliant, elegant, eloquent, without being able to
compose a correct sentence, or spell words of four syllables. The first of
statesmen, he never devised, he never framed a measure. He was the most candid
of men, and was capable of the profoundest dissimulation. A most law-defying,
law-obeying citizen. A stickler for discipline, he never hesitated to disobey a
superior. A democratic autocrat. An urbane savage. An atrocious saint.[36]

Bewildering Old Hickory was not a man to be placed casually in any
school of political thought or identified as an exponent of any
political tradition. He seems to have reached his various political
positions, not by pressing forward with a consistent line of thought
or by looking to precedent, but by consulting his own confusing
sentiments. Although he may have stirred in some hearts the hope of
a Jeffersonian revival,[37] there was no clear intellectual pathway that
led back from the Hermitage to Monticello and the lucid reason of an
earlier day. Vernon Parrington, a professed adherent of Jeffersonian
principles, found in Jackson something quite different from ortho-
doxy:

The dramatic career of Andrew Jackson, so unlike that of Jefferson, which was
determined by a speculative temperament and founded on a critical examination
of diverse systems of society and politics, was shaped in large measure by
prejudice and circumstance. A man of iron will and inflexible purpose, he was
almost wholly lacking in political and social philosophy. His conclusions were
the reactions of a simple nature of complete integrity in contact with plain
fact. . . . There was no subtlety in his mental processes. . . .[38]

36. Parton, *The Life of Andrew Jackson,* 1: vii.
37. Some of Jackson's southern supporters seem to have expected him to return to the
fondly remembered days of Jefferson and to "the *Old Constitution,* that antiquated relict of
'87" (*National Intelligencer,* 14 March 1829).
38. Vernon L. Parrington, *Main Currents in American Thought,* 3 vols. (New York:
Harvest Books, 1954), 2: 140. On Parrington's Jeffersonian bias, see ibid., 1: vii.

Political sentiments produced in such a manner could assume a coherent structure only in retrospect. And even in retrospect, there appear to be some jarring discontinuities in Jacksonian thought. The same political temperament that caused men to wax nostalgic over the nation's simple, early days and called their attention to the alarming deterioration of republican virtue—so ominous for the future of republican institutions—could also produce serene confidence that the republic was favored by Providence and was being carried by divine hand to a state of felicity and contentment. This simultaneous longing for a beloved past and a blessed future is not the product of a well-ordered political philosophy; it is the emotional response of men who are distressed and unhappy with the present and are searching in any direction for an escape from it.

Jackson and his lieutenants dominated their era, not by providing it with a consistent system of political principles or a program of action, but by establishing an emotional bond between themselves and the citizens of the age. The Jacksonian persuasion was more evocative than prescriptive. It told men how they felt, but seldom revealed exactly what could be done about it. Such an ill-defined body of beliefs and sentiments would not have been likely to provide much distinctive guidance for Jacksonian administrators. Jacksonism may have been different from the political creeds that preceded it, but the ideology of Jacksonian Democracy does not offer a very promising explanation for the administrative innovations of the Jackson men—at least not by itself.

Yet while the Jacksonian creed did not precisely define the kind of national salvation it demanded, it did call attention to the general conditions that were conceived to be the symptoms of depravity. The Jackson men thought that speculation, fraud, and the appetite for easy wealth were the early signs of imminent damnation. These were some of the things that made the present unattractive to Old Hickory and his followers. Although the Jacksonian ethos may not have exercised much direct influence over Jacksonian administrators, it does seem to identify the kinds of things that would have captured their attention. And the conditions which monopolized their attention may also have influenced their administrative actions. The ideology of Jacksonian Democracy probably did not cause Jacksonian bureaucracy, but it may have been a symptom or a reflection of the same conditions that produced the distinctive qualities of Jacksonian administration.

The social backgrounds of the Jacksonian administrators suggest that we should look for these conditions in particular areas of American society. The overwhelming majority of the high-level Jacksonian bureaucrats had legal backgrounds, and changing conditions in the legal profession may have been partly responsible for generating a new administrative style in the federal establishment. A relatively large proportion of the Jackson men came out of the West, and we may find the makings of bureaucratic change somewhere on the frontier. Finally, Old Hickory's righteous opposition to innovations in political economy indicates that new doings within the American business community may have helped to produce something new in the federal government. In addition, most lawyers of the day were also active businessmen of one kind or another. In short, we may be able to learn something about the sources of Jacksonian administrative innovation by an examination of business and the bar, especially in the West.

II

THE STRUCTURE
OF
SOCIAL INSTITUTIONS

The intrusion of the rabble into the reception chambers of the White House may well have made a man like Justice Story feel a bit uneasy and "glad to escape from the scene as soon as possible." The apparent invasion of the frontier rustics left many of John Quincy Adams' adherents wondering what would become of Washington's social grace and gentility. Yet if these well-bred aristocrats felt uneasy in the presence of the masses, it was no less true that the ordinary people felt uneasy with them. Indeed, Americans of the middling classes seem to have felt uncomfortable even with one another. They did not know how to behave, but they were most anxious to learn.

Accordingly, books on etiquette found a ready market in Jacksonian America. In the late 1820s, these primers of politeness began to be distributed in large quantities throughout the country. During the decade of the 30s and up to the Civil War, aspirants to the genteel classes could choose from about three new etiquette manuals each year. In these volumes, gentlemen might learn that wearing one's hat indoors tended "to vice and immorality." For the benefit of younger gentlemen, and ladies, textbook writers quickly added chapters on "Politeness" and "Manners in the Street and on the Road" to the standard educational diet.[1] Ordinary people readied themselves to match the members of the American establishment courtesy for courtesy.

It is paradoxical that the same generation which produced a faith

---

1. Arthur M. Schlesinger, Sr., *Learning How to Behave* (New York: Macmillan Co., 1946), pp. 17–20.

in the power of unadorned nature and the naked human will should also generate a concern for the nice conventions of social intercourse. Yet the etiquette books were but one inconsistency in Jacksonian society. "Consider the seeming paradox," writes Stanley Elkins,

> of how by that time, in the very bright morning of American success, the power of so many American institutions had one by one melted away. The church had fallen into a thousand parts. The shadow of an Anglican church, disestablished in the wake of the Revolution and its doom forever sealed by the yearly anarchy of the camp meeting, was all that remained in the South of ecclesiastical authority; and in New England the Congregational church, which had once functioned as a powerful state establishment, was deprived of its last secular supporters early in the century. It was not that religion itself was challenged—quite the contrary— but that as a source of organized social power and internal discipline the church had undergone a relentless process of fragmentation. Religious vitality every- where was overwhelming, but that vitality lay primarily in demands for individ- ual satisfaction which took inevitable and repeated priority over institutional needs.[2]

As it was with religion, so it was with almost all the giants of the society. Social institutions that had previously designated right stan- dards of conduct were no longer virile enough to do so, and it is not surprising that many Americans looked to manuals of etiquette rather than to their social betters for rules of ladylike and gentle- manly behavior.

Habits were changing. The infant industries of the nation, recog- nizing that prosperity lay in the direction of mass markets, did what they could to popularize luxuries, to generate a longing for material comforts among the working classes. And so, one economic historian has claimed, they undermined the virtuous frugality and asceticism of the ordinary people. The common man yielded to a "hedonism encouraged by highly productive and commercial aggressive factory manufactures."[3]

As an economic and spiritual consumer, the American citizen was not what he once had been. Nor was he the same political consumer. No more did he pay his allegiance to old institutions. The tributaries of influence and prestige which had fed the power of the Congres- sional Caucus were drying up one by one. Regional elites could no longer command the loyalties of lowly citizens. In New England, writes Moise Ostrogorski, "the politico-social hierarchy which Puri- tanism had set up and which was the outcome of an alliance between

---

2. Stanley Elkins, *Slavery* (New York: Universal Library, 1963), pp. 28–29.
3. Victor S. Clark, *History of Manufactures in the United States* (New York: McGraw- Hill, 1929), p. 579.

the magistracy, the clergy, property, and culture, was collapsing."[4]

The old political, spiritual, and economic goods were unable to dominate the market as they once had, and the old methods of production did not seem suitable to new craftsmen. "The inhabitants of the United States," noted Alexis de Tocqueville, "are never fettered by the axioms of their profession; they escape from all the prejudices of their present station; they are not more attached to one line of operation than another; they are not more prone to employ an old method than a new one; they have no rooted habits. . . ."[5]

The upholders of tradition did not despair at the sight of a society with "no rooted habits." There remained the hope that old sources of unity might once again exert their power. From vantage points within society's conservative institutions, some men perceived that the lapse in fealty to old standards of conduct was only momentary. In Worcester County, Massachusetts, Joseph Willard, a local lawyer, looked out over his assembled colleagues seven months after Andrew Jackson's inauguration. It was the hundredth anniversary of the county bar, and Willard urged his fellow attorneys to

dwell on these occasions: they will be found of value as a point of union hereafter to be more diligently sought for, as the circles of time and space widen, and receive more within their embrace. They will be found of value as stirring up to life and action the sympathies that exist in those following the same pursuit; the feelings now indeed almost in a state of repose, but which need but a little quickening influence to render them healthy and vigorous. They will call out that *esprit de corps* that renders the profession in verity but one body, suffering and rejoicing together. . . .[6]

The county bar, observed Willard, had grown from a small body to a host, and it was difficult to instill in such a large collection of men a sense of loyalty to the profession. "It is time, then, that stated meetings should be had, with the same general purpose as the present, binding us more closely together, and furnishing a tribute of respect for that profession which is the common mother of our peace and joy." And, above this respect for the profession, the lawyers

4. Moise Ostrogorski, *Democracy and the Organization of Political Parties*, ed. Seymour M. Lipset, 2 vols. (New York: Vintage Books, 1964), 2: 18.
5. Alexis de Tocqueville, *Democracy in America*, trans. Henry Reeve, 2 vols. (New York: Vintage Books, 1954), 1: 443.
6. Joseph Willard, *Address to the Members of the Bar of Worcester County, Massachusetts* (Lancaster, Mass.: Carter, Andrews & Co., 1830), p. 4.

were to place their obligations to society. The attorneys, said Willard, ought to enhance the reputation of the legal profession by their "sacrifice of the selfish principle" in efforts to advance the good of mankind.[7]

The increasing lack of cohesiveness which Willard perceived among his colleagues was not confined to the bar of Worcester County. Everywhere, an increase in the number of lawyers was straining the professional loyalties that held them together and the moral standards that governed their conduct.[8] As early as 1818, the *Niles Weekly Register* reported that New York lawyers were "as plentiful as blackberries."[9] And in some sections of the country, it was futile to "call out that *esprit de corps*" which rendered the legal profession a unified institution.

In the West, the lawyers' devotion to the "mother of their peace and joy" was overcome by unflinching dedication to personal gain. Their sense of fraternity, when it existed at all, was not grounded upon common tradition or devotion to the profession, but upon pride in the special talent of attorneys for turning their abilities into cash and prestige. What the lawyers admired in one another was not the willingness to "sacrifice the selfish principle" for the good of mankind, but technical proficiency and, most of all, success. John Caton, an early Chicago lawyer, took pride in his own ability to foster the spirit of litigiousness among his neighbors; it was good for business.[10] And the colleagues of Usher F. Linder, attorney general of Illinois, were in awe of him not because he did right, but because he did well. He could secure convictions for the innocent and gain acquittals for the guilty:

Notwithstanding the fact that the merits of the case were all with the plaintiff, the jury, without leaving their box, returned a verdict for the defendant. I was so dazed by the adroitness, the eloquence, and the masterly ability of Linder, that I was never able to remember much that was said. Indeed, I don't know how he could very well say anything in such a case that would be likely to stamp itself upon the memory distinctly. I think he gained the case by ridicule, by the most brilliant displays of rhetoric, and by dramatic effect.[11]

John Caton and Usher Linder were not isolated points of weakness in an otherwise noble institution. The desire for personal aggrandize-

7. Ibid., pp. 4–5.
8. See Elkins, *Slavery*, pp. 29–30.
9. Quoted in Charles Warren, *History of the American Bar* (Boston: Little, Brown & Co., 1911), p. 301.
10. John Caton, *Early Bench and Bar of Illinois* (Chicago: Chicago Legal News Co., 1893), pp. 5–15.
11. Usher F. Linder, *Reminiscences of the Early Bench and Bar of Illinois* (Chicago: Chicago Legal News Co., 1879), pp. 16–17.

ment to which they succumbed was an impulse that swept the whole profession. Because advocates were "as plentiful as blackberries," competition among lawyers for cases and fees became somewhat sharper than it had been, and in the West, though there was usually no surfeit of attorneys, the unsettled conditions of frontier life made for an unsettled profession. The great westward migration of lawyers seems to have carried many of them well beyond the outer limits of professional ethics.

The American bar, of course, had never been entirely free of shysters and pettifoggers. In the years immediately after the Revolution, the legal profession, its ranks depleted by the departure of Tory lawyers, briefly opened the practice of law to many young men with little or no professional training. In some cases, their professional scruples proved to be as deficient as their education. But the bar had recovered quickly from its early laxity, and along the eastern seaboard, in one state after another, bar associations were organized or revived to regulate the profession. These organizations typically included every member of the bar who was practicing in a particular county, district, or state, and their decisions were binding on all members. The early bar associations exercised control over prelegal education, professional training, admission to practice, and the "deportment" of attorneys.[12]

The authority of the professional associations was not unchallenged. From the Revolution onward, the legal profession faced intense popular animosity, and there was steady pressure to "deprofessionalize" the practice of law—to allow litigants to represent themselves, to lower requirements for admission to the bar, and even to suppress the legal profession entirely. In spite of public enmity, the post-Revolutionary legal profession managed to establish itself as a prestigious, influential, and unified institution with a high degree of control over its own internal affairs. But public hostility gradually took its toll, and as the adherents of Andrew Jackson were moving into positions of authority, the bar associations were being ousted from authority. One by one, they lost control over the practice of law and either disbanded or resolved themselves into "voluntary" organizations which had no supervisory power save, in some cases, the power to oversee the management of a law library. After the 1830s, "discipline by the profession itself or by a professional organization . . . simply ceased to function."[13]

12. Anton-Hermann Chroust, *The Rise of the Legal Profession in America,* 2 vols. (Norman: University of Oklahoma Press, 1965), 2: 30, 34–35.
13. Ibid., pp. 49, 154–55.

The collapse of the legal profession as a self-regulating institution occurred just as the forces of Jacksonism were establishing themselves in politics. In fact, it has been suggested that there may have been a direct connection between the two events—that the "spirit of Jacksonian democracy" was responsible for demolishing professional restrictions and controls that were perceived to bar common men from the practice of law. Jacksonian Democracy may well have contributed something to the dismantling of the organized bar, but the process of decay seems to have begun well before the Jacksonian democratic spirit came into focus. In Worcester, Massachusetts, Joseph Willard was already talking about the decline of professional unity and discipline only seven months after Old Hickory's inauguration.[14] In the West, where professional organizations seldom had the chance to gain a foothold, the signs of deprofessionalization became perceptible even earlier. Standards for admission to practice were being eroded throughout the decade of the 1820s.[15] In Missouri, 1816 seems to have marked a turning point of sorts in the history of the bar. Thereafter, "a number of men with limited educational backgrounds were admitted to the Missouri bar, perhaps as many as one fourth being almost totally destitute of the rudiments of the English language and possessing only a superficial knowledge of the law."[16]

The legal profession was not suddenly thrown into disarray by an uprising of common men resentful at the undemocratic exclusivity of the bar. The process of deterioration was a gradual one, and it was not brought about entirely by forces external to the profession. It must be remembered that when state legislatures abolished the regulatory authority of the organized bar during the 1820s and 30s, a substantial proportion of the legislators—in some cases, a majority— were lawyers. In the post-Revolutionary era, the legal profession had been able to marshal its internal resources to ward off popular assaults. In the 1830s, it could not. The difference seems to have been less in the vigor of the external attacks than in the profession's ability or willingness to withstand them.

Before and during the age of Jackson, therefore, the legal profession lost its capacity to enforce internal discipline, and lawyers, especially in the West, were left free to pursue private gain without the hindrance of professional oversight and supervision. The condi-

---

14. See above, p. 33.

15. Chroust, *The Rise of the Legal Profession in America*, 2: 106.

16. William Francis English, "The Pioneer Lawyer and Jurist in Missouri," *The University of Missouri Studies* 21, no. 2 (1947): 95.

tion of the bar in Mississippi during the late 1830s is illustrative of the results. Here, as elsewhere, currency catastrophes had the courts brimming with litigation:

Rumors soon went out that lawyers in Mississippi were far too few in number to cope with the litigation in progress, and that many of them rapidly were accumulating overgrown fortunes. The effect of such intelligence was electrical .... Attorneys came in great numbers almost by every stage-coach which came into the state, and by every steamer which descended the Mississippi river. Many came only with the intention of sojourning in the land of promise for a short period, leaving their families behind them, whilst others came to take up permanent residence. Many of the newcomers were men of learning and worth, and deserved all of the success which they afterwards achieved. If there were a few others of a different description, the fact is not at all to be wondered at. That, in such a state of things as has been described, too much avidity for the accumulation of wealth should have, to some extent, made itself apparent even among the members of the legal profession in Mississippi; that sometimes fees were demanded to an amount a good deal beyond the services actually rendered; and that there were instances of gross oppression in the collection of money by execution, should, perhaps, occasion no great surprise.[17]

Nor should it come as any great surprise that the same kinds of conditions which disturbed the serenity of the legal profession should also have sent a wave of disorder through the affairs of commercial men. Like the American bar, the American business community had become bloated, until it could scarcely be called a community at all. It was true that the mercantile and counting houses of the Northeast still carried the names of old families. And the old families were still wealthy. But in addition to these giants of private enterprise, there were now many businessmen of lesser stature whose affairs extended far inland from the eastern harbors.

An entrepreneurial fever had spread like an epidemic through the population. "Everybody is speculating," wrote one French visitor, "and everything has become an object of speculation. The most daring enterprises find encouragement; all projects find subscribers."[18] Americans, observed Tocqueville, were "constantly driven to engage in commerce and industry." Love of wealth was at the bottom of everything they did.[19] And increasingly, Americans seemed willing to do just about anything in order to achieve wealth. Money was "considered a sufficient enough end in itself to sanction

17. Henry S. Foote, *The Bench and Bar of the South and Southwest* (St. Louis: Soule, Thomas, & Wentworth, 1876), pp. 54–55.
18. Michel Chevalier, *Society, Manners, and Politics in the United States* (Boston: Weeks, Jordan & Co., 1839), p. 305.
19. Tocqueville, *Democracy in America,* 1: 240, 247.

various shady practices," and men had even begun "to praise these questionable acts as 'sharp' dealings or examples of 'Yankee ingenuity.' "[20] Some time between the War of 1812 and the days of Andrew Jackson, says Douglas Miller, "America changed from a tenacious, traditional society, fearful of innovation and not given to seeking riches by speculative shortcuts, to a shifting, restless, and insecure world bent on finding quicker ways to wealth than the plodding path of natural increase."[21]

Yankee cupidity had some impressive results. On the banks of New England rivers, industrial installations—massive for their day— rose up to turn out yard after yard of cotton cloth. Their managers grew wise in the ways of machinery, and their owners became accustomed to handling of large enterprises. But for all their entrepreneurial prowess, the captains of New England's infant textile manufactures never really escaped from the "tenacious, traditional society" of colonial men of commerce. Like their predecessors, the textile entrepreneurs of the 1820s and 30s constituted a close-knit community of wealth. The corporations were all owned by members of the same coterie of capitalists, who adjusted their products to avoid competition with one another, traded patent rights on which they as a group held a monopoly, and sold their output through the same channels.[22] The factory towns which they brought into being were probably more like feudal demesnes than modern industrial complexes. The company-owned barracks for the factory girls at Lowell, Massachusetts, and elsewhere may have helped to keep the young ladies virtuous, but their existence and the restrictive atmosphere which they represented were hardly consistent with a modern industrial age.[23]

Some New England capitalists, at least, managed to maintain a grip on the past, but even they felt that it was slipping away. As the established mercantile families of Boston shifted their wealth from shipping to the newer investment opportunities in manufacturing, transportation, and banking, they grew apprehensive about the social changes that their own financial activities would be likely to produce. Not the least of these apprehensions were their misgivings

20. Douglas T. Miller, *Jacksonian Aristocracy: Class and Democracy in New York* (New York: Oxford University Press, 1967), p. 22.

21. Douglas T. Miller, *The Birth of Modern America* (New York: Pegasus, 1970), p. 21.

22. Clark, *History of Manufactures in the United States,* pp. 457–59; Frances W. Gregory, "The Office of President in the American Textile Industry," *Bulletin of the Business Historical Society* 26 (September 1952): 123.

23. Chevalier, *Society, Manners, and Politics in the United States,* pp. 200–201.

about themselves. There was the danger that the quickening pursuit of wealth might strain New England morality to the breaking point. The multitude of new money-making opportunities could prove to be so absorbing that a man might lose sight of "higher aims."[24]

During the first half of the nineteenth century, Boston businessmen seem to have fallen away from the old Calvinist conviction that earthly riches were the outward sign of inward grace.[25] For some, God and Mammon could not be reconciled so easily. It was plain, after all, that this was a time when vicious men could achieve riches without grace. Wealth gave no assurance of spiritual well-being; indeed, its pursuit could destroy one's spirit. Timothy Flint, after an absence of ten years, returned to New England in 1825 to find his people changed and their future clouded. "You perceive in New England," he wrote, "that the wits of the people are doubly sharpened in all the arts of money-getting. Have we not to fear, that this rage for travelling, this manufacturing and money-getting impulse, and the new modes of reasoning will overturn your puritan institutions?"[26] Boston consciences were troubled. William Appleton, one of the wealthiest of the Boston businessmen, chastised himself repeatedly in the pages of his diary: "I feel that I am quite eaten up with business; while in Church my mind with all the exertion I endeavored to make, was flying from City to City, from Ship to Ship, from Speculation to Speculation. . . ."[27]

But if their own intensified business activities discomfited the consciences of Boston capitalists, these inner turmoils were mild compared with the consternation they felt when they beheld the world of commerce outside their own tight circle. There was New York, for example, where the extravagance of the financially successful "border[s] on insanity. It is at war with general health, morals, and prosperity. It is, indeed, nearly allied to, if not the fruitful parent of, the mighty frauds, peculation, forgeries which are almost daily uncovered in that great city."[28]

New York capitalists seem to have seldom been bothered by the pangs of conscience that nagged William Appleton and other Boston-

24. Paul Goodman, "Ethics and Enterprise: The Values of the Boston Elite, 1800–1860," *American Quarterly* 18 (Fall 1966): 438.
25. Ibid., p. 439.
26. Timothy Flint, *Recollections of the Last Ten Years* (Boston: Cummings, Hilliard & Co., 1826), p. 389.
27. Quoted in Cleveland Amory, *The Proper Bostonians* (New York: E. P. Dutton, 1947), p. 81.
28. Quoted in Goodman, "Ethics and Enterprise," p. 450.

ians of his era. They pursued wealth and displayed it with considerably less restraint than did the New Englanders. It was not because the New York business elite was composed of reckless adventurers who had only recently become rich. As in Boston, most of the wealthy New York capitalists during the Jacksonian era came from families that were already relatively prosperous.[29] But the aristocracy of wealth in New York was not so firmly founded on an older aristocracy as was Boston's elite. Important segments of the New York colonial elite, whose wealth was based on extensive landholdings, failed to make the transition to newer types of enterprises as easily as the Boston shipping magnates did. Throughout the Jacksonian period, the economic and social prominence of New York's landed gentry declined.[30] And perhaps the deterioration of this established aristocracy helps to explain why New York's financial elite was less cohesive, exclusive, and disciplined than Boston's. The commercial community in New York was much more heterogeneous than its New England counterpart. A relatively large proportion of its leading businessmen were not members of old New York families, but outsiders who had come to Manhattan to make or enlarge their fortunes. Their business ethics were about as varied as their backgrounds, and even some of the most prominent mercantile houses of New York were deeply implicated in financial scandals.[31] Not only the heterogeneity but also the increasing size of the city's business elite may have diminished the efficacy of ethical restraints. In 1820, there were only about one hundred men in New York City whose personal property was assessed at more than $20,000. By 1845, there were more than nine hundred fifty persons whose assessed wealth exceeded that amount, twenty-one of whom were millionaires.[32]

The city was filled with men whose absorbing ambition was to join the ranks of the fortunate twenty-one. As the rich got richer and exhibited their wealth more extravagantly, the economic aspirations of the nonrich seem to have grown more intense. Alphonso Taft, a young lawyer from Connecticut who was looking for a place to practice his profession, observed the crowd of New York "adventurers" with distaste. "The notorious selfishness and dishonesty of the

29. Edward Pessen, "The Egalitarian Myth and the American Social Reality: Wealth, Nobility, and Equality in the 'Era of the Common Man,' " *American Historical Review* 76 (October 1971): 1012–13.
30. Miller, *Jacksonian Aristocracy*, pp. 62–69.
31. Robert Greenhalgh Albion, *The Rise of New York Port, 1815–1860* (New York: Charles Scribner's Sons, 1939), pp. 235–42, 310–11.
32. Miller, *Jacksonian Aristocracy*, p. 122.

great mass of men you find in New York," he wrote, "is in my mind a serious objection to settling there. You find selfishness everywhere, I know, but it is the leading and most prominent characteristic of New York. . . . Money is the all in all."[33]

Taft moved on to Cincinnati, where the competition may have been a bit less ferocious, but not because Cincinnatians were less concerned about making money. If anything, the scramble after wealth was more widespread there than in New York. In the population of 1820, for example, 7 percent of Cincinnati's adult white males were directors or officials of banks—a large proportion by any standard. These men, moreover, were almost perfectly representative of the town's male inhabitants. The bankers' social backgrounds did not distinguish them from their fellow Cincinnatians. Nor did their business activities set them apart from their neighbors. Almost none of the community's bankers worked at the job full time. They were lawyers or farmers or merchants as well as bankers.[34]

The Cincinnati financiers seem to have been typical of western men of affairs. Part-time businessmen were becoming numerous in American society. "What astonishes me most in the United States," wrote Tocqueville, "is not so much the marvelous grandeur of some undertakings as the innumerable multitude of small ones. Almost all of the farmers of the United States combine some trade with agriculture; most of them make agriculture itself a trade." And Tocqueville noted that part-time business enterprise was especially prevalent in the West.[35]

Even in the western towns, the intensification of business activities did not lead to a substantial equalization of wealth. Communities like Cincinnati, Pittsburgh, and Louisville were in the process of developing their own financial elites during the Jackson period. [36] But while only a few men actually rose through business ventures from lowly origins to great wealth, almost everyone was trying to do so. Where commerce and manufacturing had once been the concern of a few, they were now the preoccupations of many. Yeoman farmers—the supposed backbone of the old republic—were, according to Tocqueville, abandoning agriculture to seek the quicker financial

---

33. Quoted in Chroust, *The Rise of the Legal Profession in America*, 2: 117.

34. Harry R. Stevens, "Bank Enterprisers in a Western Town," *Business History Review* 29 (June 1955): 139–56.

35. Tocqueville, *Democracy in America*, 2: 166.

36. Pessen, *Jacksonian America*, p. 53; Richard C. Wade, *The Urban Frontier: The Rise of Western Cities, 1790–1830* (Cambridge: Harvard University Press, 1959), pp. 105–6.

gains of business enterprise.[37] The business of the United States was becoming business, and Americans threw themselves into it with a vengeance. "In general," wrote Michel Chevalier, a Frenchman traveling in the United States,

the American is little disposed to be contented; his idea of equality is to be inferior to none, but he endeavors to rise only in one direction. His only means, and the object of his whole thought, is to subdue the material world, in other words, it is industry in its various branches, business, speculation, work, action. To this sole object every thing is made subordinate, education, politics, private and public life.[38]

Chevalier might have added both craftsmanship and traditional morality to the list, for when almost everyone was occupied with some private, part-time scheme for the accumulation of wealth, the quality of goods and services as well as business ethics was likely to suffer. Where men practiced many different trades on a part-time basis, it was possible for Tocqueville to meet a number of interesting and intelligent adventurers "who have successively been lawyers, farmers, merchants, ministers of the Gospel, and physicians." But a nation filled with jacks-of-all-trades paid the inevitable price.[39] And it may have been that weak attachments to several different lines of work brought a deterioration not only in craftsmanship but in the craftsman as well. A man who was not wholly dependent upon a single trade would feel relatively little compulsion to preserve his reputation in that occupation—particularly when the measure of his honor was the ability to accumulate a fortune.

Very few of these ambitious operators ever did accumulate fortunes. Those who became extravagantly rich during the Jacksonian era were, for the most part, those who had been relatively rich to begin with. The distribution of wealth became no more democratic, and it may even have become more undemocratically concentrated.[40] This does not mean that business continued as usual, for while the captains of commerce remained captains, they were now surrounded by a huge, scattered fleet of small craft over which they exercised little or no direct control. In places like Boston, it was not that the old business community was destroyed but that it was now

37. Tocqueville, *Democracy in America*, 2:163–64.

38. Chevalier, *Society, Manners, and Politics in the United States*, p. 277.

39. Tocqueville, *Democracy in America*, 1: 443.

40. Lee Soltow, "Economic Inequality in the United States in the Period from 1790 to 1860," *Journal of Economic History* 31 (December 1971): 822–39; Jackson Turner Main, "Trends in Wealth Concentration Before 1860," *Journal of Economic History* 31 (June 1971): 445–47.

enveloped in a much more widely diffused and poorly organized network of business activities. In other places, like New York, new business communities came into being that were less well-ordered than the tightly knit one in Boston. And in the West, thousands of would-be millionaires scrambled after the main chance. If the wealthy speculators could reap windfalls overnight, so could they.

While visitors like Tocqueville and Chevalier could afford to wax enthusiastic about the exuberance and ingenuity of American business, domestic writers like Jacksonian economist William Gouge could only observe morosely that the

practices of trade in the United States, have debased the standard of commercial honesty. Without clearly distinguishing the causes that have made commerce a game of haphazard, men have come to perceive clearly the nature of the effect. They see wealth passing continually out of the hands of those whose labor produced it, or whose economy save it, into the hands of those who neither work nor save. They do not clearly perceive *how* the transfer takes place; but they are certain of the fact. In the general scramble they think themselves entitled to some portion of the spoil, and if they cannot get it by fair means, they take it by foul.[41]

Others saw that the new condition of American business might have consequences that would reach beyond the business community itself. Looking back on the Jacksonian period from the vantage point of the Civil War, one middle-aged American observed that the political corruption of the mid-nineteenth century "was preceded, perhaps, and certainly aided by laxity in what may be called financial morality. In my boyhood, dishonesty in places of trust was very rare. For many years it has been very common; the store-keepers . . . found all checks so ineffectual that they calculated on a certain percentage of losses from the dishonesty of their assistants, and discharged them only when they became too extravagant."[42]

The Jacksonians came to power in a society momentarily disordered. The voices of established institutions had grown faint, and with their decline came a weakening of traditional restraints on social behavior. It was an age of untrammeled competition and strong ambitions, a time when men seemingly became less dependable than they once had been. Even a political technician like Martin Van Buren seems to have sensed the change in moral climate and taken it

41. William Gouge, "The Artificial Inequality of Wealth," in Edwin C. Rozwenc, ed., *Ideology and Power in the Age of Jackson* (Garden City, N.Y.: Anchor Books, 1964), p. 115.
42. Thomas Low Nichols, *Forty Years of American Life, 1821–1861* (New York: Stackpole Sons, 1937), p. 57.

seriously. In a personal notebook that he kept during the 1820s, filled with practical political maxims and summaries of current events, Van Buren copied down a single extract from Bishop Berkeley: "A revolution or an invasion alarms and puts the people on its defence ... a corruption of principle works its ruin more slowly perhaps, but more surely."[43]

Whether it was really true that men had grown less good, it is not possible to say. But in Jacksonian society, there were clearly more opportunities for men to go wrong and fewer obstacles in the way of corruption. Commercial and territorial expansion had opened vast new prospects for money-making enterprises, and members of the business community and the legal profession took advantage of these opportunities. In fact, almost everyone seems to have been taking advantage of them. The United States, according to one member of the Senate, was a "country in which so large a portion of the people consider the acquiring of a fortune the only rational object of pursuit,—in which so great and so exclusive an importance is attached to money, that, with a few solitary exceptions, it is the only means of arriving at personal distinction. . . ."[44] And to observers like William Gouge, it appeared that men no longer cared exactly *how* they arrived at such distinction. Any means for taking hold of opportunity was acceptable—or so it seemed.

The apparent deterioration of moral restraints upon ambition and greed was no simple matter of virtue succumbing to temptation. Temptations were certainly plentiful; but it could hardly be said that the citizens of the age were indifferent to the moral depravity which seemed about to engulf them. The temperance crusade, which took shape in this era, and the camp meeting were but two of the more dramatic manifestations of a general concern with private and public morality.[45] With much optimism and vigor, many people were trying

43. Notebook, 182(?), Martin Van Buren Papers, Library of Congress, Washington.
44. Francis J. Grund, *Aristocracy in America*, 2 vols. (London: R. Bentley, 1839), 2: 240.
45. In 1826, the Reverends Calvin Chapin, Justin Edwards, and Lyman Beecher founded the first national temperance society in the United States, the American Society for the Promotion of Temperance. It is interesting, first, that Edwards, the chief organizer of the society, launched a propaganda campaign that emphasized the spiritual evils of Demon Rum. Most earlier temperance literature had spread the news of alcohol's physical effects, not its damage to the soul. The Edwards approach was, therefore, quite in keeping with the prevalent tone of moral regeneration. Moreover, Edwards' greatest distinction seems to have been his talent for organization. In this respect also, he was representative of his age. Such talents seem to have been prominent during the Jackson era—other examples being the New England textile manufacturers and, as we shall soon see, several Jacksonian administrators. Concerning the temperance movement, see Herbert Asbury, *The Great Illusion* (Garden City, N.Y.: Doubleday & Co., 1950), pp. 33–35.

to do something about the perceived degeneration of American behavior, and not the least of these reformers were the Jacksonians, who moved forward under the banner of "republican virtue."

With so many amateur moralists at large, one might suspect that the moral crisis of the Jacksonian age was imaginary, conceived by righteous fanatics who longed for a satan to battle. It was an appeal to old-fashioned virtue, after all, which had helped to sweep Andrew Jackson into the White House. Surely a nation in which there existed such widespread loyalty to the old standards could not have reached the verge of moral disintegration. But there was something substantial in the Jacksonian dread of virtue's collapse.

Although morality still had its fervent supporters, it had lost its old connections with social power. Institutions like the legal profession and the business community had become watery fellowships, overgrown and no longer capable of enforcing even internal discipline. The American bar, which had once been organized in a string of tight-knit communities along the eastern seaboard, now extended far into the interior. It was no longer tight-knit. The nation's business affairs were no longer confined to a small and compact group of merchants and bankers. The commercial community, too, had lost its solidity.

The old standards of honesty and propriety were no longer buttressed by the bar and the business community. In America during the early 1830s, support for standards of right conduct came primarily from the inchoate moral sentiments of unorganized citizens. Few organized institutions existed through which punishment might be regularly imposed upon those culprits who offended the moral sense, but not the written laws, of a community. One substitute for these reliable structures was the lynch mob. In brief and unpredictable outbreaks of hysterical indignation, communities in Mississippi, Maryland, Illinois, Massachusetts, New York, and elsewhere visited their wrath upon gamblers, frauds, claim-jumpers, Catholics, negroes, and abolitionists. It was an age, according to John Quincy Adams, of "Lynch's law; that is mob law."[46]

These were the conditions under which Andrew Jackson and his political retainers rose to power, and these conditions can be expected to have influenced their exercise of power. To the federal establishment, Old Hickory brought the representatives of enfeebled

46. *The Diary of John Quincy Adams, 1794–1845: American Political, Social, and Intellectual Life from Washington to Polk,* ed. Allan Nevins (New York: Longmans, Green & Co., 1928), p. 462; on the prevalence of rioting and lynching, see *Niles Weekly Register,* 12 July 1834, 22 August 1835.

social institutions like the legal profession and the business community. More than four-fifths of Jackson's higher civil servants had been attorneys, and almost all had engaged in some business activities as well. These were men who were likely to have encountered during their own careers some concrete manifestation of illicit ambition, social disorganization, or alleged moral depravity. Perhaps they had even dallied with fraud or dishonesty themselves. In any case, most of them would be wise to the failings of the age.

More important, the social conditions of the era would present these executives with a special set of administrative problems. In the absence of the old institutions' regulatory power, it would be necessary for civil servants to find new mechanisms for securing peaceful, reliable compliance with laws and administrative directives. The federal establishment could no longer take advantage of its connections with the old centers of social power in order to assure general and "uncoerced" obedience to its commands. Moreover, the government was less able to rely upon the moral uprightness of the private citizens with whom it dealt. The honesty of the commercial men and the lawyers who did business with the government was less firmly supported by the internal regulatory power of the legal profession and the business community. Finally, the civil service itself would bear the imprint of the new conditions. Attorneys and businessmen who now went to work for the government could not be expected to possess the same habits of moral uprightness as their predecessors—habits taught and reinforced during the course of occupational apprenticeships which had been served within strong, cohesive professional institutions. These institutions were no longer so cohesive, and their ability to achieve internal discipline had been diminished.

In the age of Jackson, major institutions underwent major changes, and these changes offer a possible explanation for the uniqueness of Jacksonian administration. Other factors which we have considered—the social positions of Jacksonian civil servants and the unprecedented nature of Jacksonian political beliefs—seem to offer less promising ways of accounting for the Jacksonian administrative innovations. With respect to the indicators of social position, there was little difference between Jacksonian federal officials and their predecessors. At the very least, these findings cast doubt upon any explanation of administrative change under Old Hickory which rests upon such factors as class interests or class-based attitudes.

The political beliefs of the Jackson men remain eligible for inclusion among those factors which helped to produce changes in administrative practice. Belief was something that set the Jackson men apart from most of their predecessors and bound them to one another. Their creed, while not unique, did inject something new into the political struggles of the age—an emotional moral crusade. The Jacksonians' beliefs consistently turned their hearts toward the salvation of the republic. But Old Hickory's men advanced no clear-cut eschatological program, and their principles remained vague and contradictory.

It had not always been so. The major themes of the Jacksonian message had once had their clear-minded exponents. Political leaders at one time had argued coherently that government should place the virtue of its citizens before considerations of expediency, convenience, security, or efficiency. The first responsibility of the state, they had believed, was to take no action which might undermine the goodness of its people.[47] But the Jackson men did not retire to such well-prepared and well-defined theoretical positions in order to consolidate their ideas. The resulting inconsistency and imprecision of their own political thought probably reduced its direct influence upon their administrative decisions. Jacksonian political ideas were primarily vehicles for the expression of feeling, and only secondarily did they provide guidance for political or administrative action.

The creed of Jacksonism, however, did turn the attention of the faithful to the apparent moral crisis of their own age. In this crisis, the Jackson men may have found a common tie. They had come to power during a period of social disorder, a time when men seemed to have become less reliable and less upright. Behind the perceived symptoms of moral decay were declining institutions—a legal profession and a business community no longer strong enough to support and enforce old standards of conduct. Old Hickory's administrators held in common their origins in these temporarily weakened institutions. Jacksonian belief made them sensitive to the unattractive consequences of this institutional disarray. In general, the weakened condition of the old centers of social power presented the Jacksonians with a new assignment: to discover and use new instruments of social control. Somewhere, the Jackson men would have to find the means to back up republican virtue with organized power.

---

47. See, for example, "Speech of Melancton Smith, New York Ratifying Convention, 21 June 1788," in Jonathan Elliot, *Debates in the Several State Conventions on the Adoption of the Federal Constitution*, 2d ed., 5 vols. (Washington: Taylor & Maury, 1845–54), 2: 258–59.

III

SPOILS SYSTEM
AND
KITCHEN CABINET

"We do not know what line of policy General Jackson will adopt," wrote the editor of the *United States Telegraph* in 1828, "we take it for granted, however, that he will reward his friends and punish his enemies."[1] Others took it for granted as well, and before Old Hickory could settle into his new quarters at the White House, the anterooms and reception chambers of the executive mansion were clogged with "friends" seeking their rewards, largely in the form of federal offices, for real or imagined services to the Old Hero during his election campaign. Jackson would soon be obliged to make good on old promises; the infamous spoils system lay not far in the future.

By the time of Jackson's presidential victory, a miniature spoils system had already been established in almost every state of the North and the West, and where state governments were not yet geared to rotation in office, there existed political factions eager to introduce this device.[2] It was not entirely Jackson's fault, then, that a phalanx of office seekers awaited him in Washington. In the crowds of hopeful place hunters that stormed the White House, there was concrete evidence of widespread public sentiment concerning the proper way in which to staff the federal civil service.

But the sentiment of the public was also Jackson's sentiment. He stamped the official seal of his administration upon the theory of rotation,[3] and his practice of spoilsmanship indicated that he in-

1. *United States Telegraph* (Washington), 2 November 1828.
2. Carl Russell Fish, *The Civil Service and the Patronage* (New York: Longmans, Green & Co., 1905), p. 103.
3. James D. Richardson, *A Compilation of the Messages and Papers of the Presidents,* 10 vols. (Washington: Government Printing Office, 1899), 2: 448–49.

tended to "reward his friends and punish his enemies"—just as the editor of the *Telegraph* had predicted. Thus the theory of rotation was recruited to the service of Old Hickory's ambitions and those of the Jacksonian coalition. The president launched his administration in a spirit of lusty partisanship.

The opposition partisans were quickly roused to anger at the prospect of being "proscripted" out of public office. The Adams-Clay press cut short the period of grace that today is usually granted to new administrations and hastened to the attack—in a way that only journalists of the 1830s and 40s knew how.[4] When they grew tired of assaulting the spoils system, they set upon other, less spectacular Jacksonian novelties that smacked of partisan machination. The Kitchen Cabinet, a symbol of conspiratorial political maneuvering, became a popular target for the journalistic salvos.[5]

But it was not only partisanship that underlay these early Jacksonian innovations. It must be remembered that the Kitchen Cabinet and the spoils system, although they had the appearance of novelties, were grafted onto an existing administrative structure, and they incorporated some of the characteristics of an old administrative tradition. It is this tradition—the tradition of "personal organization"—that we shall examine now, along with its embodiment in the Jacksonian practice of partisan administration.

From their predecessors, the Jackson men inherited the superintendency of a square, grassy piece of real estate near the middle of Washington. At the center of this plot stood the White House, and at each corner of the presidential lot, there was a drab, brick building. Together, these four masonry structures housed almost all the headquarters offices of the various executive departments.[6]

In many ways the stark, orderly arrangement of these buildings reflected the simplicity, the size, and the administrative shape of the executive branch itself. As the White House dominated the drab official edifices, so the president dominated his administration. He stood at the center of the federal establishment; the affairs of the executive departments were within easy reach of his office, and the minute details of administration were never more than a stone's

4. See, for example, *National Intelligencer*, 26 March 1829.
5. Ibid.
6. Ben: Perley Poore, *Perley's Reminiscences of Sixty Years in the National Metropolis*, 2 vols. (Philadelphia: Hubbard Bros., 1886), 1: 44.

throw away from him. Modern students of public administration are sometimes startled at the small matters which in those days so frequently managed to slip through the slender ranks of government officialdom to pass across the president's desk. The placement of a privy at the War Department headquarters, the relocation of a customhouse, and numerous petty personnel problems all managed to distract Andrew Jackson from his monumental Bank War and the vexing constitutional questions of the day.[7]

The discovery of such intimate connections between Jackson and the crannies of bureaucracy has convinced at least one writer that Old Hickory was guilty of a cardinal sin of administration—the inability to delegate authority.[8] And Jackson certainly gave every evidence that he intended to keep most of the public business within his own grasp. The Old Hero was reluctant to settle political and administrative matters in conference with his cabinet, for, as Martin Van Buren said, such councils "were too apt to be used to screen the General from proper and often most salutary responsibility." As a military commander and a president, Jackson had insisted that all business pass under his own sharp eyes.[9] He could tolerate no intermediate level of management between himself and the brass tacks of public enterprise. Cabinet members became mere administrative assistants, who carried out his will when his hands—but not his mind—were occupied elsewhere.[10]

Old Hickory's penchant for the personal supervision of inconsequential business was not new to the executive branch, and the unsophisticated administrative arrangements which allowed him to exercise his presidential authority over privies and minor clerks were not Jacksonian innovations.[11] The general's behavior was in harmony with the government's Federalist heritage, its tradition of "executive energy."

The Federalist administrative regime was intended to invigorate the executive branch so that the president might counteract a power-

7. Leonard White, *The Jacksonians: A Study in Administrative History, 1829–1861* (New York: Macmillan Co., 1954), pp. 71–72; Albert Somit, "The Political and Administrative Ideas of Andrew Jackson" (Ph.D. dissertation, Department of Political Science, University of Chicago, 1947), pp. 133–36.

8. Somit, "The Political and Administrative Ideas of Andrew Jackson," p. 134.

9. *The Autobiography of Martin Van Buren*, ed. John C. Fitzpatrick, vol. 2 of the *Annual Report of the American Historical Association, 1918* (Washington: Government Printing Office, 1920), p. 250.

10. See White, *The Jacksonians*, p. 85.

11. Leonard White, *The Jeffersonians: A Study in Administrative History, 1801–1829* (New York: Macmillan Co., 1951), pp. 70–71.

ful legislature. The scheme required that executive officers—and especially the chief executive—have complete control over their agencies, bureaus, and departments and that they not be shielded from "proper and often most salutory responsibility." The administrative arrangements which proceeded from these intentions were marked by close adherence to the "unity of command" principle. But the administrative rubric does not fully describe the nature of Federalist organization. Command was not only unified; it was personal. Authority and responsibility for the affairs of an agency were concentrated in a single human being. The functioning of a bureau or department depended less upon its formal organizational apparatus than upon the personality and preferences of its chief. Indeed, formal organizational apparatus hardly existed. To a considerable extent, the agency was the creature of its chief—his character, his commands, and his personal tastes.[12]

Whether the Jackson men were conscious of this administrative tradition is doubtful. Neither Jackson nor any of his cabinet members had ever before seen service in the federal government's civilian bureaucracy. No previous administration could boast such a uniform deficiency in on-the-job-training. What there was of administrative experience among the chief Jacksonian civil servants had been obtained elsewhere. Jackson himself had learned the ropes as a military man. It was here, claims Albert Somit, that he acquired a taste for unity of command.[13] But men of affairs might strike up an acquaintance with the same administrative principle in their civilian pursuits as well. The alma maters of Jacksonian college men were of the same organizational species as the departments and offices of the federal government,[14] and the businesses, law firms, and plantations over which Jackson men had presided were also laid out according to the same simple administrative pattern. All these enterprises were constructed according to an unstated plan which has since been labelled "individual entrepreneur organization."[15] It was a scheme of administration in which an enterprise was headed by a single man, whose personal virtues and shortcomings would be reflected in the successes and failures of his organization. He monopolized the organization's

---

12. Ibid., pp. 140, 188, 190–91, 269.
13. Somit, "The Political and Administrative Ideas of Andrew Jackson," pp. 118–19.
14. John S. Brubacher and Willis Rudy, *Higher Education in Transition* (New York: Harper Bros., 1958), pp. 351–52.
15. Louis H. Haney, *Business Organization and Combination*, 3d ed. (New York: Macmillan Co., 1934), pp. 47–49.

capacities for creativity, innovation, and adaptability.[16] In individual entrepreneurship as in government agencies, the personal character- istics and preferences of administrative chieftains carried more weight than formal administrative arrangements.

The qualities of individual entrepreneurship were well suited to the fast and fluid business affairs of the 1830s. The lone entrepre- neur needed no special permission from the state to pursue his fortune; he required a minimum of time and energy to establish his business. And there was a certain simple virtue in this personal form of organization; in such enterprises, "a fairly exact relation exists on the average between effort and ability on the one hand and gain on the other. The judgment, energy, skill, and determination of the individual entrepreneur are put in direct relation to his profit or loss."[17] Such considerations are clearly harmonious with the pri- mary impulses of the Jacksonian persuasion—the emphasis upon unaided human will and a just reward for honest labor. And perhaps notions such as these lay unarticulated in Andrew Jackson's mind as he insisted on personally supervising even the most trivial business of the executive branch.

Yet, had Jackson and his administrators looked back only two generations in the history of the republic, they might have found an explicit justification for this administrative style. "Regard to reputa- tion," the argument went, "has a less active influence when the infamy of a bad action is to be divided among a number than when it is to fall singly on one."[18] Hence, the concentration of responsibility in individual men could be expected to produce devoted and ener- getic administrators. This idea is simply the mirror image of the one stated above; instead of emphasizing the rewards of individual entre- preneurship, it calls attention to the undivided punishments that may fall upon the shoulders of an erring administrator. Such an observa- tion is consistent with the Jacksonian concern for personal morality, integrity, and individual responsibility. But it was also a point ad- vanced by Alexander Hamilton, whose place among the Jacksonians' intellectual ancestors was compromised by his brainchild, the United States Bank. For the Jackson men, whose slogan proclaimed that

16. Michel Crozier, *The Bureaucratic Phenomenon* (Chicago: University of Chicago Press, 1964), p. 186; see also chap. 10.
17. Haney, *Business Organization and Combination,* pp. 47–49.
18. Clinton Rossiter, ed., *The Federalist Papers* (New York: New American Library, 1961), p. 111.

"the world is governed too much,"[19] it would not do to express an intellectual debt to the foremost proponent of central power.

Instead, they might have been expected to follow the Jeffersonian example. Here, at least, they could find an ancestor who, like themselves, aimed to give government back to the people. But Jefferson had provided no justification for the Jacksonian form of organization. Wherever possible, he had attempted to disperse administrative duties, scattering responsibilities as broadly as he could. [20] In the previous political thought of the republic, then, there was no suitable rationale for the "personal" character of Jacksonian administration.

But the Jackson men seemed to need no rationale for their unpretentious administrative style. The taste for individual entrepreneurship was simply an organizational habit, acquired during the course of business careers and strengthened by a certain inchoate appeal—an appeal best summarized by Alexander Hamilton, hardly a Jacksonian.[21] In his emphasis upon "regard for reputation," Hamilton seems to have expressed the administrative preferences of his generation of social notables, but he also crystalized the organizational sentiments of the age that followed his own. It was an optimistic, entrepreneurial era, whose citizens, disinclined to entrust their fortunes to the workings of fate, to an impersonal economic system, or to massive social forces, liked to believe that success followed good character and that failure could be attributed to personal, not social, causes.[22] Their arrangements for the handling of business matters reflected this emphasis upon aspects of character. Men seldom pondered the fine points of administrative organization,

19. James Parton, *The Life of Andrew Jackson,* 3 vols. (New York: Mason Bros., 1860), 3: 260.

20. See Lynton K. Caldwell, *The Administrative Theories of Hamilton and Jefferson* (Chicago: University of Chicago Press, 1944), p. 136.

21. An alternative explanation attributes "personal" bureaucracy to the scale of the Jacksonian enterprise. The luxury of personal control, it is argued, could be permitted to a president or an agency head as long as the federal bureaucracy remained a small, intimate affair (White, *The Jacksonians,* pp. 533–34). As the nation and its business grew, administrative details could no longer be handled at the center of the federal establishment, and it was absolutely necessary that the president and his immediate subordinates divest themselves of some responsibilities. The retrospective character of this explanation seriously impairs its usefulness. To most modern scholars of bureaucracy, the division of labor appears valuable because it facilitates the handling of a large volume of business. It does not necessarily follow that the unitary arrangements of the Jacksonian age were designed to handle a small volume of business

22. Sigmund Diamond, *The Reputation of the American Businessman* (Cambridge: Harvard University Press, 1955), p. 22.

since personal qualities like frugality and diligence would insure success. Good men made good organizations.

The same sentiment was evident in the handiwork of the Jacksonian generation's federal administrators. It was the "personal" character of their archaic organizational pattern which distinguished it from later and more complex ventures in the construction of bureaucratic machinery. Authority was concentrated in the hands of the agency head; government relied upon his "regard for reputation" to insure the successful conduct of his bureau's business and seldom depended upon formal administrative arrangements to produce efficiency. The administrative chief could look over the shoulder of every clerk in his office; he probably knew them all by name and was well acquainted with the merits and deficiencies of each. The channels of administrative authority carried not only his orders but his personality as well, and his commands were gauged to the capabilities of those subordinates who were to execute them. The "distribution of duties among officers and clerks," reported Postmaster General William T. Barry in 1830, "has ever been founded on the adaptation of the individual to the service to be executed,"[23] and Barry gave no indication that he thought this arrangement inappropriate. Chains of command were connections of a personal sort, and administrative arrangements were not rigidly formal, but flexible and informal, bearing the marks of individual personalities, aptitudes, and loyalties.

But personal organization was not, for all its intimacy and simplicity, completely idyllic. It was as susceptible to disruptions as any human enterprise, and the obvious solution to such malfunctions was not to tamper with the formal structures of offices and bureaus, but to root out the disruptive personalities. Personal harmony was essential to an organization whose structure and operation were dependent upon personal characteristics, and harmony could be maintained only by assuring that all the subordinates of an administrative chieftain were at one with him, that their loyalties to him were unquestionable.

It is in this light and not only against the raucous background of politics and patronage that we should inspect the notorious spoils system and the Kitchen Cabinet. Old Hickory's exercise of spoilsmanship, it will be remembered, had prompted the enemies of Jacksonism to launch an unmerciful political barrage in the general's direction. The theory of rotation, it was charged, had rendered the

23. *American State Papers: Post Office* (Washington: Gales & Seaton, 1834), p. 253.

public service vulnerable to the basest sort of partisanship. The president had inaugurated an iniquitous practice,

resulting in the engenderment of abuses and enormities, vastly exceeding those professed to be reformed; such as the creation of new and useless offices, sinecures, party pensioners, and charity incumbents; the multiplication of defalcations and frauds to a frightful extent . . . with a general dilapidation of public morals, and the abandonment of useful pursuits, under the seductive and reiterated proclamation of the government Press, that General Jackson would "punish his enemies and reward his friends."[24]

Even as neutral an observer as Michel Chevalier could be taken in by the Whig propaganda. "President Jackson," he reported, "has filled all the customhouses and post offices with his creatures. . . . The President has now at his command an army of 60,000 voters, dependent on his will, whose interests are bound up with his, and who are his forlorn hope."[25]

In fact, the Jacksonian proscription was a good deal less dramatic than either the Whigs or many historians have charged. Old Hickory did not cleanse federal administration of all Adams-Clay adherents. Nor did he pack the bureaus and offices with his own henchmen. The best available estimate indicates that Jackson dismissed from office less than a thousand of the bureaucrats who had served under John Quincy Adams—about one-tenth or one-eleventh of the government's total personnel.[26] Senator Thomas Hart Benton, a portly orator from Missouri, claimed that throughout Jackson's administration a majority of the officeholders in Washington remained opposed to Jacksonism.[27] Although it is impossible to determine political attachments from the federal registers of the period, the evidence in these volumes appears to be consistent with Benton's statement. Of the Washington bureaucrats whose names appear on the employment rolls of 1828, about two-thirds were still serving the public in 1831. And included in the absent third were not only those who had been dismissed by reason of their political attachments but those who had

24. Robert Mayo, *Political Sketches of Eight Years in Washington,* (Baltimore: Fielding Lucas, 1839), p. 12.
25. Michel Chevalier, *Society, Manners, and Politics in the United States* (Boston: Weeks, Jordan & Co., 1839), p. 199.
26. Erik M. Eriksson, "The Federal Civil Service under President Jackson," *Mississippi Valley Historical Review* 13 (March 1927): 528–29.
27. Thomas Hart Benton, *Thirty Years' View,* 2 vols. (D. Appleton & Co., 1854), 1: 160. Undoubtedly many of the bureaucrats who served under Adams were loyal Jackson men. It was therefore unnecessary for Old Hickory to make a clean sweep of the federal establishment.

died, left their posts voluntarily, or been expelled for other than political reasons.[28]

There is, in fact, some doubt among students of the spoils system whether political reasons really underlay many of the Jacksonian removals. "In regard to appointments," writes Carl Russell Fish, "as in all other matters, Jackson was independent, and would willingly sacrifice party welfare to the calls of friendship or of personal whim." Old Hickory would not dismiss an officer by virtue of mere political principle; personal loyalty was the criterion for continued tenure, and Fish suggests that the unexpected moderation of the spoils system was due to its personal character. Had Jackson not so often been led by his personal feelings, he would have been more systematic in the prosecution of the removal policy, and he might have expelled every Adams man from the civil service.[29]

There is also the possibility that Jackson was not just unsystematic but that some unstated administrative considerations lay behind his "calls of friendship and personal whim." It has been suggested, in fact, that the entire spoils system had a deeper purpose than the partisan one usually attributed to it. Rotation in office, says Lynn Marshall, was one aspect of an effort to create a new system of organization in the national government, one in which "individuals could be placed or replaced without upsetting the integrity of the whole. Men were fitted to this system, not it to men. It was the administrative counterpart of the interchangeability of machine parts." In short, the proposal for rotation in offices masked a Jacksonian attempt "to increase efficiency by ignoring pre-existing social criteria like 'character' and 'respectability' and defining office impersonally, entirely by rules and regulations."[30]

The spoils system, according to this view, was not simply a means of packing the federal establishment with Jackson's own henchmen. It was an instrument of bureaucratic depersonalization. And there are certainly enough hints in the public statements of the Jackson men to suggest that the practice of spoilsmanship did represent a break with the old tradition of personal organization in government. There was Jackson's own belief, for example, that "the duties of all public offices are, or at least admit being made so plain and simple

28. Estimates compiled from employment lists in *The National Calendar* (Washington) 6 (1828) and 9 (1831).

29. Fish, *The Civil Service and the Patronage*, pp. 106, 117, 125.

30. Lynn Marshall, "The Strange Stillbirth of the Whig Party," *American Historical Review* 72 (January 1967): 455–57.

that men of intelligence may readily qualify themselves for their performance. . . ."[31] Old Hickory seemed to look forward to a time when the personal characteristics of the officeholder would not define the office, when one administrator could be exchanged for another without any disruption of public service.

Like many other aspects of Jacksonism, however, the character of the spoils system was ambiguous, perhaps even self-contradictory. On the one hand, it pointed the way toward the depersonalization of public office. But at the same time, it signified an abiding attachment to the old belief that administrative organizations were mere reflections of the individual human beings who composed them. Administrative change was to be achieved, after all, not by reworking the formal structures of government agencies, but by expelling those administrators whose personal attitudes or dispositions were inconsistent with the Jacksonian regime. The spoils system was a transitional phenomenon, which could be adapted equally well to the old administrative order or to the new one that was to follow it.

Approximately the same observations may be made with respect to the Kitchen Cabinet—another administrative innovation that drew fire from the Jacksonians' enemies. It has been suggested that this presidential advisory body foreshadowed a modern, bureaucratic mode of organization because its members were men who were not likely to leave a personal imprint upon the organizational apparatus that they operated. They were not recognized leaders with distinctive reputations, but colorless, "socially marginal" figures who did their work in obscurity. The "faceless functionaries" of the Kitchen Cabinet were Jacksonian prototypes of the twentieth century's organization men, and the Kitchen Cabinet itself supposedly represented a critical step toward impersonal administration.[32]

But the Kitchen Cabinet also had an entirely different aspect. Though it may have been an impersonal collection of "faceless functionaries," it was also the personal creation of Andrew Jackson himself, who was anything but faceless. The Kitchen Cabinet was the president's personal organization, and while its colorless members may not have shaped it in any distinctive way, Old Hickory certainly did. In fact, in the operations of the Kitchen Cabinet it becomes possible to observe Jackson's administrative style in what was probably its purest form, for it was here, in the organization which he had

31. Richardson, *A Compilation of the Messages and Papers of the Presidents,* 2: 449.
32. Marshall, "The Strange Stillbirth of the Whig Party," p. 450–52.

created as an adjunct to his own office, that Old Hickory's administrative preferences could operate with relatively little restraint—but not without notice.

Even Jackson's political allies found it difficult to accept his insistence that he must be surrounded by personal friends and cronies. When James A. Hamilton arrived at Gadsby's Hotel to assist in the drafting of Jackson's first inaugural address, he found the general in the midst of his Tennessee companions. "The General's misfortune," wrote Hamilton, "is, that his confidence is reposed in men in no degree equal to him in natural parts, but who have been of use to him heretofore in covering his very lamentable defects of education; and as he is unwilling to make these defects known to any others, he is compelled to keep these gentlemen about him." [33] Proud Old Hickory could disclose his rusticity only to his closest friends. The men who clustered about him understood his failings, and their purpose was to compensate for these deficiencies. They were appendages of his personality, who insured that the Old Hero's public appearance would not be marred by his bad grammar or his atrocious spelling.

But Hamilton was mistaken about Old Hickory's inability to disclose his faults to men outside that tight little circle of Tennessee friends. It was not long after Jackson took up residence at the White House that he began to refurbish his collection of personal advisers. Major William B. Lewis, a Tennesseean and one of Jackson's closest companions, moved into the White House with his chief, but he seems to have been assigned to tasks of less importance than the framing of inaugural addresses.[34] Lewis's brother-in-law, Major John H. Eaton, had been another of the president's Tennessee council, but as a member of the official cabinet, his business was now with the Department of War, and it is probable that this fact made him less frequently available for personal consultation.

Strangers and near strangers now moved into the strategic spots at the president's elbow. General Duff Green had first met Jackson only four years earlier, when the two men chanced to share a flatboat on a ride down the Ohio River. Jackson had persuaded Green to give up the editorship of the St. Louis *Enquirer* to beat the Jackson drum in Washington, as editor of the *United States Telegraph,* and early in 1829 the Missouri journalist was drafted for the president's unofficial

33. *Reminiscences of James A. Hamilton,* (New York: C. Scribner & Co., 1869), p. 104.
34. *Correspondence of Andrew Jackson,* ed. John Spencer Bassett, 7 vols. (Washington: Carnegie Institution of Washington, 1926–35), 5: 275 n.

cabinet. There, he joined Isaac Hill, crusty editor of the New Hampshire *Patriot*. Hill had been waving the Jackson banner and needling New England's elite for some time. "Every state in New England," he had written, "is now governed by the same aristocracy that ruled in 1798. . . ." And it was high time for a change of aristocracies. The scourge of Concord had not been one of the president's boon companions, but he was called from New England to Jackson's side in 1829. Daniel Webster, for one, was not sorry to see him go.[35] The new set of advisers was completed later in Jackson's tenure by the addition of Martin Van Buren; William T. Barry, an unsuccessful candidate for the Kentucky governorship; and Amos Kendall, a financially insolvent editor from the same state.

Kendall was to become the sinister and invisible mystery man of the new administration. He was, according to an account of 1835,

one of the most remarkable men in America. He is supposed to be the moving spirit of the whole administration; the thinker, planner and doer; but it is all in the dark. Documents are issued of an excellence which prevents their being attributed to persons who take the responsibility of them; a correspondence is kept up all over the country for which no one seems to be answerable; work is done, of a goblin extent and with goblin speed, which makes men look about them with a superstitious wonder; and the invisible Amos Kendall has the credit of it all.[36]

Men did not always look about themselves with superstitious wonder, but they did recognize that Kendall had special importance to the President: ". . . It is generally believed in Washington," wrote Governor John Floyd of Virginia, "that there is a good understanding among members of the cabinet that the wretch of a printer, Amos Kendal [*sic*], fourth Auditor of the Navy has more influence with the President than any other man. . . ."[37] Floyd sensed too that the existence of the Kitchen Cabinet had brought about a reshuffling of power. No more could one assume an identity between appearances and reality. The president had become a mere figurehead, for "[t]hese miserable reptiles, William B. Lewis, John Eaton, Van Buren, and Barry manage the whole affairs of the United States."[38]

35. Bray Hammond, *Banks and Politics in America* (Princeton: Princeton University Press, 1959), pp. 330–31; Eric M. Eriksson, "President Jackson's Propaganda Agencies," *Pacific Historical Review* 6, no. 1 (1937): 52; Parton, *The Life of Andrew Jackson,* 3: 180; and William Graham Sumner, *Andrew Jackson as a Public Man* (Boston: Houghton Mifflin Co., 1883), p. 141.
36. Harriet Martineau, *Retrospect of Western Travels,* 3 vols. (London: Saunders & Otley, 1838), 1: 235.
37. Charles H. Ambler, *The Life and Diary of John Floyd* (Richmond: Richmond Press, 1918), p. 133.
38. Ibid.

In short, the personal organization of the White House establishment had gone awry. By Floyd's estimation, and by Daniel Webster's, the "pages on the back stairs" now molded the actions of their
chief.[39] The nation was being governed by committee. But these
were the lopsided assessments of Jackson's enemies. Other observers,
no less hostile to the members of the Kitchen Cabinet, were more
sensitive to the dominating eminence of Old Hickory. The functions
of Jackson's sub rosa cabinet were seen to be less weighty than either
Floyd or Webster had perceived and more similar to those performed
by that outworn Tennessee advisory board. Virginia Congressman
Henry A. Wise reported secret conferences late at night in Jackson's
bedroom, in which Amos Kendall was not "the moving spirit of the
whole administration," but simply Old Hickory's

chief scribe and amanuensis, to write the broadside editorials of the *Globe* [the
Jacksonian journalistic mouthpiece] under his dictation and instruction, but not
with his diction. He [Jackson] was a better thinker than his scribe, his scribe a
better writer than he. He would lie down and smoke and dictate his ideas as well
as he could express them, and Amos Kendall would write a paragraph and read
it. That was not the thing; many times the scribe would write and rewrite again,
and fail to "fetch a compass" of the meaning. At last by alteration and
correction, getting nearer and nearer to it, he would see it, and be himself
astonished at its masterly power.[40]

Although the Kitchen Cabinet may have contained more talent
than Jackson's early collection of cronies, it is likely that this later
body served many of the same functions as the Tennessee council,
and its members—even Amos Kendall, "the thinker, planner and
doer"—were just as much dominated by Old Hickory's "masterly
power." The White House establishment was, in effect, an adjunct of
Jackson's personality, intended to compensate for his personal deficiencies and to extend his personal influence. It may be significant
that Jackson did not leave the organization of the Kitchen Cabinet to
chance. It was not composed of old friends who happened to follow
him to Washington, but of men purposefully recruited because of
their demonstrated loyalty and because they possessed skills—largely
literary—which Jackson lacked. Their chief function, it seems, was to
employ these skills to broadcast Old Hickory's personal qualities and
sentiments to the nation at large. Here was an emphatically personal
organization which had not come into being fortuitously or "natu-

39. Charles Wiltse, *John C. Calhoun,* 1st ed., 3 vols. (Indianapolis: Bobbs-Merrill,
1944–51), 2: 37.
40. Henry A. Wise, *Seven Decades of the Union* (Philadelphia: J. B. Lippincott & Co.,
1881), p. 117.

rally," but apparently by conscious intention. And the intention had been Old Hickory's. Evidently, the president held a preference for the informality, unity, and personal concord which were possible in a personal organization composed, for the most part, of relatively obscure men whose fortunes were directly dependent upon his own. Jackson could find little of this unity and personal loyalty within his official cabinet.

In spite of his efforts to staff his regular council with personal friends, Jackson had been compelled by political necessity to appoint a few men whose fortunes were not wrapped up with his own— Calhoun supporters like Treasury Secretary Samuel D. Ingham and Secretary of the Navy John Branch. None of the cabinet's Calhoun-ites were of such political stature that they might have challenged Jackson's authority or put him in the shade, but their presence within his official family made Old Hickory a bit wary of his formal advisory panel. Between the president and his cabinet there was not the same personal harmony that existed between Jackson and his informal council, and until Jackson could be assured of the un-divided loyalties of his regular advisers, he preferred to rely upon his unofficial political bodyguards. He depended upon them not only for their advice and communications skills but for their ability to strengthen his grasp on the executive branch. The Kitchen conferees acted occasionally as personal administrative agents of the Old Hero; they cruised about the executive branch tinkering with the adminis-trative machinery.

In mid-1829, for example, a Post Office Department clerk com-plained that "Amos Kendall and Isaac Hill are at times PMG [post-master general] or cause their incumbent to perform their acts." The two editors were in the habit of substituting themselves for the official managers of the mails in order to distribute Post Office patronage.[41] As Jackson's administrative emissaries, they tampered with the composition of the federal bureaucracy so as to suit the tastes of their chief; they usurped the regularly delegated powers of a department head in order to assure that the general would not be screened "from proper and often most salutary responsibility."

Jackson was not inclined to rely upon those official administrative arrangements which declared him to be the supreme commander of the executive branch. He aimed to assert his headship by insuring

41. Dorothy G. Fowler, *The Cabinet Politician* (New York: Columbia University Press, 1943), p. 10.

that federal officers pay him their personal loyalties. Old Hickory exhibited this tendency in the establishment of his own private Kitchen Cabinet. It was impossible, of course, that *all* civil servants be his personal acquaintances or liegemen or that some direct connection be established between the White House and every government clerk or crossroads post office. Personal administration could not survive on so grand a scale, but it could be reproduced in offices, bureaus, and departments below the presidential level. And it was.

It may be significant that members of the Kitchen Cabinet took the lead in bringing personal administration to the lower regions of the executive branch. Not long after he was appointed secretary of war, John Eaton informed his head clerk, Charles J. Nourse, that "the chief clerk of the department should to his principal stand in the relation of a confidential friend. Under this belief, I have appointed Doctor Randolph, of Virginia. I take leave to say, that, since I have been in this department, nothing in relation to you has transpired to which I could take the slightest objection, nor have I any to suggest."[42] There was nothing of partisan politics in this dismissal—nor in Amos Kendall's request that he be given full authority to appoint and dismiss the clerks who labored under him in the Treasury Department's Office of the Fourth Auditor. Jackson granted Kendall's request, but the Kentuckian fired only two of his sixteen subordinates, and those on grounds of bad character, not bad politics.[43] Jackson was subsequently most scrupulous in his observation of the agreement with Kendall. In 1834, Old Hickory wrote to the fourth auditor concerning the transfer of a new clerk into Kendall's office, and he was careful to point out: "I can not interfere to impose a clerk on your bureau contrary to your wishes."[44]

Such aspects of the Jacksonian appointment policy hint that the spoils system involved something more than packing administrative offices with political partisans. There was indeed much of this in the Jacksonian removal policy, but there was also a reinforcement of personal organization—an attempt to establish and preserve personal harmony between the head of an agency and his subordinates. If it is

42. Quoted in *Niles Weekly Register,* 9 May 1829.
43. *Autobiography of Amos Kendall,* ed. William Stickney (Boston: Lee & Shepard, 1872), pp. 311–17.
44. Jackson to Kendall, 25 October 1834, *Correspondence of Andrew Jackson,* 5: 303.

true that Jackson fashioned the spoils system to accomplish such "nonpolitical" ends, we should find evidence of these purposes in offices other than those headed by Old Hickory's intimate advisers. Such administrators, as Albert Somit points out, might have been permitted to supervise appointments and dismissals in their own agencies only because Jackson considered them to be politically trustworthy. What appears to us as "personal administration" may in fact have been political administration thinly disguised.[45]

There were, however, a number of major administrators who were not of Jackson's political circle. In the Treasury Department, several Adams incumbents remained undisturbed. Peter Hagner, who entered the public service in 1793, was third auditor, as he had been since 1817 and would be until his death in 1849. Joseph Anderson, the first comptroller, had held his post under three presidents before the Jacksonian entourage trooped into Washington. Anderson would continue to serve until 1836. The first and fifth auditors, along with the commissioner of the General Land Office, were also federal employees of relatively long tenure,[46] and their tenures grew longer still in the administration of Old Hickory. Under these five gentlemen labored about half the headquarters staff of the Treasury Department: 72 of the department's 144 subordinate employees. If Jackson's spoils system had been intended simply to staff the civil service with his political henchmen, the rate of dismissal among these 72 clerks and messengers should have been about as high as that in any other agency of the Treasury. It might be reasoned, in fact, that the rate of removal for these officers should have been even higher than that for the agencies headed by Jackson appointees. Jackson's penchant for close supervision might have impelled him to fill the bureaus of the five politically uncommitted executives with his own friends, thereby enabling him to keep a tight rein on the activities of officers like Hagner and Anderson.[47]

If Jackson's motives were not entirely political, if he aimed to infuse the federal establishment with the personal intimacy of individual entrepreneurship, the rate of dismissal for the five Treasury bureaus should have been lower than that for the Treasury offices to which he appointed new administrative chieftains. Old Hickory,

45. Somit, "The Political and Administrative Ideas of Andrew Jackson," p. 162.

46. Ben: Perley Poore, *The Political and Congressional Directory* (Boston: Houghton, Osgood & Co., 1878), pp. 226–30.

47. Concerning the political neutrality of these bureaucrats, see White, *The Jacksonians*, pp. 350–51.

according to this hypothesis, regarded bureaus and offices as the personal trusts, if not the personal property, of their administrative heads. If the head of an agency were not dismissed, his immediate subordinates could not be removed either. They constituted a unit, bound up with personal attachments and loyalties. The office itself was a creature of these ties and of the administrative idiosyncrasies of its personnel. Its operation depended upon the good character of its chief and the personal loyalty of his subordinates. These agencies were not composed of interchangeable parts; a president could not simply remove one handful of officials and replace them with another.

The findings in table 4 indicate that this second interpretation comes closer to the truth than the first. The percentage figures presented here are 1829 turnover rates for Treasury Department offices—one for offices that continued to be headed by Adams incumbents and another for those that were supervised by Jackson appointees. The figures do not tell us how many employees were dismissed. We know only the proportion of officers who departed from the public service and nothing about their particular routes of departure. Some were fired; some resigned, and some died. It is fairly clear, however, that the clerks and messengers who worked in offices headed by Adams incumbents, with a departure rate of only 9.3 percent, remained relatively undisturbed during the period of Jacksonian spoilsmanship. But subordinate employees in the bureaus headed by Jackson appointees had slightly better than a one in four chance of leaving the public service, by one route or another, between January and December 1829.[48]

Where one of the Adams incumbents continued to serve as the head of an office, the operation of the proscription—the spoils system—was restrained. It was necessary, given the characteristics of personal administration, to preserve the integrity of these agencies. The subordinates of an executive were *his* men, and they could not

48. The authority to appoint these subordinate employees was not in the hands of the individual bureau chiefs. All the clerks and messengers in the Treasury Department were given their appointments by the secretary of the treasury, and the authority to appoint these lowly bureaucrats may have rested in a higher place than the secretary's office. The *United States Telegraph,* at least, hinted that the real power lay elsewhere. "The President does not appoint the clerks or subordinate officers in any of the Departments; but if any chief of any Department appoints to office an unfaithful or unworthy clerk, and refuses to remove him upon the suggestion of the President, the President is vested by law with the power to remove the head. . . . This is a natural consequence of the obligations imposed upon the President to see the laws faithfully executed" (*United States Telegraph,* 19 March 1829).

Table 4

Subordinate Personnel Turnover in Treasury Offices, 1829[a]

Treasury Office	Percent Leaving Their Positions	Base N
Offices headed by Adams incumbents	9.3[b]	72
Offices headed by Jackson appointees	26.4[c]	72

[a]Data Compiled from U.S., Congress, House of Representatives, *Executive Documents,* House Document 28, 21 Cong. 1 sess. (1830).

[b]One clerk included in this total transferred to Office of Solicitor of Treasury.

[c]Two clerks included in this total transferred to Treasurer's Office.

simply be removed and replaced with strangers. But where the head of an office was a newly appointed Jackson man, the same restraint was not likely to operate; in fact, the desire to create personal harmony between a chief and his subordinates may have impelled Jackson and his lieutenants to be especially vigorous in the practice of spoilsmanship—at least in those bureaus where new executives were appointed.

Outside Washington, in the customhouses, land offices, and post offices of the nation, a majority of the federal officials who had served under Adams continued to labor undisturbed. And this is as we would expect it to be. Because the capital's department heads and bureau chiefs rarely encountered these bureaucrats of the hinterland, there was no compelling reason to establish harmony between the two groups, and we would accordingly expect the spoils system to have passed rather lightly over collectors of customs, postmasters, and land officers. This seems to have been the case. Of more than 8,000 deputy postmasters, for example, only 491 were removed by Jackson.[49] In the case of the field officers, however, it is difficult to reach any clear-cut conclusions concerning the practice of spoilsmanship, for they could be eliminated from the public service by means other than formal dismissal. Many of these administrators had been appointed for four-year terms, and Jackson might have avoided some of the hostility that followed every application of the removal policy by simply biding his time until the expiration of the field administrators' commissions. Jackson, however, seems not to have made very extensive use of this quiet expedient for ridding the government of Adams appointees. Of eighty-four registers and receivers in the dis-

49. Eriksson, "The Federal Civil Service Under President Jackson," pp. 526–27.

trict land offices, for example, Old Hickory renewed the commissions of approximately half, and only five public land officers who had received their appointments from Adams were replaced by new appointees when their commissions expired.[50]

Although the spoils system may have been powered by partisan considerations, its operation was guided and in some places restrained by the requirements of personal organization. Of course, such requirements as were imposed by this penchant for personal administration would hardly have been new to the executive branch. The single-headed organization of bureaus and offices, which this administrative tradition demanded, had always been characteristic of the federal establishment.[51] Arrangements for the handling of public business had always been marked by a vesting of responsibility in human beings, not in "mechanical" administrative systems. It was always a personal sort of responsibility.[52] As for the proscription, it too had its precedents. The proportion of government employees removed by Thomas Jefferson was very nearly equal to that dismissed by Andrew Jackson. Even the venerable George Washington had dabbled a bit in spoilsmanship.[53] What, then, was unique about the Jacksonian brand of personal administration?

What Old Hickory and his lieutenants contributed to personal organization was not new, but antique. Although institutions like the spoils system and the Kitchen Cabinet may have contained a potential for bureaucratic impersonality, this potential was not immediately realized by the Jacksonians. They regarded their early administrative handiwork, not as an attempt at modernization, but as the restoration of something old and respectable. They aimed to purify the federal establishment of all its new-fangled complexity, to restore "the government to its original simplicity in the exercise of all its functions."[54] When Jackson embarked on his presidential career, he

50. *The National Calendar* 6: 153 and 9: 77–79; U.S., Congress, Senate, *Journal of the Executive Proceedings of the Senate* (1829–37).

51. Lloyd M. Short, *The Development of National Administrative Organization in the United States* (Baltimore: Johns Hopkins Press, 1923), p. 23.

52. Carl Russell Fish, *The Civil Service and the Patronage* (New York: Longmans, Green & Co., 1905), pp. 1–2.

53. Ibid., pp. 11–14; Paul P. Van Riper, *History of the United States Civil Service* (Evanston, Ill.: Row, Peterson & Co., 1958), p. 20.

54. Jackson to the Hawkins County (Tenn.) Committee, quoted in *Niles Weekly Register*, 9 October 1830.

accordingly directed each of his cabinet members to make "a strict examination into the state of his Department and a report to the President, stating what retrenchments can be made without injury to the public service, what offices can be dispensed with and what improvement made in economy and dispatch of business. . . ."[55]

But Jackson's attempt to restore republican simplicity to the federal government involved more than just economizing on expenditures. The government's "original simplicity" had been identical with Hamiltonian unity of command, and it was apparently Jackson's aim to restore this old unity. He sought to strengthen the administrative arrangements of personal organization—arrangements that had grown slack and weak.[56]

Under John Quincy Adams, elements of unseemly discord had been allowed to creep into the executive branch. Jackson's predecessor had gone as far as to offer cabinet posts to his political enemies, and he could tolerate the presence of suspected traitors within his official family.[57] But Old Hickory could brook no disharmony, actual or potential. So careful was Jackson to construct an easily dominated cabinet that even his political allies were provoked to note their disappointment with the composition of this advisory body: "We should suppose that one pretty good rule was for the Chief Magistrate to consider offices not as made for himself, the gratification of his own feelings and the promotion of his own purposes, but as a public trust to be confided to the most worthy."[58] The cabinet shake-up precipitated by Jackson's falling-out with John C. Calhoun was just one manifestation of the imposed harmony with which Old Hickory's intimates were already familiar. The dismissal of Secretary of the Treasury William Duane was another. Duane had refused to accede to Jackson's decision to remove all government deposits from the United States Bank, and he announced his reservations to Jackson. The general returned the secretary's memorandum with a short note: "Having invited free and full

55. Quoted in Albert Somit, "Andrew Jackson as an Administrative Reformer," *Tennessee Historical Quarterly* 13 (September 1954): 204.

56. The old unity which Jackson perceived in the youthful federal bureaucracy of the Republic's early days was probably partly imagined. Washington's cabinet, after all, had been anything but unified; the presence there of Hamilton and Jefferson made perfect harmony impossible.

57. See Fish, *The Civil Service and the Patronage*, p. 72; Francis P. Weisenburger, *The Life of John McLean: A Politician of the United States Supreme Court* (Columbus: Ohio State University Press, 1937), p. 72.

58. Thomas B. Ritchie to Martin Van Buren, 27 March 1829, quoted in *The Autobiography of Martin Van Buren*, p. 246.

communication of your views before I made up a final opinion on the subject, I cannot consent to a further discussion of the question."[59] Duane continued to discuss it, but not for long. Two days after the return of his memorandum, he received another note from the president: "Your further services as Secretary of the Treasury are no longer required."[60] Such demonstrations of presidential intolerance led one New York Whig to note in 1834 that the president, "since he came into office in 1829, has had four secretaries of state, two of war, five of the treasury, three of the navy, and three attorney generals. Tyrants are fickle in their choice of servants."[61]

The alleged tyranny of Old Hickory might be dismissed as mere presidential idiosyncrasy were it not that we have already observed similar and related phenomena among lesser members of his administration—instances in which federal officers seemed intent upon the preservation of personal harmony in the executive branch. The general's administrative quirk is notable, too, because he attempted to give such organizational characteristics as administrative unity a permanence which would allow them to survive his own presidential tenure. In his early, tentative tinkerings with the formal structure of the executive branch, Jackson clearly disclosed his fondness for unity of command and a certain devotion to administrative autocracy. In his first State of the Union Message, Old Hickory recommended a reorganization of the Navy Department that would have abolished the Board of Naval Commissioners, a body which had steadily absorbed functions and powers rightfully belonging to the secretary of the Navy. With one stroke, Jackson would have restored the secretary to the superintendence of the department and assigned each of the commissioners to direct a particular subdivision of the Navy's business. "Under such an arrangement," claimed Jackson, "every branch of this important service would assume a more simple and precise character, its efficiency would be increased, and scrupulous economy in the expenditure of public money promoted."[62] Old Hickory would also have rid the government of an administrative arrangement inconsistent with the principle of undivided responsibility, and he would have created a situation more congenial to the operation of personal administration, in which the head of a department might truly call his agency his own.

59. Jackson to Duane, 21 September 1833, *Correspondence of Andrew Jackson,* 5: 204.
60. Jackson to Duane, 23 September 1833, Ibid., p. 206.
61. *The Diary of Philip Hone,* ed. Bayard Tuckerman, 2 vols. (New York: Dodd, Mead & Co., 1889), 1: 120.
62. Richardson, *A Compilation of the Messages and Papers of the Presidents,* 2: 460.

Another innovation suggested by Jackson would have brought the debt collecting activities of the government under the supervision of the attorney general. These responsibilities had hitherto been assigned to one of the accounting offices of the Treasury, where, said Jackson, "A want of legal skill habitually and constantly employed in the direction of the agents engaged in the service" had left many of the government's debtors quite free of their obligations. By transferring debt collection to the attorney general, Jackson hoped "that this branch of the public service" would "be subjected to the supervision of such professional skill as will give it efficiency." It was not only professionalism, however, that Old Hickory was after, but an opportunity to concentrate administrative responsibilities in a single man. When Congress responded to this request for legal expertise by creating a new office in the Treasury Department—the Office of the Treasury Solicitor—a dissatisfied General Jackson complained that he did not feel this concession was "calculated to supersede the necessity of extending the duties and powers of the Attorney-General's Office."

On the contrary, I am convinced that the public interest would be greatly promoted by giving to that officer the general superintendence of the various law agents of the Government, and of all law proceedings . . . in which the United States may be interested, allowing him to devote his undivided attention to the public business.[63]

Old Hickory's recommendation gave voice to several presidential complaints about the conduct of public business. First, Jackson wanted the attorney general to be given duties heavy enough and a salary generous enough to justify full-time devotion to the public business. Until 1814, the attorney general had not even been granted an appropriation to maintain an office in Washington. While other government offices labored in the capital, the government's legal counsel remained at his home, sending his opinions to the president by mail and appearing in person only when it was necessary to present a case before the Supreme Court. In Jackson's time, the attorney generalship was still regarded as a part-time job. The office carried a salary lower than any cabinet-level post because it was expected that its incumbent would supplement his government salary with an income from private practice.[64] But if the attention of the attorney general were divided between his own affairs and those of

63. Ibid., 2: 527.
64. Short, *The Development of National Administrative Organization in the United State,* pp. 184–95.

the government, his sense of responsibility for the public business was not likely to be very strong. His reputation would not stand or fall according to his public performance; he could always redeem or ruin himself by his private activities. A part-time attorney-generalship was thus inconsistent with the demands of a personal organization, whose mainstay was "regard for reputation."

A second of Old Hickory's complaints concerned the division of responsibility for the government's legal affairs among a number of federal officers. Such an arrangement, like the one described above, was not likely to produce a lively sense of stewardship for the legal business of the republic. If Jackson wanted the job done well and faithfully, it had to be done by one man. Finally, the establishment of personal concord between a chief and his subordinates would seem to require that men of the law—district attorneys, federal marshals, and the like—be supervised by other men of the law, not by an accountant in the Treasury Department, and this was what Jackson recommended.

Whether all these ideas ran through the general's mind it is impossible to know. But it is improbable that he thought in terms of administrative principles—personal organization, unity of command, and unifunctional departmentalization. The Jacksonian metier was not, as Leonard White points out, the abstract manipulation of administrative theory. Jackson and the Jackson men depended upon experience to guide their administrative tinkering,[65] and most of this experience had been acquired in the personal organizations that flourished in a booming, individualistic business economy. The personal administration of the public business was, in effect, reinforced by the popularity of individual entrepreneurship—a private version of personal administration—in the nation's business community.

Like the operation of the spoils system and the Kitchen Cabinet, Jackson's early recommendations for administrative reorganization clearly reflected this personal pattern of organization. The efforts to concentrate responsibility in individual men, to fuse the personal reputations of these men with the fortunes of their agencies, to establish harmony between each chief and his subordinates—these were all earmarks of personal administration. But recommendations of this variety soon disappeared from Jackson's annual messages. The suggestions for remodeling the Navy Department and the attorney generalship were first enunciated in 1829. When Congress did not

65. White, *The Jacksonians*, p. 551.

frame appropriate responses to these recommendations, Jackson repeated them in his annual message of 1830. The legislators remained unresponsive, and Jackson never presented these reorganization plans again. His later efforts at rearranging the executive branch were of a different character than these first, "personal" schemes. Something deflected Jackson's intentions from that initial commitment to return "the government to its original simplicity in the exercise of all its functions." Jackson and his administrators, fresh from smallish conquests in private finance and only recently reminded of the virtues of individual entrepreneurship, attempted to put new vigor into the temporarily disarranged personal organization of the federal establishment. And then, paradoxically, they discarded this administrative scheme.

IV

PERSONAL ORGANIZATION IN JACKSONIAN SOCIETY

Personal organization was an administrative scheme without complexity or formality. In a sense, it was no administrative scheme at all. Men who headed organizations simply performed their functions according to their own aptitudes and preferences, and these personal inclinations, as well as the nature of the relationship between chiefs and subordinates, determined administrative structure and procedure. Private enterprise's version of this unselfconscious organizational design has come to be known as "individual entrepreneur organization." In government, "executive energy" was the term that designated this administrative style. But both governmental and private varieties were cut from the same branch. In both fields, administrative organization was fitted to the administrators and not the other way around.

In a personal organization, individual character played a crucial role, and the character of the organizational chief was more important than any other. In the absence of impersonal bureaucratic rules, the chief's personality and imagination gave his enterprise form and direction. His subordinates seem to have been tied to him, and to the organization through him, by personal loyalty, friendship, and, not infrequently, kinship.

Generations before the heyday of Jacksonism, personal organization was the stock-in-trade of American business administrators. Just how it came to be so broadly accepted remains uncertain, but it was clearly popular. Private businessmen occasionally voiced administrative sentiments that bore a striking resemblance to the ones that Jackson articulated within the government. "I have a great horror," wrote one Boston entrepreneur, "of divided responsibility, preferring one common man, who has got to take all the credit or blame, to half a dozen geniuses, who put it off on somebody else."[1] The imprint of personal organization could be observed in almost all the private enterprises of the early nineteenth century. In 1809, its influence was evident in an installation of button and comb factories at Meriden, Connecticut, which were "all carried on to a great Extent by a Native, who . . . set them all up on principles of his own."[2] Indeed, almost all businessmen seem to have established their enterprises on principles of their own and not according to any abstract administrative plan. Organizations were similar to one another only in that they all reflected the whims, preferences, imaginations, and idiosyncrasies of their respective chiefs.

But the inclinations and preferences of organizational executives were surely not without some degree of uniformity. The executives of mercantile and financial houses were members of a business community, after all, and the influence of their colleagues undoubtedly limited the range of their behavior. By the time of Jackson, however, the regulatory capacity of the business community had been diluted. As Alexis de Tocqueville observed, the nation had become cluttered with an "innumerable multitude" of small enterprises. Almost every farmer supplemented his income from agriculture with earnings from some business venture. Many of these new businessmen seemed to be beyond the reach of regulation. In the nation's capital, small-time urban entrepreneurs set up shop within a stone's throw of government offices. With at least as much guile and gusto as modern manufacturers, these enterprisers hawked everything from hair oil to tooth powder. The advertisement pages in Washington newspapers of the period attest to the imagination and avarice of these businessmen.

Throughout the countryside, the best known small businessman was the picturesque Yankee peddler, who did not need to employ the raucous, attention-getting devices of urban advertising. He could confront his customers personally. The traveling salesman could practice his sharp dealing and unload his shoddy goods without the aid of gaudy commercial announcements. Rural folk were happy to have him descend upon their homesteads, with his junk jewelry,

1. Quoted in Paul Goodman, "Ethics and Enterprise: The Values of the Boston Elite, 1800–1860," *American Quarterly* 18 (Fall 1966): 441.
2. Elias Boudinot, *Journey to Boston in 1809,* ed. Milton Halsey Thomas (Princeton: Princeton University Library, 1955), p. 19.

wooden nutmegs, soapstone "soap," and the cheap wooden clocks
that always seemed to stop running shortly after he had departed for
the next farmhouse.

There were other lapses from morality more jarring and less
forgivable than the distasteful tricks of Washington merchants and
wandering peddlers. During the long, hot summers of the 1830s,
ominous news reached the capital, of riots in New York, Baltimore,
Boston, Philadelphia, Charleston, and Richmond. These were bloody,
vicious affairs—hardly in the gentlemanly tradition of the Boston Tea
Party. And the gentlemen too had changed. Philip Hone, a prominent
New York Whig with a sharp eye for civil disorder, noted that

the practice of duelling has increased to such a degree in the South and West,
and is marked with such savage ferocity and deadly determination, as to form a
stigma on the national character. It seems impossible to carry on a political
election, which is in any degree warmly contested, without an excitement of
feeling leading to quarrels amongst the most active partisans, and most frequently between the candidates themselves, which nothing but blood will
settle.[3]

such was the range of apparent social depravity faced by the
Jackson men—from the affable fraud to the destructive rioter to the
gentlemanly murderer. All these marched in the wake of declining
social institutions—a waning political oligarchy, a disorganized business community, and churches in frenzied disarray. And there beside
them walked the Jacksonian administrator. He was not insulated
from the era's social disjointedness. He led his private life amid the
hot-tempered politicians, the shrewd merchants, and the fast-dealing
farmers. He shared their ambitions and their habits, and as we shall
soon see, it was personal organization which helped him to transfer
these "private" things to public administration.

Amos Kendall, "the moving spirit of the whole administration,"
was one of these Jacksonian civil servants—and one of those responsible for some of the most significant Jacksonian bureaucratic innovations. The son of a Congregationalist deacon in Dunstable, Massachusetts, Kendall had sought his fortune as a New England school-
teacher, a frontier lawyer, a Frankfort, Kentucky newspaper editor,
and even as a playwright.[4] In none of these capacities had he been
able to make a comfortable living, and in 1829 he joined the anxious
politicians who herded together in the hotels and boardinghouses of

3. *The Diary of Philip Hone*, ed. Bayard Tuckerman, 2 vols. (New York: Dodd, Mead, &
Co., 1889), 1: 178–79.
4. *Autobiography of Amos Kendall*, ed. William Stickney (Boston: Lee & Shepard,
1872), *passim*.

Washington during the months before Old Hickory's inauguration. Here the Kentucky journalist was initiated into a new kind of profession—office seeking. The quest for lucrative government jobs had become almost as much a matter of private profit and loss as selling tooth powder or peddling junk jewelry. This, at least, was the perspective from which Kendall seems to have regarded his entry into the public service.

When he first arrived in Washington, Kendall had not planned to remain for the swearing-in of his hero; he was eager to return home to his wife, Jane, and his family. But the editor's finances were in such a sorry condition that he had to keep in mind other considerations than the domestic warmth of his Frankfort fireside:

There is no doubt that such an office will be offered to me here as I cannot in justice to myself and family refuse to accept. I do not yet know precisely what it will be, or what will be the salary attached to it. The only doubt . . . is, whether it will be a principal clerkship with a salary of $2,000, or an auditorship with $3,000. Of course, I prefer the latter, and it is the opinion of my friends that I can get it, provided I will remain here until the arrangements of the new administration are completed. Although I dislike extremely to remain from you and my children for so long, yet the prospect of securing $1,000 a year by it . . . ought not to be thrown away.[5]

In mid-February, Kendall had his first interview with Andrew Jackson. The general told him nothing that he did not already know—that he was being considered for a chief clerkship or perhaps an auditorship. Ten days later, he talked again with the president-elect. Jackson, "after saying many flattering things of [Kendall's] capacity, character, etc.," observed that he had told a friend that Kendall was "fit for the head of a department" and should be put as "near the head as possible."[6]

In this ambiguous remark, Kendall found cause for optimism. Since an auditor was fewer ranks removed from the head of a department than was a chief clerk, it was clear that Old Hickory intended him to fill the more lucrative position. But then there came almost three weeks of silence—no news, no rumors, and no interviews with the president-elect. It was not until two weeks after the inauguration that Kendall heard anything more about the possibilities of government employment—and then only as a piece of gossip. Word reached the Kentuckian that the second and fourth auditorships were to be offered to Major William B. Lewis and himself, but the specific

5. Ibid., p. 278.
6. Ibid., pp. 283–85.

allotment of the offices had not yet been decided upon. Kendall paid
a visit, not to Jackson, but to Lewis, and the two westerners agreed
that Kendall was to get the fourth auditorship; Lewis, the second.
Four days later, Kendall received his commission.[7]

The editor's appointment sent a ripple of partisan alarm through
the columns of the *National Intelligencer,* journalistic stand-by of
Washington's Adams-Clay adherents. In making places for newspapermen like Kendall and Isaac Hill, the *Intelligencer* argued, "the President of the United States has been deceived and misled, by injudicious and unsafe counsellors, into measures totally repugnant to
public opinion. . . ."[8] Kendall and Hill had been among the more
aggressive of Jackson's partisans during the hand-to-hand combat of
the election campaign. It was they who had defended Old Hickory's
good name and slandered the reputations of his enemies. One should
not place the public business in the charge of such violent political
warriors.

Kendall, perhaps by his own design, managed to reappear in the
pages of the *Intelligencer* just a few days after his debut. In order to
return the fourth auditorship to "its original simplicity in . . . all its
functions," Kendall had first canceled all his predecessor's newspaper
subscriptions. He thus tempted even the opposition press to give
notice to the presidential retrenchment policy. This, at least, was the
effect of his action. The *Intelligencer* pouted: "We are always very
glad to discontinue sending this journal to any one whom it likes not,
and therefore owe no ill-will on this score to the Fourth Auditor. We
announce the fact to our readers merely to show what *sort* of
retrenchment is to be made in the public expenditures."[9] Three days
later, the editors of the *Intelligencer* had evidently conceived a debt
of ill-will to Amos Kendall. In a full-scale assault upon the spoils
system—which had scarcely begun—the fourth auditor was singled
out for a particularly large dose of journalistic abuse.[10]

Through all the political squabbling, Kendall maintained the
stance of a man uninterested in politics, a private citizen who
happened to have found employment with the government. In June
1829, he wrote home to a Kentucky newspaper colleague:

I have long desired the day when I could retire from political turmoils. My
enemies forced me to remain in the field many years longer than I designed. I do

7. Ibid., pp. 308, 287.
8. *National Intelligencer,* 26 March 1829.
9. Ibid., 28 March 1829.
10. Ibid., 31 March 1829.

not think I am ambitious, or that I have even inordinately coveted office or distinction. This place offered me here I have accepted as a means of enabling me to retire into the bosom of my beloved family, educate my dear children, and spend my years in the full enjoyment of domestic affection.[11]

Kendall may not have been completely sincere when he declared his intention to retire into the bosom of his family, but he did at first manage to remain reasonably faithful to the role in which he had cast himself. No longer engaged in public political turmoils, he plunged into his administrative duties, assuring the president that he would "manage the office on the same legal and moral principles that [he] managed [his] private affairs, and if ever satisfied that such a rule was impracticable in administering a public office, [he] would resign and go into private life."[12] Obviously, Kendall did not expect that personal standards would prove inappropriate. He believed that there was no essential difference between standards of private and public conduct. The public business was best managed when men were personally honest, diligent, and upright. Good administration could not be secured by sketching fresh lines upon an organization chart; one gained honesty and efficiency by seeing to the moral character of public servants.

Accordingly, the fourth auditor directed his reformative energies to his employees and not to the formal structure of his office. When he had been at his new post for a few weeks, Kendall felt himself sufficiently well acquainted with the administrative ailments of his bureau to draft his first bureaucratic proclamation, which he addressed to the sixteen clerks who labored under him:

1. Every clerk will be in his room, ready to commence business, at nine o'clock A.M., and will apply himself with diligence to the public service until three o'clock P.M. . . .

3. Newspapers or books must not be read in the office unless connected directly with the business in hand, nor must conversation be held with visitors or loungers except upon business which they may have with the office. . . .

5. The acceptance of any present or gratuity by any clerk from any person who has business with the office, or suffering such acceptance by any member of his family, will subject any clerk to instant removal.

6. The disclosure to any person out of the office of any investigation going on, or any facts ascertained in the office, affecting the reputation of any citizen, is strictly prohibited without leave of the Auditor.

11. Quoted in *Niles Weekly Register,* 6 June 1829.
12. *Autobiography of Amos Kendall,* p. 308.

7. No person will be employed as a clerk in this office who is engaged in any other business. . . .

8. Strict economy will be required in the use of the public stationery or other property. No clerk will take paper, quills, or anything else belonging to the government for the use of himself, family, or friends.[13]

In things both great and small, Amos Kendall saw to it that his clerks adhered to strict standards of private morality, that they would not draw unearned profits from their public positions, and that they would not divide their interests between the concerns of their employer and any private business ventures. The fourth auditor demanded of his subordinates a complete devotion to the business of the agency.

In other offices too, Jacksonian bureaucrats imposed the strict, puritanical rule of republican virtue—as they saw it. And the *National Journal,* another organ of the Adams-Clay press, objected to the new administrative style. Duff Green's *United States Telegraph* delivered the Jacksonian reply:

They [the *Journal*] asserted that "free born, free thinking, free acting man, was turned into a mechanical automaton." We maintained "that public business was attended to, and performed faithfully by those paid out of the public money for it, and that there was none of that slowness, dissipation, or gambling now, that there had been formerly."[14]

The introduction of Jacksonian codes for administrative behavior had, the *Telegraph* claimed, brought new efficiency to the executive branch:

No man who has had much business in the Departments, but must admit there was a strong necessity of a change of some sort in the manner of doing business. There was a looseness and indifference which struck every new officer, with astonishment, and which the people here have been enabled in some degree to appreciate by witnessing the increased attention to business of the old clerks, &c. But few of them are now seen sauntering about the streets and public places in office hours. . . .[15]

Sauntering and other reprehensible activities were not even to be permitted when a government employee had put aside quill and ledger to take a rest from his public labors. He was a member of a personal organization, and there could be no fine, dehumanizing distinction between such actions as he chose to take in his public capacity and those which he took as a private citizen. His superiors

13. Ibid., pp. 319–20.
14. *United States Telegraph,* 11 May 1829.
15. Ibid., 6 May 1829.

relied upon his good character, and private vices—whether they interfered directly with his public performance or not—could not be permitted to depreciate his personal worth. These private failings were a frequent cause for Old Hickory's interference in trivial personnel matters. To Secretary of State Edward Livingston, for example, Jackson announced a personnel policy of his administration:

"That where any officer under the Government, (clerk or others) contracted debts and failed to pay them, and has taken the benefit of the insolvent debtors act, that he should be forthwith removed"—the debt being contracted under this administration. It is reported that a Mr. Ruggles in the Patent office, has been guilty of a violation of this rule. Please have enquiry made as it appurtains to your department, and if truly reported, as to him, or any other, Let them be removed.[16]

Mr. Ruggles was removed.

Old Hickory directed the postmaster general to launch another "enquiry" into the personal habits of government employees. A Mr. Payne and a Mr. Taylor, both clerks in the Post Office Department, had "been reported to be of dissipated habits" and had been observed cavorting "in the streets and Billiard Room and behaving in a manner unbecoming gentlemen, officers of the Government."

That such a disgraceful conduct may be hereafter prevented the postmaster general, whilst engaged in these enquiries will extend it to all clerks in the post-office Department, that those clerks behaving in a sober and proper manner and the Government, may be relieved from the imputation of acts, and the sanctioning of acts, so injurious to the morals of the country, by promptly removing all guilty of such improper conduct from the employ of the Government.[17]

The machinery of personal organization was well prepared to cope with the more obvious vices of subordinate employees. The intimate, personal connections between administrative officers made the surveillance of personal behavior a relatively easy task. But it was more difficult to police the moral characters of field administrators, and this difficulty was aggravated by a peculiar vulnerability of personal organization. Just as good men made good organizations, so bad men made bad ones. If the head of an office were corrupted, there was no

16. Jackson to Livingston, 6 August 1831, *Correspondence of Andrew Jackson*, ed. John Spencer Bassett, 7 vols. (Washington: Carnegie Institution of Washington, 1926–35), 5: 323.

17. Jackson to Kendall, 21 May 1835, Andrew Jackson and Amos Kendall Correspondence, Library of Congress, Manuscript Division, Washington.

device to prevent his contaminating the entire agency. It was, after all, his own domain. The case of Samuel Swartwout is one that clearly illustrates this deficiency of personal administration and also the difficulties that were encountered in supervising the federal field establishment.

In 1829, Swartwout was one of these lucky politicians who found that the new administration owed him a debt. In that year he had written with some optimism to one of his close friends: "Whether or not, I shall get anything in the general scramble for plunder remains to be proven, but I rather guess that I shall; perhaps Keeper of the Bergen lighthouse."[18] And indeed, Swartwout's hopes were well founded, but not nearly grand enough. Old Hickory, indulging one of his personal whims, perhaps, appointed his New York friend collector of customs in that city—among the most profitable posts that the president could bestow upon one of the faithful. And Swartwout was to make it even more profitable than it was intended to be. Martin Van Buren, perhaps, foresaw this possibility when he advised the Old Hero concerning Swartwout: ". . . His selection would in my judgment be a measure that would in the end be lamented by every sincere and intelligent friend of your administration. . . ."[19] It was a prophetic understatement. Eight years later, when Swartwout retired from office and sailed for Europe, the Treasury Department found a shortage in the accounts of the New York collector which amounted to more than one and one-quarter million dollars, a sum equal to more than five percent of the entire yearly budget of the federal government. Before the investigation of Swartwout's defalcation had progressed very far, one of the investigators, Federal District Attorney William Price, joined the ex-collector in London with another $80,000.[20] Irate congressional committees confronted embarrassed federal administrators with the evidence of the sensational defalca-

18. Quoted in Carl Russell Fish, *The Civil Service and the Patronage* (New York: Longmans, Green & Co., 1905), p. 114.

19. Van Buren to Jackson, 23 April 1829, *Correspondence of Andrew Jackson,* 4: 26. C. C. Cambreleng, one of Van Buren's political colleagues from New York, seems to have prompted Van Buren's statement of opposition to the Swartwout nomination. Cambreleng's estimation of Swartwout's likely performance as customs collector was even less charitable than Van Buren's: "I do not know a man less fitted to be entrusted with such a vast discretion and authority. Should he be appointed to that highly responsible office I should look with apprehension at the result" (Cambreleng to Van Buren, 15 April 1829, Martin Van Buren Papers, Library of Congress, Manuscript Division, Washington).

20. U.S., Congress, House of Representatives, *Committee Reports,* House Report 313, 25 Cong. 3 sess. (1837), p. 8.

tion, and "swartwouting" entered the national vocabulary as a synonym for embezzlement.[21]

Throughout Swartwout's tenure, no one in Washington had seriously suspected that he was dipping into the public monies. But his associates in New York seem to have been well aware of his shoddy character. James A. Hamilton, district attorney for Southern New York, had been irritated that Swartwout "was so entirely ignorant of the laws which regulated his duty . . . that he required the district attorney's services in resolving questions and difficulties from day-to-day." In fact, Hamilton claimed that he had to appear at the customhouse every morning in order to help the collector untangle the mess he had created during the previous afternoon. One morning, while he was waiting for Swartwout to arrive, Hamilton watched a customhouse clerk make out a check for $5,000 to the private account of the collector. When Swartwout came in, "taking his accustomed seat at his table, he read the check, endorsed it, and looking around the circle of persons standing outside the rail, went over to a gentleman [Hamilton] knew well as a brother and delivered the check to him. . . ."[22] Hamilton reported the irregularity to Jackson, but Swartwout had apparently quieted all fears of embezzlement. He seems to have been expert at smoothing the ruffled feelings of his Washington superiors[23] —so expert, in fact, that Secretary of the Treasury Levi Woodbury was forced to admit before a House committee that "whilst Mr. Swartwout remained collector, suspicions do not seem to have been excited at the Department that he was guilty of any default, unless it may be that the balance of money in his hands, when he was renominated to the Senate in 1834, appeared to be too large. . . ." But Swartwout had been able to overcome even the senatorial reservations.[24]

Although the Treasury Department had been oblivious to the extended pilfering of which it was the victim, the employees of the New York Customhouse had been eyewitnesses to Swartwout's crime. Had they chosen to enlighten his superiors in Washington, the collector might have found his powerful conciliatory skills of no

21. Ben: Perley Poore, *Perley's Reminiscences of Sixty Years in the National Metropolis,* 3 vols. (Philadelphia: Hubbard Bros., 1886), 1: 128.
22. *Reminiscences of James A. Hamilton* (New York: C. Scribner & Co., 1869), pp. 173–74.
23. See, for example, Swartwout to Jackson, 27 March 1830, *Correspondence of Andrew Jackson,* 4: 130.
24. House Report 313, 25 Cong. 3 sess. (1837), p. 2.

avail. Joshua Phillips, one of the customhouse clerks, told a House Committee that he and Swartwout had often discussed the collector's real estate and stock speculations, which had been financed by Treasury funds. They had also talked about Swartwout's "prospects of being able to make good his deficiencies, and have a large fortune left." Phillips had not told anyone of Swartwout's defalcation because, he said, "I was Mr. Swartwout's clerk, and would not betray the secrets of my employer."[25]

Nathaniel Schultz was seventy-three years old and the auditor of the New York Customhouse. He had seen collectors come and go since the administration of John Adams, and he too had been aware of Swartwout's embezzlement. But he had kept this knowledge to himself.

> ... We clerks in the custom-house consider ourselves as in the service of the collector, and not in the service of the United States. The "collection law" does not seem to regard the clerks of the Collector as in the service of the United States, as the markers and weighers, &c., who are appointed by the Treasury Department. We have always thought ourselves the private assistants of the collector. It was my duty to render the accounts *truly*, and credit the United States *truly*, as I did; but not to inquire into the *private* transactions of the collector.[26]

Swartwout had been able to make his office his own private barony. In this he was aided by that complex of administrative attitudes and practices which constituted personal organization. It was Swartwout, for example, and not the Treasury Department, who appointed the customhouse clerks. He also nominated all the "markers and weighers, &c.," and these nominations were approved as a matter of form by the Treasury secretary. In his own post, he resembled a Roman tax farmer more than a modern civil servant. The collector's salary, for example, came not from the Treasury Department, but from the fees he collected and from a commission on the duties paid at his port. In other words, the collector paid himself, and he paid his office expenses from his own salary, not from a government appropriation.[27] The customhouse was, therefore, something of a private organization, quite beyond the reach of the secretary of the treasury.

25. Ibid., pp. 362–63.
26. Ibid., pp. 421–22.
27. Laurence Schmeckebier, *The Customs Service* (Baltimore: Johns Hopkins Press, 1924), p. 5.

The privacy of public office was well established throughout the federal field establishment. The personal character of administrative organization made it unlikely that anyone would draw fine distinctions between public and private functions. The units of administration were not offices or job descriptions, but human beings, and it was difficult to bisect a bureaucrat so that his private interests could be held at arm's length from the public interest. Such abstractions were infrequently resorted to in the age of Jackson; nice distinctions between public service ethics and personal morality were seldom made. These conditions made for an easy fusion of public and private affairs. In Washington, private business tended to be absorbed by public. A government employee was a public servant among other public servants, and he could be closely supervised by his bureaucratic superiors. His personal financial affairs and his behavior in the street became proper subjects for the attention of his employers.

But in Chocchuma, Mississippi, or Zanesville, Ohio, a civil servant was a private citizen among other private citizens. Very often, his public duties occupied only part of his time and a subordinate position in his attention. Joseph Ficklin, postmaster of Lexington, Kentucky, since 1822, went right on with his job as editor of the *Kentucky Gazette* while transacting the business of the government in an office adjoining that of his newspaper.[28] Postal inspector James Holbrook found the postmaster of one New England village dispensing molasses in his general store, which also served as the local post office.[29] In these field offices, the public business became private, and occasionally even official regulations contributed to this tendency. Land officers, for example, were required by the Treasury Department to take up residence on the spot at which they did business.[30] The public duties of a government employee might thus conceivably be mingled even with his home life.

By itself, this blending of public and private bore no signs of outrageous corruption or inefficiency, but it was an inviting chink in

28. Tom L. Walker, *History of the Lexington Post Office from 1794 to 1901* (Lexington, Ky., 1901), p. 25.

29. James Holbrook, *Ten Years among the Mail Bags* (Philadelphia: H. Cowperthwaite & Co., 1855), p. 273.

30. See U.S., Congress, House of Representatives, *Executive Documents,* House Document 313, 25 Cong. 3 sess. (1837), p. 198.

the government's administrative armor. In an era of shaky moral standards, the indistinct division between public and private helped to make the public service susceptible to the prevalent private vices. This easy mixing of public and private, coupled with the inherent vulnerability of personal organization to the ravages of bad men, rendered the federal offices open to sloppy administration and peculation.

It was not at all surprising that bureaucrats in the field should have looked indifferently upon such injunctions as those issued by Amos Kendall to his clerks. Postmasters, customs collectors, and land officers from Louisiana to New England cared little about objections to their "sauntering about the streets ... in office hours." And if a public land officer wanted to chat with his friends while he worked, there was no one to stop him. Thomas Flood, register of the land office at Zanesville, Ohio, frequently invited his friend Charles C. Gilbert into his office, where the two could sit by the fire, read their newspapers, and talk. Gilbert had his own office right next door, but since his business was land speculation, he found it advantageous to spend his time where the action was liveliest.[31] The affairs of Gilbert and Flood became so intermixed that Elijah Hayward, commissioner of the General Land Office, finally asked the president to dismiss the register at Zanesville. Among other things, Flood had assisted Gilbert in defrauding innocent, and often illiterate, purchasers of public lands; he had also facilitated Gilbert's speculative activities in military bounty land scrip, and he had rigged public auctions so that Gilbert could buy choice parcels of land at minimum prices. And Flood, of course, did not render all these services without compensation.[32]

Other land officers were similarly inclined to turn a profit from their posts. In 1834, Secretary of the Treasury Roger B. Taney had written to the land officials in Mississippi: "... It has been represented to the department that some of the receivers of public money in Mississippi have been engaged in trading on the banknotes they receive in payment of the public lands, by exchanging them for banknotes of inferior value. I hope there may be some mistake in this business. ..." But there was no mistake. R. H. Sterling, one of the Mississippi receivers, reported that he had indeed obliged a few

31. *American State Papers,* 8 vols. (Washington: Gales & Seaton, 1832–61), *Public Lands,* 7: 274.
32. Hayward to Jackson, 26 October 1833, General Land Office, Miscellaneous Letters Sent, National Archives, Washington, lbk. 4 (n.s.), pp. 150–51.

people, including a Tennessee congressman, by accepting some bank-notes slightly more exotic than standard United States currency, but he argued that every note which he had accepted was as sound as a dollar. For his services, Sterling had received a "small discount." [33] Two years later, Secretary Woodbury questioned Sterling about a settler's complaint that the receiver had refused to accept a twenty dollar note from the Bank of Virginia unless he was paid a two dollar "discount." Sterling's response was irate: "I consider it mean and niggardly in him, after the favor which I extended to present me at the Treasury Department as a petty *shaver*." And Sterling was right. He was no petty shaver, for he retired from the public service owing the government almost $11,000.[34]

The most popular profit-making activity among the land office receivers appears to have been speculation in the same public lands that they were supposed to have been selling to the public. By itself, this was nothing new. Ever since the government had begun to sell off the public domain, public land officials had dabbled in land speculation.[35] But during the Jacksonian period, an increasing number of the local land officers began to use the government's own money to finance their speculative ventures. The most spectacular case of this variety was probably that of W. P. Harris, another of the Mississippi receivers. Harris was, according to his friend Representative John Claiborne, "unblemished in all the relations of life." But he resigned from office after losing more than $100,000 of the government's money in speculation, and he recommended that his friend Colonel Gordon D. Boyd be named his successor. Boyd was apparently a more judicious investor than Harris, for he lost less than half as much. In an often quoted report, the government investigator who looked into Boyd's case observed that "the man seems really penitent" and that his dismissal would accomplish nothing:

I am inclined to think, in common with his friends that he is honest, and has been led away from his duty by a certain looseness in the code of morality, which here does not move in so limited a circle as it does with us at home. Another receiver would probably follow in the footsteps of the two. You will not, therefore, be surprised if I recommend his being retained, in preference to another appointment; for he has his hands full now, and will not be disposed to speculate any more.[36]

33. House Report 313, 25 Cong. 3 sess. (1837), p. 148.
34. Ibid., p. 154.
35. Malcolm J. Rohrbaugh, *The Land Office Business: The Settlement and Administration of American Public Lands, 1789–1837* (New York: Oxford University Press, 1971), pp. 32–33.
36. House Report 313, 25 Cong. 3 sess. (1837), p. 189.

A "certain looseness in the code of morality" seems to have beset most land office activities. Strung out along the frontier, from Michigan to Louisiana to Florida, the Land Office's district administrators were relatively secure from the prying eyes of Washington bureaucrats. But, so blatant were the frauds and irregularities in which these field administrators indulged that it cannot have made much difference to them whether the commissioner of the General Land Office was a thousand miles away in Washington or next door. Littlebury Hawkins, receiver at Helena, Arkansas, had reportedly made open proposals to his neighbors that one of them join him in a partnership to speculate in public lands with public money; his clerk took bribes; he frequently stole into the register's office to mark as sold those tracts which he wanted reserved for himself; and he was accused of entering fraudulent claims for his friends.[37]

Elsewhere, public officers did not even maintain the pretense of public service. At Crawfordsville, Indiana, Samuel D. Milroy had been appointed register of the land office, but he did not bother to comply with the Treasury Department regulation that required him to reside at his office. Instead, he delegated his official duties to his son, a speculator in currency and land scrip. "It is with much pain," reported a government investigator,

that I am compelled to say, the character of General Samuel D. Milroy, derived from sources entitled to full credit, is that of an arbitrary, overbearing, passionate, and reckless man, exceedingly abusive of whomsoever he may dislike, and by no means calculated, as a public officer, to win the good will and affections of the people to the Government, for the mildness, patience, and impartiality with which the public service is performed. My own personal observation has convinced me that this personal delineation is not exaggerated. . . .[38]

Milroy was dismissed. His successor, a man named Tyler, was more cautious, but certainly no more upright. Tyler was one of that legion of Washington place hunters, and he was apparently deep in debt. When Jackson awarded him an appointment, Tyler requested that his good fortune be kept secret, for he wanted to make some advantageous bargains with his despairing creditors before he left for Indiana. If they were aware of his new source of income, their terms might be demanding. Commissioner Hayward reluctantly gave his consent, warning Tyler that his Washington affairs must be closed and the performance of his duties begun by 1 September 1833. Tyler

37. Hayward to Inspector Lewis Randolph, 13 May 1835, General Land Office, lbk. 6 (n.s.), pp. 17–22.
38. *American State Papers: Public Lands*, 7: 193.

dawdled in the capital until mid-September, arrived at his new post later in the month, and promptly demanded his salary for the whole month.[39]

In many of the Land Office's outposts, there was no glaring indication of fraud or embezzlement, but much evidence of plain indifference to public duties, of incompetence, or very often of both. An inspection of the land office at Tallahassee, Florida, found bookkeeping five years in arrears, and at St. Augustine, it was two years behind.[40] After a particularly aggravating stay in Ouachita, Louisiana, one government investigator reported to his Washington superiors: ". . . In the hands of these gentlemen, in common with most of the land offices I have visited, the journal and ledger, from the manner in which they are kept, are worse than useless. Ignorant of the art of bookkeeping, they do not make their entries according to the established forms. . . ."[41] And things could get even worse. "The journal has been wretchedly kept, with few exceptions, since the opening of the office," reported an examiner in Fort Wayne, Indiana. "The register permitted a small boy, his nephew, to *learn to write* in the journal, and the penmanship is such as never ought to disfigure a public record."[42]

In the face of such laxity, the "personal" apparatus of Jacksonian administration could do very little. The administrative machine operated by virtue of personal connections, personal supervision, and personal loyalties. And, because these ties could not be extended to the periphery of the public service—to the frontier land offices and village post offices—the arrangement collapsed. The end came when "a certain looseness in the code of morality" penetrated the civil service. Previously, the behavior of public officials had been regulated not only by government inspectors and proclamations from the Treasury Department but by sturdy religious, economic, and professional institutions. When these regulatory institutions weakened, as they did during the 1820s and 30s, bureaucratic reliability seems to have deteriorated as well. Under John Quincy Adams, the first rash of peculation spread through federal offices. Tobias Watkins, Kendall's predecessor as fourth auditor of the treasury, left the public service with a shortage of $3,300 in his accounts; the collector at Perth Amboy, New Jersey, helped himself to $88,000 of the govern-

39. Hayward to Taney, 7 October 1833, General Land Office, lbk. 4 (n.s.), pp. 142–43.
40. *American State Papers: Public Lands,* 7: 181–82.
41. Ibid., p. 213.
42. Ibid., p. 190.

ment's money and left the United States for Canada; Asa Rogerson, collector at Elizabeth City, North Carolina, took more than $32,000 and fled, and the collector at St. Marks, Florida, was discovered to have been engaged in smuggling. Altogether, the Jackson men claimed to have discovered frauds amounting to more than $280,000—and this in the Treasury Department alone.[43]

It is notable that John Quincy Adams was shocked and hurt to find that such things had occurred during his regime.[44] His astonishment is one sign of the difference between the state of mind which prevailed in his own administration and that in Jackson's. Under Adams, public officials seem to have been trusted to regulate their own activities. Their moral dependability was taken for granted. The Jacksonian administrators trusted no one and took pains to see that each clerk, postmaster, land officer, and customs collector was as closely supervised as possible. In short, they were more sensitive to that moral unreliability which proceeded from institutional disintegration, and, expecting the worst, they took every opportunity to inspect the behavior of civil servants who labored far from the watchful eyes of their Washington superiors.

In the General Land Office, the chief provision for scrutinizing the performance of field administrators was the system of annual examinations. These inspections were older than the Land Office itself, having been initiated in 1804, when the business of administering the public domain was still supervised by a clerk in the secretary of the treasury's office. At first, these examinations "were ... annually made rather as a matter of form." The department would appoint some respected citizen who lived in the vicinity of a district land office to take a day off from his private labors and look in on the affairs of the register and receiver. Frequently, the examiner was a friend and political ally of both officers, and it was not uncommon for him to know nothing at all about the proper manner in which to conduct the business of a land office. The report which he sent to Washington was, in most cases, completely useless. In 1815, Secretary of the Treasury Alexander Dallas made some minor revisions in this empty ceremony, which rendered it a somewhat more effective device for regulating the activities of local land officers. In that year, he dispatched a clerk from the General Land Office in Washington to

43. Erik M. Eriksson, "The Federal Civil Service under President Jackson," *Mississippi Valley Historical Review* 13 (March 1927): 531–32.

44. *Memoirs of John Quincy Adams, Comprising Portions of His Diary from 1795 to 1848,* ed. Charles Francis Adams, 12 vols. (Philadelphia: J. B. Lippincott, 1876), 8: 141.

examine the district offices in Ohio and the territories to the west. In the following year, he returned to the appointment of private citizens, but with the requirement that they must not be neighbors of the bureaucrats whose offices they examined.[45]

In the years after Dallas's revision, the regulatory muscle of the General Land Office grew flaccid from neglect. George Graham, Land Office commissioner under John Quincy Adams, allowed the inspections to become, once again, perfunctory ceremonies, and he came close to abandoning the system altogether. In 1827, he had reported to the Senate: ". . . It may not be actually necessary to examine all the Land Offices annually, yet I think that beneficial effects would result from the occasional examination of them." An occasional inspection, of course, would not have been nearly sufficient to curb the rich variety of profit-making schemes and miscellaneous abuses which could be conceived by registers and receivers. But, faced by a stingy Congress, Graham felt obliged to cut costs, and he seems to have regarded the Dallas examination system as expendable, even if it meant returning to the old friends-and-neighbors inspection policy.[46]

The commissioner's indifference to the investigatory system cannot be attributed to a special nobility of character that prevailed among his subordinates in the field—a probity and diligence that made inspection unnecessary. One of Graham's field officers was Charles C. Gilbert, who, when his days in the public service were finished, would continue to share the fireside of the register's officer at Zanesville—and, it will be remembered, he received more than warmth by his presence there. One of Graham's examiners was General Samuel Milroy, subsequently the "arbitrary, overbearing, passionate, and reckless" register of the land office at Crawfordsville, Indiana.[47] And a more careful investigation would probably turn up a few more Jacksonian frauds in Graham's field establishment. It is conceivable that these gentlemen became dishonest with the change in administrations, but it is far more likely that their vices, though active, went undetected during the Adams administration. Throughout the Adams tenure, the policing of land office operations was at best superficial.

Each of the local land offices was staffed by two administrators—a register and a receiver. The register's job was to record which parcels

45. House Document 44, 17 Cong. 1 sess. (1822).
46. House Document 235, 20 Cong. 1 sess. (1828), p. 5.
47. See ibid., p. 6; *The National Calendar* 6 (1828): 150.

of land had been sold; the receiver was responsible for handling the money that was collected in these sales. The law required that the receivers' books be examined once a year, and Commissioner Graham was prepared to do that much, but not much more. He instructed his investigators to count the cash in each receiver's office and to spot check bookkeeping entries against the register's records of lands sold. The register's books were to be inspected for neatness and checked against entries made on maps of the land district.[48] With that, the examiner rode off to the next land office. It is not inconceivable that he may have left in his trail several ingenious peculators, who had concealed their fraudulent activities by some imaginative bookkeeping. More probably, the examiner would have missed all those shady activities which did not involve crude embezzlement. Such vices as currency speculation or auction rigging would probably have escaped his notice altogether. The examination went no further than a superficial check of the books and records of registers and receivers. The transactions of a whole year had to be audited in three days or less.

The details of these administrative rituals may be profitably compared with the inspection liturgy conceived by Elijah Hayward, Andrew Jackson's Land Office commissioner. From start to finish, Hayward designed his examination system with an eye to the most perverse and ingenious frauds. "In the discharge of your duties . . .," the commissioner began his instructions to investigators,

you are requested not to communicate the fact of your appointment to any person until you arrive at the respective Offices . . . and this letter of instructions you will not communicate to any person whatever, not even the officers themselves, as the object of your mission is to ascertain *facts*, without any disclosure of motives or objectives.[49]

Hayward's aim was to take the registers and receivers completely by surprise, and since the mode of examination was to be concealed from the field officers, they could not prepare for it by any manipulation of official records. That, at least, was the intention.

The Jacksonian inspector began his investigation in much the same way as his predecessors had, but once begun, the examination was apt to take as long as a week. Like the earlier inspections, the Jacksonian examination included a survey of books, ledgers, and

48. Instructions to Land Office Examiners, 24 February 1826, General Land Office, lbk. 16 (o.s.), pp. 337–42.
49. Hayward to Inspector Charles Biddle, 15 May 1833, General Land Office, lbk. 4 (n.s.), pp. 99–102; quotations in the next two paragraphs are from ibid.

journals and a balancing of accounts. But it was a much more thorough process than the previous policing of district office book-keeping. Entries were examined to see if the land officers had obeyed the Treasury Department's instruction circulars; an inventory was made of all office furniture belonging to the government, and a report on its condition was sent to Washington; a list was compiled of every tract of land purchased by the register and receiver, and in addition to these and other details, the examiner was to forward any piece of information which he might "deem it proper for the govern-ment to be advised of."

With the completion of these copious surveys, inventories, and audits, the examination was over—at least it must have appeared so to the land officers. But it was yet too early for the undetected peculator to breathe easily. Hayward had further instructed his bureaucratic espionage agents to "make every necessary enquiry to become acquainted with the general conduct and demeanor of the several Land Offices, so as to ascertain whether it is such, towards those who transact official business with them, as comports with a prompt and faithful discharge of public duty...." This done, the examiner was to look into the personalities of the field administra-tors:

I have also to request you to enquire in a guarded and unsuspicious manner into the respective characters of the Registers and Receivers, and report thereon as to their official conduct, as gentlemen of honor, probity, impartiality and fidelity, and in doing so you will carefully conceal from all persons your motives and objectives. . . .

Hayward's policing of his agency's field establishment was not restricted to books and ledgers but extended beyond the interior of the district land office to the surrounding neighborhood and even penetrated into the field officers' private affairs, their personal vices and virtues. Just as Washington clerks might be dismissed for finan-cial irresponsibility or intemperance, so might these bureaucrats of the hinterland be removed.[50]

Hayward used the examination system in an attempt to exercise the same sort of authority over the conduct of field administrators as he had over his two dozen clerks in Washington. The investigators acted as the traveling eyes and ears of the commissioner, to detect the smallest hint of fraud or personal unreliability among the local officers. But annual inspections, which were all that the law allowed,

---

50. See, for example, Jackson to Secretary Ingham, 16 March 1830, *Correspondence of Andrew Jackson*, 4: 127.

were not sufficient to maintain the kind of personal supervision that smooth-running personal organization required. Men like Samuel P. Milroy, W. P. Harris, and R. H. Sterling could not be kept on the straight and narrow path by the investigator's yearly visit. Even the rigorous inspection system devised by Elijah Hayward could not counter all the fraudulent and deceptive practices of the public land officials. On some occasions, for example, local receivers who had dipped into the office cash managed to evade detection by borrowing money, which they used to conceal their shortages. As soon as the inspector moved on to the next land office, the money was returned to its lenders. Effective personal supervision could not be achieved through a yearly, impersonal inspection, and the fact that local land officers were political appointees with powerful friends certainly complicated the job of policing their behavior.[51]

In a personal organization, much depended upon the strength and character of the administrative chieftain. If he were wicked, like Samuel Swartwout, he could indulge his private greed with a minimum of interference from his clerks and assistants. They were his liegemen, and his evil contaminated both them and the tissue of the organization. But personal administration might be subjected to the ravages of moral disintegration even if the agency executive were an honest and upright man. Elijah Hayward, unable to extend his personal control to the fringes of his bureau, could not regulate the behavior of his field officers.[52] Broad barriers of distance separated these local officials from the puritanical rule that prevailed among their Washington brethren. Hayward's authority grew impotent as it approached the far corners of his domain, and corruptible administrators became available for corruption.

Even when administrators worked in a Washington office under the surveillance of some respectable administrator, there was no guarantee that they would conduct the public business without knavery. Such agencies might still be vulnerable to peculation and to the righteous wrath of congressional investigating committees. Postmaster General William T. Barry found himself at the head of just such a department.

The unfortunate Major Barry had probably never much cared for

51. Rohrbaugh, *The Land Office Business,* pp. 284–89.
52. There is some reason for doubt concerning even Hayward's uprightness. On at least two occasions, Jackson admonished Hayward for excessive drinking (see Jackson to Woodbury, 15 August 1834, Levi Woodbury Papers, Library of Congress, Manuscript Division, Washington).

his assignment in Washington. After a defeat in the Kentucky gubernatorial election of 1828, he had applied to Old Hickory for a seat
on the Supreme Court. In his neighborhood, Barry was regarded as
something of a legal scholar, and he evidently believed that he could
leave his mark beside those of Marshall and Story. The major was at
first granted this request, but, by some complex appointment shuffling in the early days of the Jackson administration, the Supreme
Court vacancy fell to another applicant, and Barry found himself in
the cabinet. Here, he distinguished himself by being the most unobtrusive of the department heads.[53] Yet, when Jackson's opponents
in Congress laid siege to the administration, Barry was not overlooked. The major, in fact, seems to have suffered most from the
attack.

Many years after the affair had passed, Martin Van Buren recalled
how it had all come about:

> Mr. Clay's co-adjutors in the Senate . . . all contributed in blowing the trumpet
> of distrust and alarm. . . . Mr. Ewing of Ohio, a most indefatigable agitator,
> possessed of highly respected talents, and capable of almost any degree of
> physical indurance, was made chairman of the Committee on Post Offices. The
> overhauling of this department had . . . been regarded by Mr. Clay as a rich mine.
> He had been brought up with Major Barry, who had unhappily been placed at its
> head, and knew him to be an honest man, of kind and generous disposition; but
> illy qualified to resist the importunity of that class, which is always to be found
> besieging the Treasury. . . .[54]

Senator Ewing's committee launched two brief, critical reports in
the direction of the administration during the following two sessions
of Congress. The investigation of the Post Office Department was
also taken up by a select committee of the House, probably as a
measure for the defense of the department. A majority of the
representatives on this special panel were Jackson men, but they
could not prevent the minority from issuing a 150-page dissent to
their final report.

The Senate committee, "blowing the trumpet of distrust and
alarm," noted the trends which had been established during Major
Barry's regime. The major's predecessor in the Adams administration,
John McLean, had left the department with a healthy surplus—well
over $300,000, in fact. Just a few years of the major's amicable
mismanagement had thinned this margin considerably. By April

---

53. See *The Autobiography of Martin Van Buren,* ed. John C. Fitzpatrick, vol. 2 of the
Annual Report of the American Historical Association, 1918 (Washington: Government
Printing Office, 1920), p. 545.

54. Ibid., p. 744.

1834, the department's financial cushion had been reduced to a bed of nails: the Post Office was almost a million dollars in the red.[55]

Just how every dollar was disposed of, it is not easy to know, but it is fairly certain that a large part of the money ended up in the pockets of private mail contractors. In the absence of government-owned facilities for the transportation of the mails, these enterprising gentlemen supplied horses, coaches, armed guards, and postriders. They were paid from the funds of the Post Office Department, and if they were diligent, influential, and venal, they could get a great deal more than their services were worth.

The Post Office treasury could be raided in a variety of ways, and the postal entrepreneurs managed to think of most of them. They established fictitious companies which submitted bids far below those that any legitimate contractor could afford. The nonexistent firms would be awarded the contracts, and when they failed to provide performance bond, one of the "old and faithful contractors" would step forward to serve the public—at a higher price. In order to complicate the competitive bidding system, a greedy contractor could combine a number of routes under one price, thus making it difficult for the chief clerk, who supervised the letting of contracts, to compare the bids. The chief clerk, however, seems not to have minded the inconvenience. The contractors found that it was also possible to circumvent the bidding process by submitting "improved bids"—offering standard service at one price and "improved service" at another. The Post Office seems to have been interested in getting the best that was to be had.[56]

Occasionally, a contractor might combine several methods in order to achieve satisfactory results. Peck, Babcock, and Burt, one of the mail contracting companies, submitted a combined bid for five routes "at $9,050, or, with an alteration, at $11,050. It was accepted at the latter amount." The businessmen who dealt with the government could, however, demonstrate an extreme lack of imagination. One of the mail carriers managed to win a contract with a bid that combined thirty-eight routes under one price. But some of his colleagues in the business showed considerable ingenuity. In 1831, James "Land Admiral" Reeside, whose stagecoach armada made him one of the grandest of the postal entrepreneurs, submitted a $40 bid

55. U.S., Congress, Senate, *Executive Documents,* Senate Document 422, 23 Cong. 1 sess. (1834), pp. 1–3.

56. Leonard White, *The Jacksonians: A Study in Administrative History, 1829–1861* (New York: Macmillan Co., 1954), pp. 153–55.

for the thirty-one mile route between Hagerstown, Maryland, and McConnellstown, Pennsylvania. For $99, he promised the government "improved service." When he won the contract, Reeside claimed that the $40 and $99 sums had been inserted mistakenly by his clerk; they should have read $1,400 and $1,999. Reeside kept his contract at $1,900 a year, having magnanimously consented to a $99 loss on his "improved" bid.[57]

The House Committee was disturbed by all these evidences of injudicious administration, but it was far more upset by another aspect of the Post Office Department's lax management—one that had less to do with the bidding process itself. Once a contract had been awarded, it was possible for a contractor to receive "additional allowances." These payments above the contracted price for transporting the mails were granted for supposed improvements in service or special hardships encountered in providing service, and they were entirely free of the bidding process. In the absence of competitive pricing, the avarice of postal enterprisers was restrained only by the sternness of the Post Office Department. It was not a very powerful restraint. The contractors soon discovered that they could wheedle substantial price increases from the government. Stockton, Stokes, and Company, for example, won the contract for the mail routes from Baltimore to Washington and from Baltimore to Wheeling. Their original price had been $4,500 a year. Two years later, it had risen to $38,500 and, shortly after that, to about $57,000—a total increase of more than 1,200 percent.[58] The mail carriers often provided unnecessary services so that their contracts could be well padded with the additional allowances. The House Committee reported that "horse routes at once or twice a week [were] sometimes improved into post coach routes." And, apparently, there were many businessmen who never bothered to provide all the extra services for which they were paid.[59]

In the face of so many abuses, even the Jackson men on the House Committee were compelled to frame a conclusion critical of Post Office administration:

The finances of this department have been managed without frugality, system, intelligence, or adequate public utility.... The mode of preparing advertise-

57. House Report 103, 23 Cong. 2 sess. (1835), pp. 16, 28; Senate Document 422, 23 Cong. 1 sess. (1834), p. 11; Poore, *Perley's Reminiscences*, 1, 98–99.

58. Amos Kendall to B. F. Butler, Attorney General, 30 June 1835, Post Office Department, Letterbooks of the Postmaster General, National Archives, Washington, lbk. A, pp. 231–32.

59. House Report 103, 23 Cong. 2 sess. (1835), pp. 11–12.

ments for mail contracts has practically inverted the ends of the law which enjoined it. . . . The practice of granting extra allowances has run to wild excesses; some illigitimate, and therefore without apology. . . .[60]

But Major Barry was spared the embarrassment of the most serious congressional accusations. He may have been incompetent, but he meant well, and the House Committee repeatedly did "not discover sufficient reason to call in question the good faith of the Postmaster General."[61] The pernicious extra allowances were not, after all, originated by the major. They had been distributed by Postmaster General McLean, as well, and by his predecessors all the way back to 1814.[62] And the Post Office Department had looked with benevolence upon "old and faithful contractors" long before the good-hearted Major Barry had begun to handle its affairs.[63] It is likely that he assented to this liberal policy under the apprehension that it was a venerable postal precedent, and in this he may have been correct. But the precedent was applied to particular cases by an administrator who was probably less upright than Major Barry and who seems to have known how to profit from the major's weaknesses. It was the jovial Reverend Obadiah Brown who, as Barry's chief clerk, zestfully presided over the liquidation of the department's revenue.

Brown was a bureaucratic veteran. When Amos Kendall arrived in Washington, he found the Reverend Brown already established in the Post Office Department with a salary of $1,700—at a time when standard income for an ordinary clerk was only $1,000 a year. Brown and Kendall had shared a boarding house, and the Kentuckian had been amused by the Reverend's habits. "Mr. Brown," Kendall had written to his wife, "though a Baptist minister, is a cheerful, jolly man, who loves good eating and drinking and delights in a joke. He is scarcely ever serious except at prayers or in the pulpit."[64] One more thing the Reverend took seriously, and that was money. His connivance made it possible for the mail contractors to plunder the Post Office treasury.

Brown was charged with the supervision of the so-called Contract Office. It was the Reverend who drew up the advertisements for mail

60. Ibid., pp. 50–51.
61. Ibid., p. 28.
62. Ibid., p. 17; Barry to H. W. Connor, Chairman of House Select Committee, 24 January 1835, Post Office Department, lbk. A, pp. 138–39.
63. Francis P. Weisenburger, *The Life of John McLean: A Politician of the United States Supreme Court* (Columbus: Ohio State University Press, 1937), p. 44.
64. *Autobiography of Amos Kendall*, p. 288.

transportation bids and awarded the contracts once the bids were received. In this capacity, he carefully tended to the interests of old and faithful contractors, but not to those of the department. A good sample of Brown's handiwork is his solicitous handling of some contracts in which James Reeside was interested.

In 1831, the routes from Bedford, Pennsylvania, to Blair's Gap and from Bedford to Cumberland, Maryland, had been awarded to an inconspicuous contractor named James Clark. Clark had carried the mails over these routes once a week on horseback, and his price for both of them was $275. In 1832, James Reeside submitted a bid for the Bedford contracts. By the Land Admiral's estimation, the volume of the Bedford mails had increased to such an extent since Clark began his service that it would be necessary to make three trips a week on each of the two routes, and nothing less than a four-horse coach would be able to do the job. Reeside won the contract, and the price went up to $4,500. Reeside soon discovered that so much mail passed between Bedford and Blair's Gap that it would be necessary to make a daily trip between the two villages. He calculated the additional expense at $2,911.72, and Brown awarded him an extra allowance in that amount. In 1833, Major Barry may have become suspicious of Brown's activities, for he transferred the Reverend to other duties. Soon after Brown's reassignment, the Reeside contract was reduced by almost $4,000, and in 1834, the Bedford routes were returned to horseback transportation at $505 a year. In its investigation of these violent and mysterious oscillations of contract prices, the House Committee found that Reeside had never carried the Bedford mails in a four-horse post coach. They were usually transported on horseback or at best in a two-horse stage.[65]

Brown's dealings with Reeside certainly appear suspicious, but the evidence convicts the Reverend of nothing more immoral than stupidity. Other of his transactions were more damning. Sometime in 1832, Obadiah Brown became interested in a piece of real estate and a horse belonging to John T. Temple, a Post Office Department clerk. Temple, in turn, was interested in moving west, to the Michigan Territory, and he wanted to sell his property. But he did not intend to strike out for the frontier, like so many other settlers, without any assurance of a steady income—which for him meant a mail contract. While Brown dickered with Temple over the sale of Temple's property, Temple negotiated with Brown for a profitable

---

65. House Report 103, 23 Cong. 2 sess. (1835), pp. 32–33.

mail route. But the transaction was complicated by a regulation which prohibited department employees from investing in postal contracts. Temple, therefore, had to submit his bid in the name of Asahel Savery, a friend who lived in the Michigan Territory.

Until the Senate Committee unearthed the transaction, things had gone smoothly for Brown and his clerk. Temple and Savery had asked for the mail route between Green Bay and Chicago. The Reverend "accidentally" excluded that route from the customary advertisement for bids. Savery was awarded the contract at $3,500 a year, and he immediately submitted a request for an extra allowance of $1,000—in Temple's handwriting. It was granted. Brown convinced Major Barry that there was nothing improper in transferring the contract to Temple. Temple resigned and moved west.

While the contract negotiations were proceeding, Brown and Temple agreed upon a satisfactory price for Temple's horse and real estate—$3,000. But Brown did not have that much cash available, so he approached James Reeside and one of Reeside's partners, William Slaymaker. These gentlemen gave him a $3,000 "loan." Two months later, Reeside, Slaymaker, and Company received an extra allowance of $10,000 for "hardship" on the route between Philadelphia and Pittsburgh.[66]

The extraordinary fusion of Reverend Brown's private transactions with the public dealings of the Post Office was, perhaps, a logical consequence of that Jacksonian administrative policy which included the personal affairs of government employees within the public sphere. The personal mode of organization tended to muddy the distinction between public and private. This is not to say that men of the Jacksonian era were incapable of separating public from private; certainly the House and Senate investigating committees recognized that there was some sort of difference between the two and that certain mixtures of them were improper. But the state of administrative organization was not yet adapted to such distinctions.

In the Jacksonians' personal style of organization, the functions of an agency do not seem to have been clearly distinguished from the men who performed them. "The distribution of duties among officers and clerks," Major Barry had noted, "has ever been founded on the adaptation of the individual to the service to be executed." [67] Men did not simply fill positions; in a sense, they *were* positions.

66. Senate Document 422, 23 Cong. 1 sess. (1834), pp. 10–11; *Niles Weekly Register,* 29 November 1834.
67. *American State Papers: Post Office* (Washington: Gales & Seaton, 1834), p. 253.

Such habits of thought are evident even in the bureaucratic titles which dotted the federal registers of the day. There was no Audit Division for Navy Accounts, but instead an Office of the Fourth Auditor of the Treasury.[68] Not the function, but the performer of it received the attention of Jacksonian administrators and their predecessors. The focus of their administrative regime lay in the personal characters of government employees, not in bureaucratic apparatus. The principal reliance of the federal establishment was on the personal goodness of its civil servants.

But an administrative order which took its form and sustenance from the personal talents and temperaments of its administrators was susceptible to a potentially troublesome tendency—the tendency for its "public" affairs to be absorbed by the private or personal concerns of its administrators. It was no easy task to make any practical distinction between public and private functions. Some agencies met this difficulty by annexing the private segment—a man's private finances and his street behavior—to the public. Because they spoke for his personal character, these private things were perceived to be directly relevant to a bureaucrat's public performance. His official duties were shaped by his own capabilities and character. If he were corrupted, his public functions would be polluted as well.

Just as a government agency might assume authority in the private affairs of its employees, so its employees might look upon their public duties as not very different from any of their other activities. Old Hickory himself found occasion to complain about those bureaucrats among whom "office is considered as a species of property, and government rather as a means of promoting individual interests than as a means created solely for the service of the people."[69] But even in Jackson's own administration, there were civil servants who turned a profit from their offices, and others who made places in their bureaus for sons, brothers, and nephews.[70]

But nepotism and curious titles like "Fourth Auditor of the

68. The Jacksonians later attempted to change these Treasury Department titles to reflect the functions performed in each office, but the reorganization plan that incorporated these changes was never enacted by Congress.

69. James D. Richardson, *A Compilation of the Messages and Papers of the Presidents*, 10 vols. (Washington: Government Printing Office, 1899), 2: 448–49.

70. The federal registers of the Jackson period list a great many officials who appear to have been related to one another. Bureaucrats with identical surnames frequently appear within the same bureau. For a detailed treatment of kinship in the Jacksonian civil service, see Sidney H. Aronson, "Status and Kinship in the Higher Civil Service: The Administrations of John Adams, Thomas Jefferson, and Andrew Jackson" (Ph.D. dissertation, Columbia University, Department of Sociology, 1961), p. 348.

Treasury" had been part of the federal establishment since the days of George Washington. Presumably, there had also existed that same privacy of public office which was to plague Andrew Jackson. Long before Old Hickory assumed the duties of the presidency, for example, the Nourse family of Virginia had staked its claim upon the federal establishment. Altogether, about twelve of the Nourses—brothers, sons, and nephews—managed to become public servants at one time or another, and the family seems to have developed particularly strong proprietary rights in the War Department and the Register's Office of the Treasury.[71] Until the spoils system whisked many of them from the public service, no one seems to have seriously questioned the Nourses' claim to these agencies. There was nothing sinister in this arrogation of public offices by a private family.

The mixture of public and private could cut the other way as well. In the Post Office Department, for example, officials frequently found themselves exercising authority in the supposedly "private" affairs of private mail contractors. In 1803, Postmaster General Gideon Granger had attempted to arbitrate a personal dispute between two partners of a mail contracting firm.[72] John McLean, Major Barry's predecessor, had tried in 1826 to exercise some control over a contractor's choice of a place to live. The postal entrepreneurs, McLean thought, should settle down in the neighborhoods of their mail routes. "It is desirable," he explained, "that all who have any agency in the operations of this Department should, as far as practicable devote their personal attention to the same." The contractor answered, protesting, he said, "all right which you seem to claim of selecting my place of residence," and denying that "the power of the Postmaster General extends beyond the faithful performance of my contract."[73] Thus might the contractors reason, but McLean had evidently made up his mind concerning the importance of personal supervision. Duties were best performed when men felt a special, personal responsibility for them.

In none of these mixtures of public and private was any great danger perceived. But, in the Jacksonian era, it was suddenly possible for House and Senate investigators of the Post Office Department to discover evil abuses in the "intermingling of public and individual

71. Maria Catharine Nourse Lyle, comp., *James Nourse and His Descendants* (Lexington, Ky.: Transylvania Printing Co., 1897), pp. 16–123.
72. *American State Papers: Post Office*, p. 38.
73. Ibid., p. 148.

interests, of official and unofficial transactions. . . ."[74] Charges of corruption were aimed at the blending of public and private only when men believed that such mixtures might dilute the virtue of the public service. At a time when the regulatory power of private institutions—like the business community—was seriously weakened, the scale and extent of corruption in private affairs were likely to increase. The intermixture of public and private affairs, previously regarded as a relatively harmless practice, now became one of the means by which the Jacksonian era's apparent moral laxness might penetrate the federal establishment.

The merger of public and private business was in turn facilitated by a certain administrative state of mind, which we have called personal organization. The administrative arrangements that accompanied this variety of bureaucratic thinking were simple and themselves "personal." Responsibility for the conduct of public business was of a personal kind; it rested upon the shoulders of individual men and was seldom distributed among the members of a board or conceived as the collective obligation of an office or a bureau. Within the administrative units commanded by these men of responsibility labored clerks and assistants who were connected to their duties by similar, personal ties. Administrative assignments were gauged to individual character and talent, and a subordinate bureaucrat was attached to his bureau by personal connections with his chief. Administrative organization reflected personal characteristics. At many places in the executive branch, administrative structure itself bore witness to the presence of particular breeds of men with particular temperaments and talents.

Modern studies of "informal" organization indicate that administrative units are still molded by the habits and personalities of their members. But the very identification of such phenomena as informal indicates that they represent departures from something formal—an impersonal and abstract structure that has been superimposed upon bureaucratic activities. The Jacksonians and their predecessors could boast no such apparatus. Of formal structures they had little more than the Constitution and a rudimentary division of administrative labor among the cabinet departments. The essential characteristic of personal organization was this freedom from administrative abstraction. Personal organization rested, not upon sophisticated bureaucratic arrangements, but upon good character.

74. House Report 103, 23 Cong. 2 sess. (1835), p. 49.

In the absence of elaborate, formal structures, an agency could have no organizational being which transcended its officers and clerks and the personal connections between them. It was this essential humanity of administrative organization which made it particularly vulnerable to the inroads of moral deterioration. Federal agencies were susceptible to human failings. When administrators became corrupt, administration itself became an abettor of evil. Chains of command and divisions of labor depended, after all, only upon the commanders and the laborers. Evil was easily transferred from public officers to the agencies in which they served.

But the Jacksonians were not moral philosophers, and it cannot have made much difference to them whether peculation was personal or organizational—whether public sin infested only administrators or whether it also contaminated some bureaucratic abstraction called an organization. They saw only the men and not the abstractions. The important question was a practical one: how to keep public officers honest. In this connection, the superficial aspects of personal organization—like unity of command and personal supervision—became essential. We have already seen how such administrative characteristics expedited the entry of evil into the public service. Because the New York Customhouse was his private estate, Samuel Swartwout could embezzle with impunity. His clerks were his administrative valets, unable to question his actions because they were *his* men and not the government's. The field officers of the General Land Office were free to abuse the privileges of their positions because they were *their own* men. Because Elijah Hayward could not exercise his personal supervision over their activities, they could pursue their own interests to the injury of the public's. Finally, Obadiah Brown could serve the old and faithful contractors because his chief was without the personal power to command his service. Major Barry, a "good, but not a great man,"[75] was incapable of personal supervision. He was a psychological weakling.

In all three of these cases, a breakdown of personal supervision occurred. Swartwout was corrupt; Major Barry was weak; and Hayward was unable to establish the personal connections needed to bind a personal organization together. In each case, too, the spread of corruption was advanced by the informality of government organization. Because administrative organization was shaped by the personal characteristics of bureaucrats, it imposed no independent and impersonal check upon their activities. Reverend Brown could usurp

75. *Autobiography of Amos Kendall,* p. 105.

the powers of Major Barry and other officers of the Post Office Department because those powers were seldom precisely or permanently defined. They depended upon "the adaptation of the individual," and Brown chose to adapt them to his own purposes and to those of the old and faithful contractors.

Personal organization depended upon the goodness and strength of individual human beings. When institutional decline made men less likely to adhere to old standards of conduct, and therefore less reliable, personal organizations became unreliable, too. The uniqueness of the Jacksonian administrators was their sensitivity to this apparent moral decay. Executives of the Adams bureaucracy, like George Graham, seemed content to assume that their subordinates were fundamentally decent and that field administrators practiced the same standards of conduct which had prevailed for generations in the American legal profession and business community. The policing of the federal establishment was just a matter of form. Under Jackson, the administrative chiefs tended to be less certain of their subordinates' fidelity. The resolution of such uncertainties was at first a simple reinforcement of personal organization, to assure that an executive's underlings would be his own men and that employees would feel a strong personal responsibility for their public performances. Jackson's reorganization plans for the Navy Department and the attorney generalship—and even the spoils system itself—betrayed this concern. But the "personal" reorganization plans disappeared, and the Jackson men moved on to a new set of solutions.

If the personal strength of department heads could not be relied upon, it was sensible to attempt impersonal or mechanical supervision, to devise a system that would continue to operate whether Major Barry or Samuel Swartwout or Andrew Jackson stood at its head. If the moral weaknesses of civil servants were easily transferred to their public performances, the possibility of organizational corruption might be reduced by separating bureaucratic duties from the men who performed them. For, if administrative organization were conceived as a collection of job descriptions, the honesty or dishonesty of any particular bureaucrat would be relatively unimportant to the functioning of the agency. The bureau would no longer take its character from the characters of its members. And, more practically, if duties were precisely defined and limited, a corrupt administrator would find it difficult to exercise his dishonesty without restraint. Certain activities would be beyond his reach; administrative organization could transcend and counteract the human failings of the age.

V

ADMINISTRATIVE REORGANIZATION

When the tumult of congressional investigation subsided, and the dust began to settle on bulky committee reports, the Post Office Department found itself burdened with an administrative pariah, in the person of Obadiah Brown. Brown, obligingly, resigned in a huff:

I have been made an object of public animadversion for the last five years, both in the newspapers and in Congress; and though I have borne it quietly, without reply, believing it to be assigned only for political effect, it has been my settled intention as soon as it could be done with propriety, to withdraw from a field so uncongenial with my feelings.[1]

The pliant Major Barry lingered on for a few months and finally gave up his cabinet post to be appointed ambassador to Spain. The major left the capital with a pathetic pledge to Jackson that in "all time to come, whilst I live, you will find in me, although not an able, yet a sincere friend of your administration."[2] Barry never reached Madrid. In October 1835, a packet boat to New York brought the news that he had died in London.[3]

In the capital, an effort was already being made to repair the damage done by Barry's administrative ineptitude. The president had recognized the need for a thorough housecleaning in the Post Office Department, and he selected Amos Kendall to handle the job. Kendall's fidelity as fourth auditor, claimed a Jacksonian magazine,

and in every station where he was ever employed, the remarkable clearness and energy of his mind, its method and love of order, the firmness of his character,

1. *Niles Weekly Register,* 7 February 1835.
2. Barry to Jackson, [?] April 1835, Post Office Department, Letterbooks of the Postmasters General, National Archives, Washington, 1bk. A, p. 197.
3. *Niles Weekly Register,* 17 October 1835.

and inexhaustible capacity for business and mental labor, turned the thoughts of General Jackson (one of the most sagacious judges of men) upon him as a proper person to retrieve the affairs of the Post Office Department. . . .[4]

The virtues of the new postmaster general were perhaps overstated, but so were his vices. The opposition press had drawn sinister portraits of him and his allegedly malevolent influence upon the administration, "and it is some relief to the timid," wrote Harriet Martineau, "that his now having the office of Postmaster General affords opportunity for open attacks upon this twilight personage. . . ."[5] But for some loyal Jacksonians, Kendall's notoriety was cause for worry. Roger B. Taney, for example, sensed trouble: '. . . The proposed change in the Post Office Department has become known and is attracting public attention. From what I see and hear, I fear that it will be badly received by many of our friends and will create some excitement among them."[6]

Old Hickory had shrewdly selected a postmaster general who was larger than life, a political phantom whose decisions would be vested with an importance that the activities of ordinary men could not possess. Kendall's retooling of the Post Office bureaucracy would appear far more dramatic than it actually was, and the Jackson administration would be purged of the blemishes caused by previous mismanagement. This, at least, seems to have been the result of Kendall's appointment. The press paid far more attention to his organizational reforms than it had to the administrative puttering of the colorless Major Barry. Even historians of the federal establishment, like Leonard White, tend to give credit to the Kentucky editor for administrative schemes which were originally conceived by the major or his predecessors. And Kendall was not entirely innocent of promoting such misapprehensions.

He swept into the Post Office with a flourish, followed by two clerks from the Fourth Auditor's Office, and he immediately appointed Preston S. Loughborough, a boyhood friend from Massachu-

4. "Amos Kendall," *The United States Magazine and Democratic Review* 1 (March 1838): 40.
5. Harriet Martineau, *Retrospect of Western Travels,* 3 vols. (London: Saunders & Otley, 1838), 1: 158.
6. Taney to Van Buren, 25 March 1835, Martin Van Buren Papers, Library of Congress, Manuscript Division, Washington. Two months later, Taney had sharply revised his estimate of the situation. "You are aware," he wrote to Van Buren, "that I entertained some apprehensions about the manner in which Mr. Kendall's appointment as Post Master General would be received. I am now convinced that I was entirely mistaken. The appointment is popular—decidedly popular—with the great body of the people. . ." (Taney to Van Buren, 12 May 1835, Van Buren Papers).

setts, chief clerk of the department.[7] Kendall directed Loughborough to assume temporary responsibility for the department's
financial affairs.[8] On the following day he eliminated most of those
affairs by ordering postmasters to accept the drafts of no contractors
except by special arrangement with the office of the postmaster
general.[9] In short, no one was going to be paid until Kendall could
get things straightened out. With the department's financial condition frozen, Kendall occupied himself with the task of administrative
reorganization.

The department's Washington headquarters, where Obadiah
Brown, chief clerk and treasurer, had stood foursquare for the old
and faithful contractors, was the first target for Amos Kendall's
"method and love of order." For the purposes of Post Office administration, Kendall divided the nation into a northern and a
southern region—one to be supervised by each of the two assistant
postmasters general. The assistants were "to receive all applications
for changes in Post Offices and Postmasters . . . [and] prepare each
case for the decision of the Postmaster General. . . ." They were also
to superintend the letting of contracts and contract performance
within their respective divisions and each week they were to prepare
reports for Kendall. But the assistants were to be excluded from the
financial management of the department:

After closing all accounts up to 1st July, 1835, the duties of Assistants will be
confined exclusively to Post Offices and Postmasters, contractors and contracts,
it being the chief object of this arrangement to obtain a systematic, rigid, and
increasing supervision over these Agents of the Department. . . .[10]

Kendall's new scheme appeared in full in the pages of the *Niles
Weekly Register*.[11] Major Barry's organization plans had never enjoyed such publicity, and it is probable that few people noticed the
similarity between Kendall's administrative design and an earlier one
conceived by the major. Barry, too, had split the nation into northern and southern divisions, and he had charged each of the assistant
postmasters general with the supervision of one section.[12] Both

7. *Autobiography of Amos Kendall,* ed. William Stickney (Boston: Lee & Shepard,
1872), p. 337.
    8. Kendall to Loughborough, 2 May 1835, Post Office Department, lbk. A, p. 199.
    9. Loughborough to _____ , 3 May 1835, Post Office Department, lbk. A, p. 205.
    10. Amos Kendall, Postmaster General, *Organization of the Post Office Department*
(Washington, 1835).
    11. 18 July 1835.
    12. Leonard White, *The Jacksonians: A Study in Administrative History, 1829–1861*
(New York: Macmillan Co., 1954), pp. 179–80; Lloyd M. Short, *The Development of
National Administrative Organization in the United States* (Baltimore: Johns Hopkins Press,
1923), p. 180 n.

Barry and Kendall had removed the management of department finances from the jurisdictions of the assistants. But it was here that a significant difference appeared between the administrative plans of the two Kentuckians. Barry had charged his chief clerk, Obadiah Brown, with the supervision of financial operations and the general superintendence of the department.[13] Kendall declared that the "chief object" of his arrangement was "to separate the business of settling accounts from the ministerial duties of the department entirely, and this object will be kept steadily in view in the construction of every order and regulation of the postmaster general."[14] The chief clerk of the Post Office, who exercised general supervision over the affairs of the department's headquarters establishment, was therefore ineligible for financial responsibilities. Although Preston Loughborough had been Kendall's friend since boyhood, he was not to be trusted with the responsibilities which had previously been attached to the chief clerkship. Loughborough was placed by Kendall at the head of the department's "Miscellaneous Division," where he was permitted to exercise his official power over mailbags, stationery, watchmen, workmen, grounds upkeep, and mail robbers. The financial affairs of the department were removed to a "Division of Accounts," which, for the time being, remained within the personal jurisdiction of the postmaster general.[15]

In this, at least, Kendall's reorganization plan was faithful to the tradition of personal administration. It placed the burden of supervision upon himself, and it was superintendence of a personal sort. During the weeks after his appointment, Kendall saw relatively little of his own office. He wandered through the rooms of the Post Office building on E Street, to make himself "acquainted with the officers and clerks of the Department, and their several duties." Those clerks whose characters were not to his liking, he dismissed.[16] The financial affairs of the Post Office, a subject of much concern, received his special attention. No draft could be issued except by the hand of the postmaster general himself.[17] And Kendall appointed one of his trusted clerks from the Fourth Auditor's Office to handle the affairs of the Financial Division.[18] Yet it is notable that, although he took

13. U.S., Congress, House of Representatives, *Committee Reports*, House Report 103, 23 Cong. 2 sess. (1835), p. 18.
14. Kendall, *Organization of the Post Office Department*.
15. Ibid.
16. *Autobiography of Amos Kendall*, p. 337.
17. Kendall, *Organization of the Post Office Department*.
18. *Autobiography of Amos Kendall*, p. 337.

pains to surround himself with trustworthy civil servants, Kendall was disinclined to trust them. Preston Loughborough was not to exercise the financial functions which usually went with the chief clerkship, and even the head of the Financial Division was not allowed independent responsibility for the performance of his duties. He and his clerks remained within arm's reach of the postmaster general. Clearly, Kendall did not intend to rely upon personal fidelity and good character as the only assurances of good performance. He was not inclined to allow administrative arrangements to become mere reflections of the personal aptitudes, friendships, or preferences of the administrators. Not even the administrative chieftain, the mainstay of personal administration, was to be allowed the latitude he had once enjoyed—a fact that became apparent when Kendall turned his attention to the ordering of his own office.

After completing the initial steps in his managerial reform, the postmaster general paused for a careful examination of his own duties. "In relation to the subject of accounts," he wrote,

the functions of executive authority in our government may be considered as divisible into three parts:
   1. That which makes contracts and regulations and gives orders and directions out of which accounts originate.
   2. That which pays the money.
   3. That which settles accounts.

The postmaster general, Kendall argued, "unites in his own person two of these three functions." But he had not the right to appropriate the third. "It cannot be that we have such a man in our well balanced government!"[19] According to the administrative separation of powers doctrine which Kendall advanced, the postmaster general would be compelled to surrender to some independent authority his responsibility for the settlement of accounts. Congress gave its official sanction to this doctrine when, one year later, it added a Treasury Department auditor to the Post Office staff. The auditor, accompanied by about forty clerks, was to oversee the accounts of the department, with an eye to the abuses which had cropped up under Major Barry. The financial powers of the postmaster general were restricted still further by another provision of the new Post Office Law. Instead of paying the department's expenses from its current income, Kendall would be required to pay all postal revenues into the treasury, and Congress would give them back to the department in annual appropriations.[20]

19. Kendall to B. F. Butler, 6 July 1835, Post Office Department, lbk. A, p. 240.
20. U.S., *Statutes at Large*, vol. 5, p. 80.

The new postmaster general had, within a year, surrendered a significant portion of his official authority. His financial transactions were checked by emissaries from the Treasury Department. His ability to spend the money accumulated by his own department was circumscribed by the newly established system for congressional appropriations. And Kendall had not yet completed his fragmentation of authority. He next went to work on the powers of his subordinates. After a brief test of the two-region plan, Kendall discarded the arrangement and applied a set of functional divisions to the affairs of the Post Office headquarters. The old arrangement, "by burdening the assistants' minds with duties entirely dissimilar in their nature, did not seem . . . conducive to promptitude or uniformity in the administration of the Department."[21] Kendall set up three offices within his agency: the Appointment Office, to supervise the location of new post offices and the selection of postmasters, was assigned to the first assistant postmaster general; the Contract Office was to be headed by the second assistant; and the Inspection Office, overseeing the performance of mail contracts and the behavior of postmasters, was to be managed by a third assistant, who had been added to the department's staff by the Post Office Act of 1836.[22]

Kendall's functional divisions distributed even more widely the activities and responsibilities of the departmental headquarters. After the postmaster general's second reorganization, for example, no one man could assume direct supervision of both the making of mail contracts and their subsequent fulfillment. It would thus be difficult for a civil servant like Obadiah Brown to look out for the interests of old, faithful, and unscrupulous contractors.

The administrative separation of powers doctrine, which Kendall had enunciated in his plan for the Post Office audit, was extended to the country at large in a grand system of bureaucratic checks and balances. In his original reorganization plan, Kendall had advised his employees in all parts of the nation that it was "the duty of all in the service of the department to see that others regard the post office laws as well as themselves."[23] And some postmasters apparently took the direction seriously; a few began to report their colleagues in the public service for such infractions as delaying the mails or using torn mailbags.[24] But Kendall's reforms went several steps further than regulation by inter-post office espionage. The duty of a post-

21. *Autobiography of Amos Kendall*, p. 342.
22. White, *The Jacksonians*, p. 280.
23. Kendall, *Organization of the Post Office Department*.
24. *Autobiography of Amos Kendall*, p. 341.

master to report the transgressions of his fellows was part of a wider program "to make postmasters and contractors feel that [the department's] eye was constantly upon them, not only collectively, but individually."[25]

Kendall's plan for keeping the department's eye on its field employers was an ingenious device which required no force of Post Office agents or examiners to put it into effect. The postmaster general's design would pit postmasters and contractors against one another in order to achieve automatic regulation, and it would save the department some of the labor that was spent in collecting revenue from its field officers. The plan began with considerations of administrative convenience:

A revenue arises wherever the mails are carried; and it would seem obviously appropriate, as well as convenient, that the services of contractors should be paid for in the sections of the country where they are rendered, and, as far as practicable, out of the income which they produce. But the practice of suffering the contractors to draw for their pay, subjected the Department to the inconvenience of collecting its funds and transmitting them to Washington to meet the drafts.[26]

Kendall suggested that the mail contractors be made to collect their payments themselves, from the post offices along their routes. They were to keep a record of the amount collected at each office, which would be sent to the department at the end of each quarter. The postmasters, too, were directed to report how much they had paid out and to whom. At the Post Office's Washington headquarters it required only the comparison of one set of reports with another to police the system. This checking of reports, significantly enough, was a function which Kendall placed within his own office.[27]

In effect, the postmaster general had harnessed the avarice of the mail contractors and put it to work for his department. The postal entrepreneurs would easily be as energetic in the pursuit of their incomes as the Post Office Department had been in its efforts to secure prompt payment of postal revenues into its treasury.[28] And

25. Ibid.

26. U.S., Congress, House of Representatives, *Executive Documents*, House Document 2, 24 Cong. 1 sess. (1836), p. 389.

27. *Autobiography of Amos Kendall*, p. 341.

28. Delinquent postmasters were plentiful during the Jacksonian tenure. In the first three years of Major Barry's regime, eighteen lawsuits were filed against postal defaulters, whose shortages ranged from a few hundred dollars to more than a thousand; see U.S., Congress, Senate, *Executive Documents*, Senate Document 73, 21 Cong. 2 sess. (1831), pp. 43–44. When Kendall assumed the postmaster generalship, he found scores of postmasters who were behind in their accounts—as is evidenced by the many stern messages to field officers found in his letterbooks.

presumably, postmasters would be less able to resist the quarterly assaults of the mail contractors than they had the pleas of Washington bureaucrats for a timely rendering of their accounts.

The primary merit of the payment system was its ability to achieve a kind of automatic supervision of the postmasters. But the contractors were not to be neglected; Kendall intended to keep them under surveillance as well. To assure that the mail carriers performed all the services for which they were paid, the postmaster general required his postmasters to submit, along with their financial reports, a record of each contractor's service during the preceding quarter, including arrival and departure times, the means used to carry the mails (post coach, sulky, or horse), and any miscellaneous infractions (such as the delivery of rain-soaked mails). Fines were to be levied against the mail carriers for each misdemeanor.[29]

There was much in Kendall's Post Office reform that had been anticipated by earlier postal administrators. The decentralization of the department's financial activities had begun under Postmaster General McLean, who had issued drafts to contractors instead of paying them from funds accumulated in Washington. It was McLean, therefore, and not Kendall, who had begun to halt the flow of cash from the department's field offices to its headquarters establishment.[30] And something like Kendall's Post Office auditing arrangement had been conceived by Major Barry within months of his installation in the building on E Street. "It was important to devise a system," Barry reported to Congress,

> by which no moneys should be received or disbursed, or in any manner come within the control of any one individual; but that all moneys should be paid into the Department by certificates of deposite in banks, and that nothing could be withdrawn from such depositories, not even by the head of the Department, without the signature of two distinct officers of the Department, each acting independently of the other. . . .[31]

But Barry's good intentions, as we have already seen, went for nought. Within his own department, he could not rely on the independence of his subordinates' actions. They labored within a personal organization, where friendship and loyalty were the mainstays of administration. Under such conditions, they could hardly be expected to serve as independent checks upon one another. In order

29. *Autobiography of Amos Kendall*, p. 393.
30. See Francis P. Weisenburger, *The Life of John McLean: A Politician of the United States Supreme Court* (Columbus: Ohio State University Press, 1937), p. 39.
31. Senate Document 1, 21 Cong. 1 sess. (1830), p. 48.

to secure an effective check upon the financial operations of the department, Amos Kendall had finally come to depend upon an outside authority—a Treasury Department auditor.

Other of Kendall's schemes were likewise preceded by the fruitless experiments of his predecessor. The functional division of responsibilities that Kendall finally imposed upon the Post Office headquarters was an arrangement that seems to have been initiated by the major. Before the arrival of Barry and the other Jacksonian administrators, almost all the business of the postal headquarters had regularly passed across the desk of the first assistant postmaster general, ancient Abraham Bradley. Bradley had been one of the first federal officials to arrive in Washington when the government set up housekeeping there in 1800. Weeks before the postmaster general put in an appearance at the new capital, Bradley had already arranged the affairs of the postal headquarters and begun its operations.[32] The department was a thing of his own making, and it remained his personal property for many years. Until 1826, Bradley supervised the letting of contracts, the performance of contracts, the behavior of postmasters, and all the financial affairs of his department. The duties which later became lodged in the Appointment Office were performed by the postmaster general himself.

While this simple arrangement remained in force, the number of post offices quadrupled, as did the total length of the nation's post roads. And, as the country's postal system grew larger, Bradley grew older. The burden of business seems to have become too weighty for the old first assistant, who was not a particularly adaptable administrator. "Having been long in the Department," remarked Postmaster General John McLean, "and conversant with its details, he [Bradley] felt a strong preference for the rules he had been accustomed to observe in the performance of his duties, and was generally averse to changes." These considerations may have led McLean, in 1826, to remove the responsibility for contracts from Bradley's jurisdiction and to assign this function to a second assistant. The change cannot have been too difficult for Abraham Bradley to accept—the new second assistant was his younger brother, Phineas. To Phineas Bradley, McLean also delegated the responsibility for selecting postal appointees and locations for new post offices.[33]

    32. Washington Topham, "The Benning-McGuire House, E Street and Neighborhood," *Records of the Columbia Historical Society* 33 (1932): 109.
    33. Senate Document 73, 21 Cong. 2 sess. (1831), p. 66; Senate Document 1, 20 Cong. 2 sess. (1828), p. 179.

McLean's reshuffling of duties did not much alter the conduct of his department's day-to-day business. Long after the change had been effected, Abraham Bradley still felt free to dabble in the affairs of the other departmental officers. No fixed bureaucratic barriers prevented the continuance of an easy and fluid shifting of duties.[34] McLean never mentioned such bureaucratic abstractions as "bureaus" or "divisions" or "offices." The appearance of these administrative structures was first announced by Major Barry in 1830.

After the forced departure of the Bradley brothers, the major found himself in a predicament. Phineas and Abraham had left behind them no systematic record of the department's business affairs. They had had the irritating habit of recording official transactions on odd scraps of papers or, worse yet, not recording them at all. For the most part, they had carried their offices in their heads, and when they left, they took their offices with them.[35] It was no easy task to unravel departmental business so that the Bradleys' duties might be passed on to some new administrator. Barry was also troubled by what he perceived as an overextension of postal service. The expansion of operations which had been ordered by John McLean was, Barry thought, too great a burden to be borne by his department's limited resources.[36]

The major launched a thorough investigation of his agency's functions, and when he was finished, in 1830, he had itemized the duties of all his subordinates. To meet the heavy burdens of business, Barry had evidently attempted to overcome a haphazard distribution of responsibilities. Every clerk had to know his duty. It had also been necessary to clarify some of the mysteries of postal management, formerly the special province of the Bradley brothers. In effect, Barry had depersonalized some of the Bradley family's trade secrets. He had rendered them "so plain and simple" that any man of intelligence might readily qualify for their performance. But, as Barry soon discovered, departmental business was more complex than he had supposed.

The major distributed the duties of the department among three divisions. To the First Division, headed by Assistant Postmaster General Charles K. Gardner, Barry assigned the Post Office's financial concerns; to the Second Division, commanded by Chief Clerk Oba-

34. See Senate Document 73, 21 Cong. 2 sess. (1831), pp. 66, 89–90.
35. See Senate Document 1, 21 Cong. 1 sess. (1829), p. 47.
36. Ibid., pp. 45–46.

diah Brown, were duties pertaining to the appointment and supervision of postmasters. A Third Division, under Assistant Postmaster
General Selah R. Hobbie, was charged with the supervision of mail
contracting and contract performance. But Mr. Hobbie, a newcomer
to the department, quickly realized that he could not make any sense
of his duties. Phineas Bradley had left the office in such haphazard
condition that it was impossible for anyone not intimately concerned
with its functions to pick up where he had left off. Major Barry
reassigned Hobbie to the Second Division and appointed Obadiah
Brown, a veteran postal employee, to supervise the letting of contracts.[37] It may have been the greatest mistake of his administrative
career.

Barry had generated some of the paraphernalia necessary for a
form of organization somewhat more advanced than personal organization, but he was unable to make his administrative arrangements
stick. The major first compromised his organizational plan by making
adjustments to compensate for the Bradley brothers' monopoly of
the fine points of postal management. Later, his arrangements gave
way completely to the ravages of Obadiah Brown. The Reverend was
able to fashion his responsibilities to suit his tastes, manipulating
both the financial and the contracting business of the department for
the benefit of himself and his friends. It is even doubtful whether
Barry himself had ever taken his new scheme seriously. In 1833,
when he abandoned it for a regional division of duties, he reported,
perhaps by accident, that he had made no previous changes in his
department's organization.[38]

Not until the appointment of Amos Kendall did Barry's organizational abstractions begin to have any noticeable effect upon the
behavior of the postal bureaucrats. Under Kendall, each administrative activity was lodged in its own pigeonhole, and there it stayed.
No haphazard shifting of responsibilities was permitted to mar the
precise division of the department's responsibilities into functional
jurisdictions. But Kendall gave more than precision to Major Barry's
sterile exercises in organizational taxonomy; he provided them with a
clear purpose. The aim of all these administrative arrangements was
the effective regulation of bureaucratic conduct—to make administrators feel that the eye of their department "was constantly upon
them, not only collectively, but individually." Kendall thus gave

37. Senate Document 73, 21 Cong. 2 sess. (1831), pp. 37–41; *American State Papers:
Post Office* (Washington: Gales & Seaton, 1834), pp. 252–53.
38. Barry to H. W. Connor, 1 January 1835, Post Office Department, lbk. A, p. 124.

rational coherence to the gang of divisions and offices that had grown up under the major, and once the purpose of these administrative arrangements became clear, they acquired a durability they had not previously enjoyed.

Major Barry, like Kendall, had begun his administrative career with the intention of bringing forceful regulation to Post Office affairs. [39] But Barry had failed to keep his object in view, and his administrative thinking became muddled. His various organizational adjustments bore no clear relationship to his purpose. On those few occasions when he carefully sketched out the functions of his divisions and offices, he neglected to state the reasons for the administrative arrangements that he described. Amos Kendall, on the other hand, had a knack for reducing complex administrative situations to their essentials. The presentation of each decision, each new plan of management, was marked by clarity and simplicity, which Kendall achieved by beginning at the very beginning. His reports went to the roots of every administrative change, and it sometimes appeared that he was not just reshaping an existent organization but building the Post Office Department from scratch. Thus, he may have given the impression that all his administrative suggestions were original, that he had begun with nothing and created an orderly bureaucratic structure. [40]

In one sense, this impression was correct. Kendall had created an abstract organizational apparatus which he superimposed upon the concrete activities of his department. It did not give way to boyhood friendships, to personal loyalties, or to men who were acquainted with the "mysteries" of postal management. And, since it did not take its shape from the characters and personal attachments of the Post Office employees, it could act as an independent regulator of these bureaucrats' activities.

While the beleaguered Post Office Department submitted to the organizational experiments of Major Barry and the wrathful onslaughts of congressional committees, Elijah Hayward's General Land Office quietly conducted business-as-usual in a building just a few blocks away. Its chief was an ordinary man, a lawyer-farmer from

39. See Senate Document 1, 21 Cong. 1 sess. (1829), pp. 45–46.
40. For a good example of Kendall's style, see House Document 2, 24 Cong. 1 sess. (1835).

Ohio, not given to those flights of bureaucratic fancy that produced sweeping plans for administrative reorganization. Hayward was more concerned with down-to-earth things. In the State Department building to which his agency had been dispatched after the Treasury Department fire of 1833, he fretted about the safekeeping of his precious land records. He devised, not new arrangements of his bureau's functions, but a scheme for the quick evacuation of all the agency's documents should a second fire ever threaten them.[41] And he had an office manager's concern for floor space. In an ungraceful act of bureaucratic aggression, Hayward's chief clerk informed Treasury Solicitor Virgil Maxcy:

> The great increase of the business of the Office is such as to render it impracticable to transact its multifarious duties without the use of the two rooms now in occupancy by your office—and I have the honor to apprize you of my having been compelled by a sense of Official duty to communicate the fact to the Secretary of the Treasury.[42]

Hayward's "great increase of . . . business" was no contrived device intended to enhance his territorial claims. His office had indeed suffered a crushing expansion of its duties. Just a few months after he became commissioner, Hayward felt obliged to advise Congress "of the present condition of the office, its arrears of business, and the improvements and provisions which are considered necessary to its proper and efficient organization. . . ." "In the year 1827," Hayward explained,

> the number of clerks was reduced from twenty-four to eighteen . . . under the erroneous impression that the latter number was sufficient for the public service. Since that time the business of the office has greatly increased and accumulated, until, with its diminished assistance, its arrears have become a serious impediment to the facilities of its operations. . . ."[43]

Congress was not completely won over by the commissioner's story, and it parsimoniously set aside $5,000, enough money to hire about five additional Land Office clerks. Hayward had requested ten.[44]

In the following year, the Land Office again began to sag under the weight of its increased duties. In 1830, Hayward's clerks had issued 7,000 land patents; in 1831, 25,000. And sufficient arrearages existed to keep fifty-five additional clerks scribbling for a whole year—or so Hayward claimed.[45] But Congress was not inclined to

41. Senate Document 9, 23 Cong. 1 sess. (1833), p. 52.
42. J. M. Moore to Virgil Maxcy, 8 September 1834, General Land Office, Miscellaneous Letters Sent, National Archives, Washington, lbk. 5 (n.s.), p. 95.
43. Senate Document 1, 21 Cong. 2 sess. (1830), pp. 60, 63.
44. Senate Document 3, 22 Cong. 1 sess. (1831), p. 63.
45. Ibid., pp. 63, 71.

put his claim to the test, and its appropriation provided only enough to pay the salaries of the five or six additional clerks already working in the office.[46] With the passage of another burdensome year, the commissioner once again presented a description of his office's distressing condition—an account which had become a regular part of the Land Office's annual report and was to remain so for another three years:

The arrears yet remain, and have increased. To what crisis it may approach, without the necessary aid for the discharge of public duty, it is not difficult to conjecture. More than three millions of people are interested in the most prompt attention, the vigilant action, and the accurate operations of this office. It is in the will of Congress, whether so large a portion of the United States, shall be deprived of that justice, which by law they are entitled to.[47]

To this impassioned plea, the legislators gave their customary response and set aside a few thousand dollars for "extra clerk hire" in the General Land Office.

It was, perhaps, something more than congressional pennypinching or indifference that frustrated Commissioner Hayward's requests. The nation's land policy was, along with national banking, the tariff, and internal improvements, one of the leading issues of the 1830s. It was thrown into the legislative cauldron late in 1829, when Senator Samuel Foot of Connecticut presented a neat and insignificant-looking resolution to his colleagues. Foot's proposal was the vehicle for one important component of Henry Clay's "American System." It would have contributed to the Union's industrial development by restricting migration to the agricultural West, and it proposed to do this by retarding the survey of the public domain. If land were not surveyed, it could not be sold. The Foot proposal thus called into question the very existence of the Land Office's large scale operations, and one of the grandest legislative battles of the decade was begun, a struggle whose culmination was the famous Webster-Hayne debate and the defeat of the Foot Resolution in the House of Representatives.[48]

But the issue was not allowed to grow stale. It reflected far too accurately the class and sectional divisions of the age, and when conflict was brewing along these divisions, the land issue could easily

46. Senate Document 3, 22 Cong. 2 sess. (1832), p. 53.
47. Ibid.
48. Roy M. Robbins, *Our Landed Heritage: The Public Domain, 1776–1930* (Gloucester, Mass.: Peter Smith, 1960), pp. 37–38; Raynor G. Wellington, *The Political and Sectional Influence of the Public Lands* (Cambridge, Mass.: Riverside Press, 1914), pp. 10–11, 28–34.

be called up to solidify ill-defined alliances. Although it was a complex matter, national land policy could be rendered so stark and simple that it might elicit massive political sentiments. Missouri's Thomas Hart Benton was the Senate's chief popularizer when it came to questions of the public domain. In the midst of the rhetorical fireworks set off by the Foot Resolution, Benton had stepped forward Missouri-fashion to raise the bedrock issues:

The manufacturies want poor people to do the work for small wages; these poor people wish to go to the West and get land; to have flocks and herds—to have their own fields, orchards, gardens, and meadows—their own cribs, barns, and dairies; and to start their children on a theater where they can contend with other peoples' children for the honor and dignities of the country. This is what the poor people wish to do.[49]

Benton aimed to help them, and he, along with some similarly inclined congressmen, countered the land proposals of the Clay men with his own suggestions. The Pre-Emption Act of 1830 was one result of Benton's labors. In effect, it issued a general pardon to all those frontiersmen who had settled illegally on the public domain. The squatters, when they could prove that they had lived on the government's land for one year and that they had somehow improved the property, were entitled to buy their homesteads at the minimum price—$1.25 an acre.[50]

As simple as Benton's intentions may have been, his suggestions were invariably complicated, and they increased Elijah Hayward's administrative burdens. The Pre-Emption Act, for example, added a torrent of squatters' affadavits to the flow of certificates and patents which demanded the attention of his employees. To his annual plea, Hayward added a complaint concerning "the numerous acts of the last session" and their influences upon his agency's business.[51]

Other annoyances were plentiful. The routine of Hayward's office could be interrupted by epidemics of Asiatic cholera or by Indian wars;[52] perhaps most distressing were the irritating effects of improvident decisions made by Hayward's predecessor, George Graham. Graham too had been plagued by arrearages, and he, like Hayward, had sought to overcome them by hiring extra help. In 1826, he

49. Quoted in Wellington, *The Political and Sectional Influence of the Public Lands*, p. 28.

50. Robbins, *Our Landed Heritage*, p. 50.

51. See Senate Document 3, 22 Cong. 2 sess. (1832), p. 53. The Pre-Emption Act was only one of the devices suggested by congressional friends of the settler. Concerning some other suggestions, see Robbins, *Our Landed Heritage*, pp. 50–54.

52. Senate Document 3, 22 Cong. 2 sess. (1832), p. 52.

Figure 1

LAND OFFICE ORGANIZATION UNDER COMMISSIONER GRAHAM, 1826[a]

Commissioner

Chief Clerk

| 7 Accountants | 1 Private Land Claims Clerk | 1 Military Bounty Lands Clerk | 6 Patent Clerks | 1 Draftsman |

[a]Constructed from the description of Land Office organization in U.S., Congress, Senate, *Executive Documents,* Senate Document 1, 19 Cong. 2 sess. (1826), p. 138.

finally brought his office's business up to date, and, as Hayward reminded Congress, Graham had thoughtlessly announced that he could dispense with the services of his half-dozen temporary clerks.[53] Congress had responded with alacrity, and what it had taken away, it was not inclined to give back—as we have already seen.

But in 1832, the legislature finally gave some feeble signs of response to Hayward's persistent pleas. The Senate presented him with a resolution requesting both information about arrears of business in the Land Office and suggestions for eliminating them. Hayward responded with a list of duties that needed to be performed and a plan for the organization of his agency. Except that it was much grander, Hayward's scheme was not very different from the one that had prevailed under George Graham and was presumably still in effect. (see figures 1 and 2). Graham's private claims clerk, who handled difficult cases of disputed land titles, was to be transformed, in Hayward's plan, into the Bureau of Private Land Claims, with a supervisory clerk and one assistant. The military bounty lands clerk, who saw to the claims of Revolutionary veterans, was to be transformed into Hayward's Bureau of Military Bounty Lands, with a supervisory clerk and three assistants. The growth of the agency, however, had led to some more substantial proposals for change. The issuance of patents, a duty which had kept six of Graham's clerks occupied, blossomed into three separate divisions in Elijah Hayward's plan. One group of clerks was to write out the patents; another, the examiners, was to check these patents for errors; and a third was to copy patents at the request of settlers who had lost them or who needed duplicates. Three different divisions of copyists, engaged in

53. Senate Document 1, 19 Cong. 2 sess. (1826), pp. 137–38.

Figure 2

COMMISSIONER HAYWARD'S FIRST PLAN FOR LAND OFFICE ORGANIZATION, 1832[a]

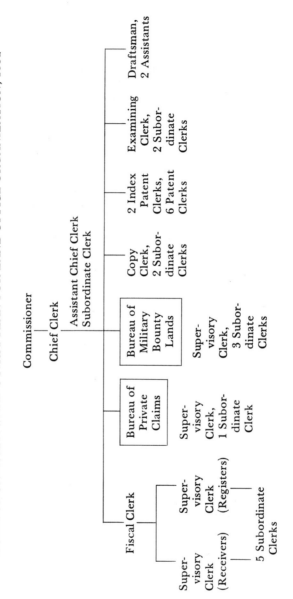

[a]Constructed from the description of Land Office organization in Senate Document 45, 22 Cong. 1 sess. (1832), p. 3.

the dreariest business which the Land Office could offer, would require the direct supervision of the commissioner or his chief clerk. And, in the case of the patent-issuing clerks, this supervision would extend to the very application of pen to parchment, for Hayward designated no supervisory clerk in this division. No middle-level managers would separate Hayward from his ordinary patent writers. This arrangement may have been dictated by the commissioner's special place in his office's patent-issuing activities: on every one of the thousands of deeds drawn up by his subordinates, Hayward was required, by law, to sign his name.

In the Land Office's financial division, Hayward seems to have envisaged some other minor changes. He apparently expected to divest himself of the responsibility of closely supervising the agency's auditing activities. He planned to remove these functions quite a bit further from his direct supervision than any of his office's other responsibilities. Beneath the fiscal clerk, who headed this bureau, duties were to be divided between two supervisory clerks. One was to oversee the auditing of the district receivers' accounts; the other, the settlement of the registers' accounts; both would share the services of the five subordinate accountants in their charge.

Hayward's plan did not amount to a full-scale reorganization. The shape of his agency would have remained much as it had been under George Graham. But even in his simple itemization of Land Office responsibilities, the Jacksonian commissioner revealed his preoccupation with the scale of his agency's operations. Those functions which had expanded most with increases in land sales were the ones Hayward seems to have reserved for his own special supervision. The issuance of patents, a routine function at best, was to have a particular claim on his attention, for it was in this area that arrearages had piled up most heavily.[54] Land Office accounting, on the other hand, was somewhat less sensitive to increases in the agency's revenue. Hayward accordingly placed this function where it would demand relatively little of his attention.

The commissioner never discovered how well his plan would have worked, for, after sending it to the Senate, he heard no more of it. Congress produced its customary appropriation for extra clerk hire, which, once again, was not enough to take care of the office's current business, much less its arrears. But the commissioner was determined not simply to sink beneath the surface of the paper

54. Senate Document 3, 22 Cong. 1 sess. (1832), p. 63.

morass, so he turned to the routine affairs of his office and attempted to take up some administrative slack by carefully rationing the time and energy of his clerks. It first occurred to him that a thoughtful reshuffling of his agency's documents might eliminate time-consuming searches for important records. Hayward set his clerks to arranging and assorting, to filing and indexing.[55] But Land Office clerks, because they were in short supply, could not always be spared for the nice business of constructing orderly indexes and files, and the commissioner had to look for other devices. He next tried to extract more work from his office force, and he informed his subordinates that he required "each and every Clerk ... to be punctual in his attendance on his duties, at 9 o'clock in the morning and to continue diligent and industrious until three o'clock in the afternoon. ..." Any absence during office hours would be reported to Hayward, and if any clerk were absent without leave for more than one day, his office would be considered vacant. No outsiders were to be permitted within the rooms occupied by the Land Office clerks unless they came on business.[56]

Hayward's schemes for handling the Land Office's booming business are notable primarily because they are so prosaic. The commissioner at first saw the solution to his problems in a simple battening down of hatches—a more efficient filing system and more clerical diligence. And his annual supplications to Congress bespeak the same deficiency of administrative imagination. Hayward sought to meet his difficulties by adding a little manpower to an existing structure and, where backlogs were particularly heavy, by applying additional supervision. There is no reason to suppose that these measures might not have done the job. Solutions of this nature had, after all, proven quite satisfactory to George Graham when he had been faced with arrearages. But other considerations than the mere press of business seem to have diverted Hayward from such conventional devices.

Early in 1833, the commissioner began to be troubled by the misbehavior of his field officers. In January, he forwarded to Secretary of the Treasury Louis McLane a citizen's complaint concerning the conduct of a register and a receiver in Louisiana.[57] A few weeks later he warily suggested that the surety bond of the receiver at

55. Hayward to John Wilson (draftsman), 2 February 1834, General Land Office, lbk. 4 (n.s.), p. 187.
56. Hayward to the Clerks in the General Land Office, 23 July 1834, ibid., lbk. 5 (n.s.), p. 73.
57. Hayward to McLane, 4 January 1833, General Land Office, lbk. 4 (n.s.), p. 37.

Crawfordsville be increased from \$30,000 to \$60,000.[58] In May, possibly on the basis of some additional citizens' complaints, he warned several of the Land Office examiners to be alert to special kinds of abuses in the district offices at Zanesville, Crawfordsville, Indianapolis, and elsewhere.[59] The examiners, armed with these warnings and with Hayward's newly strengthened inspection system, went out to test the virtue and diligence of the registers and receivers. Throughout the late summer and early autumn, the bad news came back to Washington. Hayward recommended a handful of registers and receivers for expulsion from the public service.[60] And while he was winnowing laxity and corruption from his field establishment, the commissioner found disconcerting abuses close to home. In September, he fired one of his principal clerks.[61]

Then, except for the businesslike scratch of two dozen goosequill pens, the General Land Office remained quiet for almost six months. The commissioner felt, perhaps, that he had successfully overcome the infidelity of his subordinates. He had conceived an inspection system which was more comprehensive and thorough than that of his predecessors.[62] It had already uncovered some frauds, and Hayward may have nourished the hope that these were the only frauds to be uncovered. But the new inspection system could not cope with the extensive peculations of registers and receivers—as Hayward learned in the spring of 1834. In April, the Senate Committee on Public Lands produced some evidence of frauds in a Mississippi land office.[63] A few months later, citizens' complaints and examiners' reports brought news of currency speculation in the Land Office's Alabama and Mississippi outposts.[64]

In an apparent response to the latest reports of peculation, the commissioner carried out his first actual reorganization of Land Office business. Hayward redistributed the duties of his seven accountants so that each of them would be regularly responsible for auditing the books of a particular set of field administrators. The

58. Hayward to McLane, 22 January 1833, ibid., p. 49.

59. Additional Paragraphs Inserted in the Letter of Instructions to Examiners of Land Offices, [?] May 1833, ibid., p. 110.

60. See, for example, Hayward to Jackson, 26 October 1833, ibid., p. 150.

61. Hayward to William Otis, Meade Fitzhugh, et al. (clerks), 16 September 1833, ibid., p. 137.

62. See above, pp. 90–91.

63. *American State Papers: Public Lands,* 8 vols. (Washington: Gales & Seaton, 1832–61), 7: 733–35.

64. Ibid., p. 1238; Hayward to Secretary of the Treasury R. B. Taney, 13 June 1834, General Land Office, lbk. 5 (n.s.), p. 56; Hayward to Taney, 20 June, 1834, ibid., p. 60.

Figure 3

COMMISSIONER HAYWARD'S SECOND PLAN FOR LAND OFFICE ORGANIZATION, 1833[a]

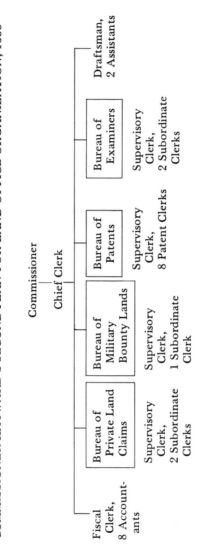

[a]Constructed from the description of Land Office organization in Senate Document 50, 22 Cong. 2 sess. (1833), pp. 8–11.

various district office accounts were to be parcelled out according to states.[65] This new arrangement at headquarters would allow for a closer scrutiny of the local land officers' financial affairs. Its adoption was the understandable reaction of an executive troubled by unreliable or dishonest subordinates in the field.

Hayward had been considering this measure for some time. Early in 1833, a year and a half before he put the new arrangement into effect, he had suggested a similar redistribution of accounting duties in one of his annual requests to Congress for additional employees. Significantly, this suggestion was made very shortly after Hayward had received the first alarms about infidelity in the district offices. [66] Not long after he had proposed this innovation to the House Ways and Means Committee, the Senate had again requested a plan for disposing of the Land Office's arrears in business. As suspicions about the reliability of his field administrators accumulated, Hayward prepared and submitted a scheme much like the one he had devised in 1832 (see figure 2), with several important exceptions. The patent-issuing activities of the agency would now be contained within two, rather than three, bureaus, and a supervisory clerk would be assigned to each of the two divisions (see figure 3). Hayward would thus place one stratum of Land Office managers between himself and the routine business of patent-writing. By reducing the number of patent-issuing bureaus, he might also diminish the demands made upon his attention by this function. With respect to the accountants' bureau, Hayward's new set of suggestions to the Senate would work in the opposite direction; here, he proposed to dispense with the two supervisory clerks who appeared in the 1832 plan. The business of checking up on registers and receivers would thus be brought one step closer to his direct supervision.

No congressional action had resulted from Hayward's 1833 proposal. For the next two years, evidence of fraud and impropriety in the Land Office field establishment continued to mount. Then, in early 1835—six months after Hayward had finally reordered the business of the accountants' bureau—he was invited to present to Congress another comprehensive plan for the organization of his

65. Hayward to the Accountants, General Land Office, 21 July 1834, ibid., pp. 70–71.
66. Hayward to G. C. Verplanck, Chairman, House Committee on Ways and Means, 7 January 1833, ibid., lbk. 4 (n.s.), pp. 39–41. Hayward had urged that the House provide for at least one clerk "to supervise the concerns of *each* land and surveying District. . . ." The clerks were not only to audit accounts but to record land patents, issue military land scrip for their respective land districts, and correspond with registers, receivers, and private citizens of the districts.

office. This time the request came from the House of Representatives. Once again, the commissioner drafted a scheme that was slightly different from his earlier designs. The issuance of patents would now be managed within one division, rather than two or three, and a few small bureaus would be added to the Land Office apparatus to handle special claims generated by new land legislation. [67] Once again, Hayward's plan of organization disappeared in the congressional machinery. Months dragged by and still nothing emerged from the legislative chambers. Congress adjourned, and Hayward quit.

Andrew Jackson named another Ohioan, Ethan Allen Brown, to preside over the clerks and documents that, by mid-1835, had come to fill the whole first floor of the State Department building. The new commissioner's appointment came just a few months after the Senate Committee on Public Lands, as a parting shot on the last day of the legislative session, had released a report disclosing extensive frauds in the land offices of Alabama and Mississippi.[68] Ethan Brown may have been better equipped to deal with these and other troubles than his predecessor had been. A former governor and senator, Brown was a more prestigious figure than Hayward, and his prominence may have made Congress a bit more respectful of his requests. In his first annual report, Brown affirmed Hayward's account of the Land Office's problems: ". . . In the representations made by my predecessor in 1833–'4 to the Secretary of the Treasury and to Congress, I have not discovered the least exaggeration of the difficulties under which the General Land Office had labored. . . ." The new commissioner suggested that decisive action be taken to remedy the situation. Referring to the annual appropriations for extra clerk hire, Brown expressed "a strong hope that Congress, perceiving the insufficiency of such temporary expedients, [would] substitute, in the course of the coming session, a scheme better suited to the weight of the circumstances that press upon and overburden this office." The extra clerks, he said, were "an imperfect and exceptionable substitute for the organic system upon which this branch of the public service ought to be established. . . ." For the purpose of putting the "organic system" in proper order, Brown said, Congress should "enact provisions whereby a more perfect supervision of labor and duty can be practised; responsibility made more

67. Hayward to Secretary of the Treasury Levi Woodbury, 27 January 1835, General Land Office, lbk. 5 (n.s.), pp. 234–35.
68. *American State Papers: Public Lands*, 7: 733–35.

sensible in the various branches of this service; and the Commissioner, in a measure, relieved of details that divert his attention from more important affairs. . . ."[69]

Congress responded, and for the first time it appeared to mean business. The House passed a resolution which requested not must information and suggestions but a draft bill for the reorganization of the General Land Office. No term so drastic as "reorganization" had previously appeared in the exchanges between Congress and the Land Office commissioner.

Brown replied some months later with a plan that extended the trends of thought that had been apparent in the successive schemes of Elijah Hayward (see figure 4). The Land Office accountants and bookkeepers were no longer to labor over their ledgers in a separate bureau, as did the other employees of the agency. Brown expanded the auditing staff and brought it into his own office, where it would be subject to his direct supervision and that of his chief clerk. The business of bookkeeping and auditing, of policing the honesty of field administrators—these, apparently, were the "more important affairs" that Brown had mentioned in his first annual report. The less important patent-writing activities of the Land Office were to be divided into two parts. The dreary and routine duties were to be assigned to a new officer, the recorder of the General Land Office. Brown explained why:

As the tedious task of signing the Patents . . . causes a more constant diversion of the Commissioner's attention from subjects of great interest than any other ordinary occupation in the discharge of his duties, I have thought it advisable that the patents be prepared under the immediate superintendence of an officer to be charged, exclusively, with that duty; by whose signature, in addition to that of the President, and the seal of the General Land Office, authenticity should be given to patents.[70]

Special or unusual patents, such as those ordered by private acts of Congress, were to be issued by the clerks in a "Miscellaneous Bureau."

Insofar as the new arrangement of Land Office functions reduced the supervisory burdens of the commissioner, it may have been an answer to the difficulties that came with an expanding volume of business. But Brown's reorganization plan cannot be fully under-

69. Senate Document 3, 23 Cong. 2 sess. (1835), pp. 2–3.
70. Senate Document 216, 24 Cong. 1 sess. (1836), p. 5. Congress had previously created a recorder of the General Land Office, but none of the earlier proposals—all had been unsuccessful—was exactly like Brown's (*Register of Debates in Congress*, 14 vols. [Washington: Gales & Seaton, 1825–37], 8: 902).

Figure 4

COMMISSIONER BROWN'S PLAN FOR LAND OFFICE ORGANIZATION, 1836[a]

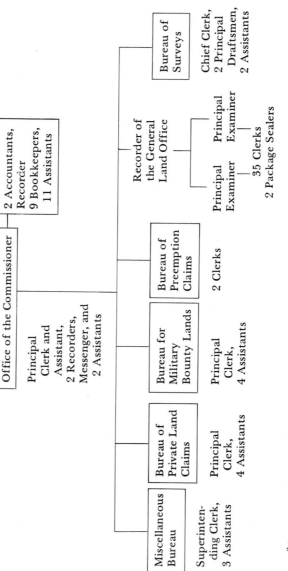

[a]Constructed from description of Land Office organization in Senate Document 216, 24 Cong. 1 sess. (1836), pp. 6–8.

stood as an answer to administrative growing pains. Elijah Hayward and George Graham had met these difficulties in an entirely different fashion—by extending the apparatus of personal organization. Hayward's first response to the expansion of Land Office operations was to remove accounting functions from his immediate purview and to concentrate his supervisory energies upon the patent-writing bureaus, where arrearages were heaviest. This was a simple, direct, and "personal" solution; the exertions of the Land Office chief followed the exertions of his subordinates. Where they worked hardest, he worked hardest. But Hayward reversed his manner of thinking when laxity, fraud, and embezzlement were discovered to have penetrated the Land Office field establishment.

Gradually, the accounting and auditing functions of his agency moved toward the center of his field of vision. Each new plan of organization would have brought these activities nearer to the concerns of his own office, and each scheme carried the dull business of patent writing a little further from his direct supervision. Ethan Brown completed the process when he brought the accountants into his own office and entrusted patent-writing to the care of the Land Office recorder.

The accounting functions to which Ethan Brown gave his personal attention were a long-neglected means for the automatic regulation of district officers' official behavior. The heart of the Land Office audit system was a checking and balancing mechanism that had been built into the administrative structures of the local land offices. The device had been designed to warn the commissioner's accountants of any gross improprieties in the conduct of local bureaucrats. The registers, who recorded the sale of land tracts, and the receivers, who recorded payments for lands, were intended to check each other's dishonest tendencies. If a receiver pocketed some public money or a register fraudulently entered a parcel of land in the name of a friend, the commissioner's auditors would notice a discrepancy between the register's records and those of the receiver. The land purchasers themselves, because they held receipts for land payments, constituted an additional check, "for, as the purchaser cannot receive a patent for his land until the evidence of payment appears on the books of the General Land Office, on the authority of the returns of sales, no attempt at collusion between officers could fail to be detected by means of this duplicate evidence in the hands of the purchaser. . . ."[71]

71. Robert Mayo, *The Treasury Department and Its Various Fiscal Bureaus, Their Origin, Organization, and Practical Operations* (Washington: William Q. Force, 1847), p.

The Land Office's accounting procedure gave no absolute guarantee that all corrupt field officers would be detected. The fallibility or infallibility of the system was not, however, its most notable characteristic. What was important in the auditing system was that it moved from the periphery to the center of the commissioner's attention. The Land Office accounting division had become the agency's nerve center.

The new prominence of Land Office accountancy and the appearance of Commissioner Hayward's rigorous inspection system were both signs of increasing uncertainty concerning the moral uprightness of district land officers. The regulation of bureaucratic behavior was fast becoming the focus of Land Office administration, and the reorganization plans proposed by Commissioners Hayward and Brown seem to have been conceived in order to make room for this new focus. There was more in these administrative readjustments than could be explained by a simple increase in the volume of public business. The increased scale of Land Office operations had undoubtedly imposed onerous burdens upon the commissioner, and Land Office reorganization was clearly intended to lessen the weight of these burdens. But, if the commissioner were freed from one set of bothersome administrative details, it was only so that he might pay greater attention to another set—the details of the Land Office accounting system, a mechanism for the preservation of decent conduct within the civil service.

When Commissioner Brown brought accountants and bookkeepers into his office, he took an important step toward the dissolution of personal organization. Until the arrival of the auditors, the commissioner, through his chief clerk, had exercised "general superintendence" over Land Office business. The agency's chief executives had presumably allowed their attention to range over all Land Office activities. They could meddle in the affairs of bureau chiefs and intervene, at any point, in the handling of the agency's business. After Ethan Brown's reorganization, the personal touch of the commissioner was not as likely to be felt at so many places in the office's operations. His time and attention were more and more taken up with the supervision of bookkeeping and auditing activities and in correspondence with field administrators. "General superintendence" disappeared from the list of his chief clerk's duties.[72] Brown had

---

205. The Land Office's system of checks and balances was not originated during the Jackson era. It had been part of the original plan for administration of the public domain.

72. See Senate Document 216, 24 Cong. 1 sess. (1836).

inscribed a faint line between the Land Office's operating divisions and its "staff," who did not directly superintend the activities of bureaucrats, but handled the flow of paper and information through the commissioner's office.

The Jackson men had looked forward to a restoration of yeoman virtue, and they had been disappointed. The federal establishment had been pockmarked by the moral shabbiness of supposed yeomen. Old-fashioned goodness seemed to have passed away with the old-fashioned men who had embodied it. It was the special property of a fondly remembered but inaccessible past. To Jacksonians and Whigs alike, it seemed that the country had lost the moral purity of its youth.

There was undoubtedly a good deal of nonsense in this conviction, but in the case of the federal civil service, there was some evidence to support it. Administrative conduct does seem to have deteriorated during the 1820s and 30s.[73] When it came to embezzlement, for example, there was certainly no federal officer in the prior history of the republic who could hold a candle to Samuel Swartwout. And although some public land officials had always dabbled in land speculation, they had once had the decency to finance these private investments with their own money, not the government's. Questionable or downright fraudulent behavior on the part of federal civil servants had become noticeably more frequent and brazen.

It is possible that the Jacksonians may have brought this trouble on themselves. Under the regime of the spoils system, after all, public office was regarded as a payment for political labor, and it was understandable that the men who earned public offices should regard them less as opportunities for public service than as sources of private profit. To make matters worse, officeholders who were political appointees generally had influential friends or were influential in their own right, and it was naturally difficult for their administrative superiors to restrain their cupidity or punish their misbehavior.[74] It is reasonable to suppose, therefore, that when Jacksonian administra-

73. Paul P. Van Riper, *History of the United States Civil Service* (Evanston, Ill.: Row, Peterson & Co., 1958), p. 11.

74. Malcolm J. Rohrbaugh, *The Land Office Business: The Settlement and Administration of American Public Lands, 1789–1837* (New York: Oxford University Press, 1971), p. 284.

tors found frauds and cheats within federal agencies, they were only discovering the consequences of Jacksonian spoilsmanship.

Of course, some of these frauds and cheats were not Jacksonian appointees, and some of the official peculation discovered during the Jackson administration had actually occurred before Jackson became president and the spoils system began to operate.[75] Certainly these instances of corruption could not be attributed to rotation in office. More important, the federal establishment was not the only institution that seemed to be troubled by an inability to regulate the behavior of its members. The legal profession, the business community, and organized religion all seem to have experienced a similar decline in the capacity to enforce internal discipline. In short, the kind of human unreliability that became evident within the federal establishment seems to have had broader dimensions than the spoils system or even the federal government.

When the regulatory authority of institutions like the legal profession and the business community was diluted, institutional standards of conduct lost force. In business, the solid seaboard merchant was joined by the shifty commercial operator; some of the seaboard merchants seem to have become rather shifty themselves.[76] Among men of the law, the scramble for financial gain was less and less inhibited by professional regulation and discipline. The effects of these changes were sure to be felt beyond the limits of the business community and the bar, for these were institutions whose day-to-day operations colored the life of the nation, and supplying most of the civilian manpower for the federal establishment was one of the ways in which they made an impression on the country at large. The behavior of federal civil servants in the Jacksonian period reflected the deterioration of discipline within these institutions.

It fell to the Jacksonian bureaucratic planners to provide for certain kinds of regulation which had earlier been achieved by the relatively unnoticed processes of institutional socialization. At one time, society had given the civil service men whose resistance to the temptations of fraud or embezzlement was taken for granted. Confidence placed in them was also placed in the institutions in which they had acquired their occupational values and habits of doing business. When those institutions could no longer be relied upon to lay down and sustain appropriate standards of behavior, the federal

75. See above, p. 89.
76. Robert Greenhalgh Albion, *The Rise of New York Port, 1815–1860* (New York: Charles Scribner's Sons, 1939), pp. 227, 256, 310–11.

establishment itself had to guarantee the good conduct of its members. In the Post Office Department and the General Land Office, the nature of these guarantees became more and more impersonal. Where the federal government had once relied on good character to assure the successful conduct of public business, it now depended on mechanical checking and balancing devices, arrangements which would make possible an almost automatic supervision of civil servants. Impersonal organization would reduce the government's reliance on "good character"—so that it could also be freed from the depredations of bad character.

The waywardness of civil servants, of course, was not the only problem that faced the Jacksonian executives, and it was not the only factor that may have influenced their administrative innovations. In particular, both William Barry and Elijah Hayward had been troubled by the increasing scale of their agencies' operations, and they both had experimented with new organizational arrangements which in some respects anticipated the "impersonal" plans of Kendall and Brown. For example, Barry and Hayward had begun to think in administrative abstractions—bureaus, divisions, offices—and they had occasionally taken the trouble to specify in writing the responsibilities of their various subordinates. These efforts were made necessary, perhaps, by the increasing size of the public enterprises that they headed. Where the press of business was great, one could not afford a haphazard distribution of responsibilities. Every clerk had to know exactly what his duties were. Administrative changes that we have regarded as products of moral unreliability in the civil service may in fact have been mere by-products of organizational growth.

Indeed, moral waywardness itself may have been encouraged by the expanding scale of public agencies during the Jackson administration. A generation earlier, for example, Samuel Swartwout would have been less able to embezzle on so grand a scale for the simple reason that the amount of money passing through his hands as customs collector in New York would not have been nearly so large. Corruption in the administration of public lands may have been nurtured by the enormous increase in land sales, which also increased the opportunities for peculation, the number of local land officers who might exploit those opportunities, and the difficulties of policing their behavior.

An increase in the scale of an organization can explain many kinds of administrative change—perhaps too many. Organizational bigness may manifest itself in so many different ways that it is relatively unenlightening to say that the transformation of an agency was triggered by an increase in its scale. It is important to know just which manifestation of bigness was responsible for the change— whether it was a simple increase in the organization's workload, or the growing difficulties of administrative communication that accompany increasing scale, or the diminishing ability to direct the behavior of subordinates, or a new disjointedness among the organization's subdivisions, or an increase in "administrative" expenses relative to operating costs. Any of these problems may be associated with organizational bigness, and any of them may stimulate administrative reform.

The reorganization plans of Amos Kendall and Ethan Brown clearly represented responses to the difficulty of supervising subordinate employees. But it cannot be denied that other aspects of organizational bigness may also have been responsible for producing administrative change. A simple increase in organizational workloads seems to have led Major Barry and Elijah Hayward to formalize the division of labor within their respective agencies. As the volume of business grew, individual clerks whose experience made them expert in the performance of different duties were each placed in charge of a handful of assistants, and the resulting work teams were called "bureaus." The veteran clerks now became bureau chiefs (although they were usually called "principal clerks"), and the agencies acquired an additional level of management between their top executives and their front-line employees.

These administrative modifications hardly represented a sharp break with the past. In fact, they amounted to little more than an expansion of the existing administrative apparatus. As long as the problems of Barry and Hayward remained problems of quantity—the extensive scope of their agencies' operations—their responses were also primarily quantitative. They attempted to meet the boom in public business by simply extending and adding energy to the administrative structures which they commanded. Barry and Hayward sought to meet their growing responsibilities by making their agencies a little bigger and a little stronger—by adding manpower and supervision where administrative burdens were heaviest. Administrative thinking seldom broke out of its old, "personal" ways. When it did deviate from the old patterns—as it may have in Major Barry's early reorganization scheme—administrative behavior quickly reverted to the old habits.

The new "middle managers" in the Post Office and the Land

Office probably relieved their chiefs of some of the bothersome burdens of personal supervision. But the chiefs and their personal assistants, the chief clerks, still exercised "general superintendence" over the affairs of their agencies. They could do this because their own functions remained largely unspecified. Within the office of the agency head, there was no regular business to conduct apart from the direction of subordinates, nothing to distract the chief from the general operations of his department. Those who conducted the business of his agency were still sure to feel his presence and the influence of his personality. Bigness alone had modified, but not destroyed, the tradition of personal organization.

Marked changes in administrative thinking and organization occurred with the discovery that civil servants could be incorrigibly unscrupulous. When reports of peculation filtered into the General Land Office, Elijah Hayward began to pay more attention to the activities of his accountants and bookkeepers—not an unconventional response. But he also gave less and less attention to the other routine operations of his agency, and finally, under Ethan Brown, these functions were removed some distance from the commissioner's personal supervision. Accountants and bookkeepers began to fill the chief's office. By the careful examination and comparison of purchase certificates, affidavits, accounting entries, deposit receipts, and the like, Ethan Brown hoped that his unreliable field administrators might be kept in check.

Amos Kendall used a similar technique to regulate the activities of his postmasters, and the office of the postmaster general, like that of the Land Office commissioner, began to swell with the addition of a few accountants and miscellaneous employees. In 1836, about a dozen postal bureaucrats were stationed in Kendall's own office. In 1830, there had been no one there but the postmaster general himself.[77] In the Post Office, as in the Land Office, the appearance

77. Kendall to H. W. Connor, 17 December 1836, Post Office Department, lbk. B, pp. 452–53. The postmaster general's "staff" was considerably smaller than that of the Land Office commissioner. In 1835, the commissioner's office contained the chief clerk and one or two correspondence clerks. In 1836, it housed more than twenty-five accountants, clerks, and bookkeepers. The growth of an executive staff was less striking in the postal bureaucracy, but its effect becomes clear if we consider the changes in the chief clerk's duties. Before Kendall's reorganization, the principal clerk had been the chief reliance of the postmaster general. He acted as the personal agent of the department head in the exercise of "general superintendence." After Kendall's administrative renovation, the chief clerk's superintendence was no longer general. He managed the Miscellaneous Bureau, which was attached to the office of the postmaster general. Here, he took care of the Dead Letter Office, building maintenance, office supplies, and similar matters. Such changes suggest the decline of general superintendence.

of an "executive staff" within the office of the agency head seems to have been a sign that general superintendence and personal supervision were on the wane. The postmaster general was now occupied with the management of an impersonal system of bureaucratic checks and balances. He had neither the time nor the need to establish within his department the older variety of personal supervision.

What was new about the administrative structures of the Jacksonian era represented, for the most part, a response to the apparent moral failings of civil servants. The nature of the response might have been different had it not been for the increasing volume of business and the increasing size of the federal field establishment. If the Post Office and the Land Office had been smaller and less expansive agencies, their heads might conceivably have countered the moral frailties of their employees, not with impersonal systems of regulation, but with more rigorous personal supervision and inspection. The size and the geographic spread of the two agencies made such nonbureaucratic remedies impractical. Instead, the Jacksonians resorted to administrative arrangements that departed from the traditional ways of the federal establishment. Administrative organization did not embody the personalities of its members; it counteracted them. Human unreliability, exaggerated by a decline in the regulatory power of social institutions, had made impersonality a necessary feature of the administrative order. Individual character was seemingly no longer worthy of organizational reliance.

The Land Office and the Post Office were the fastest growing agencies of the Jacksonian age. Both were sensitive to the expansion of the nation's business, population, and settled territory. In a sense, these agencies constitute the hard cases against which to test the proposition that the growing volume of public business was not the chief stimulus to administrative change. If organizational bigness was the factor that dominated the Jacksonian administrative changes, then its overriding importance should be clearly evident in the Post Office and the Land Office. It is not. In other agencies—the "easy" cases, perhaps—administrative bigness was not a serious problem, but reorganization plans appeared in these departments as well. The occurrence of these changes adds emphasis to the fact that mere organizational growth was not the only condition that produced administrative reorganization.

The executive departments, which had once clustered around the White House in a few drab buildings, had begun to grow more elaborate. In defiance of Old Hickory's pledge to return the government to its original simplicity, federal agencies adorned themselves with new bureaus and divisions, and new reorganization plans one after another were set out before Congress. The State Department added new bureaus on three separate occasions, in 1833, 1834, and 1836. The War Department did the same in 1832 and 1833.[78] These renovations, like those in the Post Office and the Land Office, came relatively late in the Jacksonian tenure, and it may be that they too answered a bureaucratic need whose existence became known only by sad experience—the need for rigorous supervision of unreliable civil servants. Some aspects of these reorganizations indicate that this may have been the case. In 1833, for example, a State Department reorganization plan provided for the division of functions into bureaus. The Disbursing and Superintending Bureau was to be headed by the chief clerk.[79] This merger of financial administration and supervision is one we have already seen in both the Post Office and the Land Office.

In the case of the War Department, an 1833 plan provided for the establishment of a Pension Office. Secretary Lewis Cass explained that this measure was necessary in order to achieve control of the extensive pension funds. The duties of the pension clerk, said Cass, "are not defined by law, nor are his acts recognized by law. While, in fact, controlling the disbursement of near $2,500,000 annually, he is still known upon the statute book as a clerk only . . . without the slightest allusion to the powers and duties he actually exercises." Cass was not inclined to rely on an arrangement which did not formally limit the discretion or state the responsibility of his clerk.[80]

Confidence was no longer reposed in good administrators; government relied principally upon administrative arrangements. And the fitness of those arrangements was usually determined less by considering the efficiency or expedition that they brought to the conduct of public business than by weighing their ability to withstand the depredations of corrupt civil servants. In 1836, when the House Ways and Means Committee completed an investigation of clerical duties and compensation in the Treasury Department, it reported that much of the department's excessive workload had been created by an accounting system which imposed a quintuple check on all receipts

78. Somit, "The Political and Administrative Ideas of Andrew Jackson," pp. 172–74.
79. Short, *The Development of National Administrative Organization in the United States*, pp. 115–16.
80. Ibid., pp. 136–37.

and expenditures. The committee noted that "the result of the
reciprocal checks here established" between the treasurer, the auditor, the comptroller, the secretary, and the register "is, that no
money can be received or paid out without the agency of these five
separate offices, involving the labor of one or more clerks in
each."[81] Such arrangements were clearly not intended to expedite
the onward march of an elephantine public enterprise or to make
manageable an expanded volume of business. And although the Ways
and Means Committee expressed its concern about the increasing size
of the Treasury Department's workload, it pointedly refrained from
reducing that workload by recommending a simplification of accounting procedures. When confronted with a choice between responding to the increased scale of government business and safe-
guarding against the moral frailties of public employees, the committee chose to retain the safeguards. It seems to have accorded more
importance to the dangers of official peculation than to the exi-
gencies of bureaucratic bigness.

Secretary of the Treasury Levi Woodbury seems to have had
roughly the same priorities. In 1834, when the House passed a
resolution asking him to streamline his department, he produced a
reorganization plan which would have left the cumbersome accounting system unaltered. In fact, the central feature of his plan would
have introduced an additional check against the improper use of
funds. Under the existing organizational scheme, the first comptroller of the treasury was responsible both for administering the customs service and for auditing its accounts. It was manifest to Woodbury "that no effectual check can exist where the same officer
authorizes the expenditure, and audits or controls the audit of the
account." He therefore proposed that the auditing duties of the first
comptroller be separated from the authority to supervise the collection of customs, a responsibility which would be assigned to a new
"commissioner of customs." In commenting on Woodbury's plan,
the House Commerce Committee observed that it would make possible not only a more rigorous accounting check but also a more
vigilant surveillance of the activities of customs officers. Under the
proposed scheme, the commissioner of customs would be able to give
his undivided attention to an examination "into the internal management of the several custom-houses. . . . Such an examination
would tend to produce uniformity in the manner of transacting

81. House Report 641, 24 Cong. 1 sess. (1836), p. 2.

business, and would lead to the detection and dismissal of such agents from the public service as might be found unworthy."[82]

Expressions of concern about the increased workload of the executive branch were repeatedly transformed into proposals for achieving a more secure administrative defense against official corruption. It was not mere bureaucratic bigness which seems to have preoccupied the Jacksonian administrative planners, but bureaucratic misbehavior. Secretary Woodbury's plan for strengthening the Treasury Department's safeguards against misbehavior was never enacted by Congress. But the problems that it addressed were not forgotten. Three years after the Woodbury plan was first proposed, President Van Buren sent to the members of his administration a plaintive request for suggestions about "what farther legislative provision is required to secure the proper application of the public moneys in the hands of disbursing officers, and fully to protect the public interests. . . ."[83] The response of George Wolf, first comptroller of the treasury, reflected the lessons learned from almost ten years of Jacksonian administrative experience. The government, said Wolf, must rely upon the "heart and conscience" of men in positions of public trust as the ultimate safeguard against official dishonesty. "As men, however, are sometimes selected to fill stations of the description mentioned, without possessing the qualities alluded to, it becomes necessary to make use of such artificial means as will be best calculated to guard the public against peculations. . . ."[84] The Jacksonians had already multiplied these "artificial means" in an effort to compensate for defects of heart and conscience in civil servants. It remained to be seen whether such artificial means would suffice.

82. House Report 81, 25 Cong. 2 sess. (1837), pp. 5, 7–8, 30–31.
83. Senate Document 1, 25 Cong. 2 sess. (1837), p. 708.
84. Ibid., p. 165.

VI

THE SOURCES OF
ADMINISTRATIVE
ENERGY

The business of the Post Office Department was to carry the mails, and though Amos Kendall might banish corruption from his agency and endow it with bureaucratic symmetry, his administration could not be considered successful if it did not provide for the efficient performance of the Post Office's central task. It was, then, somewhat embarrassing to Kendall when the *Niles Weekly Register* reported that the "mails were never in a worse state than they have been for some time past.... We had relied much on the *energy* of the postmaster general. The present apology seems to be a snowstorm that happened eastward of Baltimore on Sunday last—but the post office has been badly managed for a month or more."[1] "The roads," pointed out the Philadelphia *Inquirer*," are bad, and some allowances should be made; but we must also remind our readers that, despite the snow storm, little or no delay had been experienced on the railroad, which could as heretofore, have been at the service of the postmaster."[2]

But the railroad men were not quite so inclined to enter the service of the Post Office and the public as the *Inquirer* thought them to be. Long stretches of iron rail, laborers, steam engines, and rolling stock were all expensive items, and before the railway enterprisers could worry about the public interest, they had to consider their own. They had advanced into an uncharted and unproven industry and spent heavily of their investers' money, and now they had to demonstrate that they had discovered entrepreneurial gold

1. *Niles Weekly Register,* 16 January 1836.
2. Quoted, ibid., 23 January 1836.

mines. Those who expected public service from them would find that such services came high, and Amos Kendall had already made that discovery.

The postmaster general's first encounter with the magnates of steam transportation had been cool but cordial. In September 1835, Kendall had written to M. W. Hoffman, president of the New Orleans and Nashville Rail Road. The "transportation of the mails over the Rail Roads," said Kendall, "is a subject to which I have given some attention, and it is becoming one of great interest." But he could not accept Hoffman's proposal—that the government subscribe stock for construction on the New Orleans-Nashville line in return for the carriage of the mails.[3] The proposition, after all, smacked mightily of that dreadful arrangement which had once existed between the government and the United States Bank. It was a high price to pay for postal expedition.

Still, it was a tempting prospect for the postmaster general. The speed of rail transportation could mean a dramatic improvement in postal service. In his own mind, Kendall had already calculated its advantages. A letter could be entrusted to the Baltimore and Ohio Company at its Washington terminus; in two and a half hours, the message would be in Baltimore; in another six and a half, Philadelphia; nine more from there to New York, and twenty-two from there to Boston. The mails could be carried from the capital to Boston, largely free of hindering blizzards and muddy roads, in a mere forty hours.[4]

It was an exciting thought, but something of a pipe dream. Most of the rail lines which Kendall fit into his scheme for railway mail service on the East Coast were still under construction or in the planning stage. And those which had begun their operations had not yet proven themselves to be reliable enterprises. The latest development in railway technology was the implausibly named "Old Ironsides," a locomotive with the somewhat jerry-built appearance of a butter churn on wheels.[5] Its deceptively sturdy-sounding title was, perhaps, not accidentally chosen, for citizens needed some reassurance before they would entrust their goods and lives to these dangerous machines—which seemed to spend almost as much time plunging over embankments as running along the tracks.[6]

3. Kendall to M. W. Hoffman, 10 September 1835, Post Office Department, Letterbooks of the Postmaster General, National Archives, Washington, lbk. A., p. 319.
4. Kendall to Preston Loughborough, 31 October 1835, Post Office Department, lbk. A, pp. 370–71.
5. Slason Thompson, *When Railroads Were Young* (New York, 1926), pp. 60–61.
6. See *Niles Weekly Register,* 8 October 1836.

Nevertheless, Amos Kendall was determined that the nation's postal system should take advantage of this new transportation network. Out into the unfamiliar world of iron rails and steam boilers, the postmaster general sent his chief clerk, Preston Loughborough. Loughborough was instructed "to wait upon the President and other managers of the Baltimore and Ohio Rail Road and apprize them of the earnest desire of the Dept. to make an arrangement with them for the transportation of the mail [between] Washington and Baltimore on terms which shall be satisfactory to all parties and promise to be permanent." Loughborough was also directed to negotiate with other companies whose rail lines formed sections of the grand network which Kendall had sketched out in his mind.[7]

The postmaster general had also sketched out a detailed bargaining strategy, which his chief clerk was to apply in appropriate situations. Loughborough was to approach the B&O officials hat in hand and tell them how very important it was "to the business of the country and to the interests of the Post Office Department that the public mails should be transported by the most speedy means of conveyance which modern improvements can afford." And he was to assure the railroad men that the department meant to cause them as little trouble as possible. All it asked was that their engines haul a mail car from one station to another, and for this it promised "liberal arrangements with the Rail Road companies. . . ." If the price for such small services were beyond the department's means, the chief clerk was to suggest an arrangement by which the government would itself run locomotives on the rails, late at night, when the carriage of private freight and passengers would not be interrupted. "It is believed," said Kendall, "that the importance of the object will induce the public spirited men who manage this concern, to permit the government, for a suitable consideration, to use their Road . . . at hours when they may not think proper to use it themselves."[8] Should these public-spirited businessmen prove recalcitrant, Loughborough might then play the department's trump card:

It is not deemed necessary to press upon them any supposed rights which the government may have to use the Rail Roads. . . . Yet, it may be useful to call their attention to that point. The Constitution confers on Congress the power "to establish Post Offices and Post Roads." So far as it respects Roads, this delegation of power has been construed to mean that Congress may designate the Roads on which the mails shall be carried. . . . Rail Roads differ from

7. Kendall to Loughborough, 31 October 1835, Post Office Department, lbk. A, p. 371.
8. Ibid., pp. 371–73.

Turnpikes owned by private companies only in the fact that in the former case the companies own the means of conveyance as well as the Road. But if established under the authority of Congress as Post Roads, is it possible for those companies to prevent the carrying of the mail upon them?[9]

Kendall thought not, and when Loughborough reported the cool reception he had received in Baltimore, the postmaster general delivered up another offer to the stern consideration of the B&O managers—but now he called it an "ultimatum." Loughborough was to propose that the department provide fireproof boxes for the carriage of the mails. These containers would be loaded aboard the B&O's cars by postal employees and carried as though they were regular shipments of private freight. For transporting such a box once a day from Baltimore to Washington and back, the department would pay $100 per mile per year. "In making this proposition," Kendall instructed his chief clerk,

you are requested to inform the several Companies that the compensation offered is a munificent one for the service required, and having had the unanimous action of a Committee of the House of Representatives proposing to restrict the Department to three fourths of this price, I do not feel that I should be justified in exceeding the amount now tendered without the authority of Congress.[10]

But the railroad men had a somewhat different price-setting criterion than the supposed value of "the service required." Instead of the $4,000 price offered by the postmaster general, the B&O men wanted $10,000, and, so that they might easily escape the arrangement if it were not to their liking, they demanded a one-year contract.[11] Most postal contracts were four-year agreements. To Kendall's offer the B&O's Quaker President, P. E. Thomas, gave the disappointing reply:

The Board deliberatively considered the proposal . . . made for carrying the mail between the cities of Baltimore and Washington at the rate of one hundred dollars per mile . . . [and] deem the offer to be so far below the actual cost and inconveniance to which such an engagement would subject the company, that they do not feel at liberty to accept the same, and they have instructed me to make known this conclusion to thee.

But included in Thomas's "cost and inconvenience" were items which Kendall had not considered—not only operating expenses, but

9. Ibid., p. 373.

10. Kendall to Loughborough, 8 November 1835, Post Office Department, lbk. A, p. 381. Kendall had turned to the House Post Office Committee to back up his "ultimatum." It had restricted the price which he might offer the railroads to a maximum of $75 a mile.

11. Baltimore and Ohio Railroad Company, Office of the Corporation Secretary, Minute Books, Baltimore, book C, 16 November 1835, pp. 401–2.

capital investments for construction, maintenance, and safety.[12] The B&O, in effect, wanted an indirect government subsidy for railroad expansion.

Such an arrangement was strikingly inconsistent with the policy that Kendall had laid down during his first exchange with M. W. Hoffman. Although he perceived nothing improper in the government's purchase of a right to use the rails, the postmaster general found "objections to advances of money as stock or otherwise to be applied to the construction of these roads. . . ."[13] And well he might. Here again, in the B&O negotiations, was the seed of a nefarious coalition between government and vested interest. It was this kind of relationship, with its nurturing of old and faithful contractors, which had recently brought the Post Office to grief, and if that evidence were not enough, the economic machinations of Nicholas Biddle and the United States Bank were clear indications of the evils to which such alliances lent themselves. Kendall drew upon this storehouse of Jacksonian experience—perhaps even Jacksonian philosophy—and drew the line at his $4,000 offer to the B&O.

It was a line he had drawn before, the kind of boundary he had attempted to interpose between the private interests and the public duties of his clerks in the fourth auditor's office. Here again he attempted to separate the public from the private, a fact that is evident even in the minute details of his negotiations with the Baltimore and Ohio officials. In his first proposal, for example, Kendall had suggested that the B&O locomotives haul a mail car from Washington to Baltimore and back again. But it had to be a special sort of car. The postmaster general required that it be govern-

12. P. E. Thomas to Kendall, 23 November 1835, ibid., 25 November 1835, p. 403. The nature of the B&O's reservations becomes a little clearer if we consider the fact that it had already agreed to carry the mail from Baltimore to Frederick for Stockton, Stokes, and Company, a mail contracting firm. Stockton, Stokes complained about the high price they had to pay for this service, but evidently found it possible to absorb the cost in the amount which they, in turn, were paid by the Post Office Department (Baltimore and Ohio Railroad Company, 18 April 1835, book C, p. 342). It would appear, then, that the B&O was asking an unusually high price in its negotiations with the Post Office Department in order to defray part of its heavy capital expenses. In later negotiations with Kendall, the B&O officials frequently hinted at this sort of an arrangement. Their objections to the postmaster general's price offers were coupled with talk of the heavy debts which were shortly to be incurred for the "extension of the Rail Road between this and Philadelphia and between this and Richmond. . ." (see Baltimore and Ohio Railroad Company, 13 September 1836, book D). Earlier attempts to get the Federal government to provide capital for B&O expansion had been made by the railroad company's friends in Congress, but they did not succeed (*Register of Debates in Congress,* 14 vols. [Washington: Gales & Seaton, 1825–37], 9: 954).

13. Kendall to M. W. Hoffman, 10 September 1835, Post Office Department, lbk. A, p. 319.

ment owned and, rather interestingly, that it be specially made so that it could be removed from the rails and pulled through city streets to a local post office, where it would stay until the government needed it again. This was a curious provision to cast into negotiations which were already complicated by the incompatible intentions of the bargainers. A specially constructed car would probably prove to be more trouble than it was worth. Its only use would be to carry the mails from a rail depot to a city postal station—certainly no great distance in the cities of 1835. But with such a car the railroad companies might also be prevented from using public property when the government had no use for it.[14] Kendall was determined that the railroad managers should gain no more from the government than they earned by their services. He was not about to create a parasitic class of "old and faithful" railroad companies. The government could not enter into, support, or finance the private dealings of the railway entrepreneurs.

It was all very well to draw fine distinctions between public and private interests when the only objects of concern were bags of mail, contract prices, and railroad cars. But the issue was a more delicate one where human beings were involved. How was one to separate the private acts of government employees from their public duties, and what sorts of private activities were to be forbidden to federal officers? The problem was not a new one to Amos Kendall, but Senator Samuel McKean presented it to the postmaster general in a particularly troublesome way. McKean complained that postal officials in New York State had interfered in a gubernatorial election, and for this improper use of their official influence, he wished to see them punished. Coming as it did only a short time before the presidential election of 1836 and from candidate Van Buren's home state, the complaint must have represented a possible embarrassment to the Jacksonian party. Indeed, it may have been intended to serve just that purpose. Kendall handled it with the caution that it deserved.

It was difficult, he wrote to Senator McKean, to maintain "that a person accepting a public station forfeits thereby any right to canvass

14. Kendall to Loughborough, 31 October 1835, Post Office Department, lbk. A, p. 372.

freely ... which he possessed as a private citizen." According to
Kendall, the difficulty was "to draw the line between the rights of
the citizen on the one hand and the assumptions of the officeholder
on the other. To draw any distinct line," he confessed himself "after
mature reflection, utterly incompetent."[15]　But if Kendall were unable to draw a distinct line between public duty and private rights, he
could at least conceive of a rough and hazy division between the two,
and this boundary was an unusual one. While yet preserving the
public bounty of the republic against the incursions of the railroad
entrepreneurs, the postmaster general opened the way for another
sort of public-private mixture.

　　Kendall conceded that it would be dangerous to have the nation's
"eleven thousand post offices made centers of electioneering operations directed by their incumbents." But he argued that there was a
certain "legitimate influence attached to office."

It is that which arises from a faithful, prompt and polite performance of its
duties ... The office holder thus makes himself beloved in the circle which
surrounds him ... and the popularity which he gathers round him, is shared by
the administration under which he acts. This is the legitimate influence of
office....[16]

　　Legitimate or not, the kind of influence that Kendall described
was obviously intended to operate for the political advantage of the
Jackson men. And such influence is notable for its object—not
established national institutions and elites, but neighborhoods, communities, and townships. Kendall had broken off the Post Office
Department's alliance with the old and faithful mail contractors. He
had held the railroad industry at arm's length. But he sought to
cultivate the friendship of other powers. In new settlements from the
Alleghenies to the Mississippi, a great source of political energy
waited to be tapped. The local community represented an alternative
source of social solidarity and a mechanism of social regulation.

　　Here were places where a man might always find friends, people to
help him raise his house and barn and, perhaps, people to keep an
eye on his behavior. In these towns, a man had to rub elbows with
his neighbors. "A man to be popular in our new Western towns,"
wrote an English settler,

should be acquainted with everybody, shake hands with everybody, and wear an
old coat, with at least one good hole in it. A little whiskey and a few squirts of
tobacco juice are indispensable. From much of the former you may be excused

15. Quoted in *Niles Weekly Register,* 29 October 1836.
16. Ibid.

if you treat liberally to others. If there is one fool bigger than another, defer to him, make much of him. If there is one fellow a little more greasy and dirty than another, be sure to *hug* him. Do all this and you have done much toward being a popular man. At least you could scarcely have a jury-case carried against you.[17]

And if a man were *not* popular, where in these small settlements would he turn when his crops were bad or when his barn burned down? Here, certainly, was a powerful force for the regulation of social behavior, a source of power that could be useful to any federal administrator with the skill to tap it, as Kendall was already attempting to do.

The year after Kendall became postmaster general, there were three hundred newspapers publishing in the small towns of western America, and they bombarded the Union with about 13,000,000 editions annually. Many persons looked to these allegedly honest and uncorrupted rural presses as fountains of reform. The western sheets would exert a wholesome, patriotic influence upon the nation. They were "less likely to be affected by political error" than the jaded journals of the large cities, and they could, perhaps, solidify that nostalgia for the old days of republican virtue.[18] But the frontier press operated at a disadvantage. The small towns from which these journalistic establishments spread the news were themselves rather far removed from the big cities where news was being made. When word of great political happenings finally reached the frontier settlements, it was already stale. If the outlying editors were to exert their beneficial influence, they would have to receive the news as quickly as their eastern brethren.

It was clear that the responsibility for this speedy transmission of the news, if it were a public responsibility, lay with Kendall's Post Office Department. And it *was* a public responsibility. In his first annual message, Andrew Jackson had noted of the Post Office that

in a political point of view this Department is chiefly important as affording the means of diffusing knowledge. It is to the body politic what veins and arteries are to the natural—conveying rapidly and regularly to the remotest part of the system correct information of the operations of the Government, and bringing back to it the wishes and feelings of the people. Through its agency we have secured to ourselves the full enjoyment of the blessings of a free press.[19]

17. See Alice Felt Tyler, *Freedom's Ferment* (New York: Harper & Row, 1962), p. 19.

18. Julian P. Bretz, "Some Aspects of Postal Extension into the West," *Annual Report of the American Historical Association, 1909*, vol. 2 (Washington: Government Printing Office, 1911), p. 146.

19. James D. Richardson, *A Compilation of the Messages and Papers of the Presidents*, 10 vols. (Washington: Government Printing Office, 1899), 2: 460–61.

Old Hickory might muddle his biological metaphors, but Amos Kendall saw his department's duty clearly, and to that end, in midwinter, 1837, the postmaster general again dispatched Chief Clerk Preston Loughborough—this time to the West. Loughborough was to check the condition of the roads between Washington and St. Louis for the purpose of establishing a special express mail service to the journalists of the frontier.[20]

The Post Office had already proven itself a true friend of the editor. By an act of Congress, the department had been authorized to provide free carriage of news exchange slips, making possible a kind of nineteenth-century wire service.[21] And now, Amos Kendall aimed to establish a particularly warm relationship between his agency and a certain class of journalists, the newspapermen of the frontier. While he traveled through the West, Preston Loughborough was to "visit the Editors of Newspapers and enquire of them how they receive exchange slips and with what regularity their papers are received by their subscribers."[22] These solicitous inquiries after the editors' well-being may not, of course, have been completely altruistic. Editors were important people in election campaigns—as Kendall must certainly have known—and their influence upon their fellow townsmen was substantial. But it was unlike Kendall, the tough bargainer of the B&O negotiations, to be so concerned for the prosperity of private businessmen. And his proposal for western express mail was even more out of character. What the postmaster general suggested was, in effect, that the government subsidize the growth of frontier journalism.[23]

In the case of the newspaper editors, the ultimate object of federal benevolence was, once again, the new, western community. Newspapers were not big, national, mass circulation enterprises, but small community businesses. They were attached to neighborhoods, and it

20. Kendall to Loughborough, 2 January 1837, Post Office Department, lbk. C, p. 2.
21. Bretz, "Some Aspects of Postal Extension into the West," p. 147.
22. Kendall to Loughborough, 2 January 1837, Post Office Department, lbk. C, p. 4.
23. Kendall had earlier proposed an express system for the whole country. When he did, he made explicit his intention to subsidize American journalism: "By receiving the news in advance of the ordinary mails, the local newspapers would be enabled to give it to their subscribers before it could reach them through other channels, by which means their circulation would be greatly promoted" (Kendall to H. W. Connor, 16 March 1836, Post Office Department, lbk. B, p. 9). Some of the Jacksonian editors in the East did not think well of Kendall's original proposal for a nationwide express mail. Francis P. Blair, editor of the Washington *Globe,* was convinced that the higher postage rates charged for express service would make it "the rich man's mail exclusively," and he worried that it would give the "federal party" a journalistic advantage over a Jacksonian press that relied upon "our honest gray horse, democratic mail" (Blair to Van Buren, 14 July 1836, Martin Van Buren Papers, Library of Congress, Manuscript Division, Washington).

was toward these neighborhoods that Kendall directed his administrative amiability. Clearly, these overtures of friendship were aimed
at enhancing the political good will which Jacksonism enjoyed in the
towns just behind the frontier. But there was something more here.
With respect to these settlements, Kendall was attempting to dissolve
the boundary between public and private so that a merger could
occur between the administrative affairs of the federal government
and the private doings of these communities. His efforts seemed to
aim at an easy exchange of energies and resources between the two
sectors. Perhaps the federal establishment could draw from local
communities the kind of regulatory power which had once been
provided by institutions like the legal profession or the business
community.

While Woodrow Wren, Postmaster of Natchez, Mississippi, was
eating breakfast on a summer morning in 1835, several of his fellow
townsmen broke into the local post office, opened some of the mail
which had arrived during the preceding day, read it, and resealed
it.[24] Sometime during the night of 30 July, citizens of Charleston,
South Carolina, had broken into their city's post office. During the
following evening, the outskirts of Charleston were lit by bonfires
into which local citizens threw bags of mail. In New Orleans and
Norfolk, residents were roused to near hysteria. In Livingston, Mississippi, there were five hangings.[25]

Throughout the South, violent passions had been fired by thousands of insurrectionary abolitionist pamphlets which the anti-slavery
societies of New York and Boston had sent into the cotton and
tobacco country. Nor did hysteria and bloodshed deter these determined northerners from the grave task of emancipation. The New
York Abolition Society decided "not to abandon the right of transmitting, through the post office, all such tracts and papers as they
choose to flood over the country." But Samuel Gouverneur, postmaster of New York, was a bit more skittish about bloodletting than
his abolitionist neighbors. Gouverneur "boldly and fearlessly" informed the society that "during the present state of the question,"
he would "set aside in his office all abolitionist tracts, and refuse to

24. Kendall to Woodrow Wren, 10 September 1835, Post Office Department, lbk. A, p.
389.
25. *Niles Weekly Register,* 8 August 1835.

send them by mail in any direction from New York, until he had positive instructions to the contrary from the government at Washington."[26]

The rumblings of anger in North and South were now delivered to the front steps of the Post Office's E Street headquarters. The department was responsible for relieving anxiety on both sides of the Mason-Dixon Line, and in the South the task was one of special urgency. Bloody slave insurrections in Virginia and the discovery of alleged abolitionist plotters in Mississippi and Tennessee had turned southern ire into frenzied rage, and the postmaster general had to act quickly to soothe these violent sentiments.

Kendall made his decision. To the dismayed postmaster of Charleston, he wrote that the "postmaster general has no legal authority to exclude newspapers from the mail, nor prohibit their carriage or delivery on account of their character or tendency. . . ." But clearly these incendiary pamphlets imperiled the public safety, and if the law did not provide a satisfactory solution for the preservation of domestic tranquility, there was a higher answer. "We owe an obligation to the laws, but a higher one to the communities in which we live, and if the *former* be perverted to destroy the *latter,* it is patriotism to disregard them." If the postmasters at Charleston or New York found the seeds of social disorder in these abolitionist tracts, it was their public duty to refuse to deliver them.[27]

It was obvious to many that Kendall's subordinates in the field had been instructed to act beyond the legal limits of their powers. Such usurpations brought a testy response from citizens of the North. "Every petty postmaster in the country," wrote Philip Hone, "is thus made the judge of the cases which justify his interposition, and he may stop the circulation of pamphlets, newspapers, and letters too, for aught I can see to the contrary."[28] The Boston *Atlas* questioned Kendall's political reasoning: "What *higher duty* can we owe to the community in which we live, than to obey the laws which that community has framed?"[29] The postmaster general went into consultation with Old Hickory.

Jackson, himself a slave owner, addressed himself to the abolitionist problem with rustic subtlety:

26. Ibid., 15 August 1835.
27. Ibid., 22 August 1835.
28. *The Diary of Philip Hone,* ed. Bayard Tuckerman, 2 vols. (New York: Dodd, Mead & Co., 1889), 1: 186.
29. Quoted in *Niles Weekly Register,* 22 August 1835.

I have read with sorrow & regret that such men live in our happy country, I might have said monsters, as to be guilty of the attempt to stir up amongst the south the horrors of a servile war, could they be reached, they ought to be made to attone for this wicked attempt with there lives. But we are the instruments of, and executors of the law, we have no power to prohibit anything from being transported in the mail that is authorized by law.

Until Congress saw fit to change the law,

we can do nothing more than direct that those inflammatory papers be delivered to none but who will demand them as subscribers, and in every instance the postmaster ought to take the names down, and have them exposed thro the publick journals as subscribers to this wicked plan. . . .[30]

Old Hickory clearly perceived the possible consequences of his scheme. When the abolitionist monsters became known to their townsmen, "every moral & good citizen will unite to put them in coventry . . . their are few so hardened in vilany as to withstand the powers of all good men."[31] Neither were there very many fanatics who could resist the power of a determined lynch mob.

Jackson and his postmaster general thus halted the circulation of abolitionist literature in the South, but without any glaring disregard of legal obligations. Where the actions of field administrators were restrained by law, community sentiment could be recruited to execute federal policy. This was a technique of cooptation peculiarly suited to the towns of the West, where social distinctions were indefinite and a man who wanted to get along had to "shake hands with everybody." In the East, townsmen were apt to be a less homogeneous lot, and the weight of community sentiment could be held back by barriers of respectability. So it was in Beltsville, Maryland, where, long after the promulgation of the Kendall-Jackson policy, Postmaster William Belt worried about what to do with two abolitionist papers which were addressed to "a quaker Family of high respectability in the neighborhood." Amos Kendall advised him not to consult his obligation to his community, but to "look to the law for instructions and obey its mandate."[32]

Kendall himself heeded a different mandate. He could not find his instructions in the law which his "community" had framed. The community to which Boston journalists referred was not the warm, immediate fellowship of frontier farmers and townsfolk. It was the

30. Jackson to Kendall, 9 August 1835, Andrew Jackson and Amos Kendall Correspondence, Library of Congress, Manuscript Division, Washington.
31. Ibid.
32. Kendall to William Belt, 13 September 1836, Post Office Department, lbk. B, p. 186.

maker of federal law: it was national and abstract, and it had grown weak. The pillars of that community—a brotherhood of attorneys, a northeastern economic elite of nationwide prominence—had faltered. Kendall built around them and shut them out. He dealt coolly with railroad entrepreneurs and mail contractors,[33] representatives of enterprises which were not local and parochial. He would bestow no benefits upon them that they had not earned. But toward the frontier editors, Kendall was more cordial and open-handed. These were local men, spokesmen for their towns, and they guarded the gates by which news of national events might reach their neighbors. Kendall attempted to bribe these sentries. But, more important, he demonstrated a willingness to blend public and private affairs in order to gain access to whatever lay behind the village gates—and what he found there was political energy, a power to enforce decisions which administrative apparatus, by itself, could not enforce. From these tiny reservoirs of energy which dotted the nation, he hoped to draw fresh resources for the federal establishment, to renew that strength which had once been provided by common loyalties to particular values and traditions. It was yet uncertain what new values would guide the exercise of this community power. Some skeptics perceived no standards at all: "The People," wrote Philip Hone, "are to be governed by the law just so long as it suits them."[34] But others, like John Quincy Adams, saw an ominous regularity in the new style of governing. It was "Lynch's law; that is, mob-law."[35]

In the Land Office as in the Post Office, the neighborhood had become an organ of administration, and it was just as securely embedded in bureaucratic structure as the bureau or the division. District land officers frequently chose to deal with their Washington

33. In his distribution of extra allowances to mail contractors, Kendall demonstrated that his stinginess was not something which he reserved for avaricious railroad managers. In the year ending 1 July 1839, for example, the postmaster general granted only four extra allowances of more than $1,000, and in return for each of them, he demanded substantial increases of service. Major Barry had been much more generous (see U.S., Congress, Senate, *Executive Documents,* Senate Document 422, 23 Cong. 1 sess. [1834], pp. 83–119; U.S., Congress, House of Representatives, *Executive Documents*, House Document 149, 26 Cong. 1 sess. [1839], pp. 10–11, 20–21).

34. *The Diary of Philip Hone,* 1: 155.

35. *The Diary of John Quincy Adams, 1794–1845: American Political, Social, and Intellectual Life from Washington to Polk,* ed. Allan Nevins (New York: Longmans, Green & Co., 1928), p. 462.

superiors, not directly, but through community-based intermediaries—their congressmen. A land officer's request for a leave of absence or a special expense allowance was backed by the weight of the community's political power as well as the personal influence of its Washington representative when it was carried to the capital by a congressman.[36] And messages did not flow in only one direction along this slightly twisted bureaucratic channel; the commissioner often forwarded instructions to his field subordinates by means of the same communications line.[37]

Such connections between the capital and the country's neighborhoods, settlements, and townships occasionally lent themselves to the promotion of bureaucratic regulation. The community and its powers might be employed to keep field officers under continuous surveillance and to force them into paths of proper conduct. The Land Office commissioner could act on allegations contained in the Columbus (Ohio) *Peoples Press* concerning the mischievous doings of the receiver over at Bucyrus, and he could dispatch an examiner to look into the officer's behavior.[38] Congressmen recently returned from trips to their districts could be questioned concerning the conduct of the public business in the federal government's field outposts. To a Mississippi representative, Elijah Hayward wrote: "I have been informed that you visited the Surveyor General's Office in Mississippi during the last season. If so, I will thank you to advise me of the state and condition you found it, so far as your personal knowledge and observation extended."[39]

But on many occasions the Washington administrators found the local community to be an intractable force. It could be useful if its feelings were in harmony with the intentions of the capital's bureaucrats, but if neighborhood sentiment ran against administrative decisions, the federal government was at its mercy. It was during the Jacksonian regime that local communities seem to have acquired the knack for subverting federal policy. When a local officer of the federal government found his community hostile to a certain law or

36. See, for example, Hayward to Representative M. Patterson, 1 March 1834, General Land Office, lbk. 5 (n.s.), p. 1; Hayward to Representative J. Murphy, 16 April 1834, ibid., p. 28; Hayward to Representative E. D. White, 29 April 1834, ibid., p. 36; and Hayward to Representative A. H. Sevier, 13 February 1835, ibid., p. 148.

37. See, for example, Brown to Senator W. R. King, 14 June 1836, ibid., lbk. 7 (n.s.), p. 62.

38. Brown to Elijah Hayward, 13 August 1836, ibid., p. 96. After he had resigned from his post in Washington, Elijah Hayward continued his service to the Land Office as an examiner in Ohio.

39. Hayward to Representative W. C. Dunlap, 28 June 1834, ibid., lbk. 5 (n.s.), p. 66.

administrative decision, he might simply choose not to execute it.[40]
A generation earlier, such disregard for legal authority and responsibility had been uncommon. The customs collectors and district
attorneys who were charged with the enforcement of the unpopular
Embargo Act had rarely buckled under to community sentiment.
Even in New England, where the embargo was most resented, federal
administrators remained loyal to the government. If they felt that
they could not enforce the act, they resigned their posts, but seldom
did they defy their Washington superiors.[41] Jacksonian field officers
were not nearly so docile. They and their neighbors frequently
conspired to circumvent distasteful directives from the capital.

When Elijah Hayward's bookkeepers found a shortage of more
than $50,000 in the accounts of Israel Canby, receiver at Crawfords-
ville, a federal marshal in Indiana took possession of Canby's property and tried to auction it off so that the government could make
good its loss. Meanwhile, Crawfordsville's register, Samuel P. Milroy,
spread the word that "no gentleman would bid on the property"—at
least no gentleman who wanted to stay in the good graces of
overbearing General Milroy. And no gentleman did, except for some
of Canby's close friends who bought the receiver's goods at nominal
prices and immediately turned them over to his spinster sister.[42]

Not only in Crawfordsville but everywhere in the West, the auction seems to have been an ideal medium through which community
pressure could be brought to bear upon townsmen. The transactions
of the public land sales were open to the gaze of the whole neighborhood, and though a buyer might legally purchase a parcel of land, he
could not be assured of peaceful possession unless the transaction
met with the approval of his neighbors. Where the law failed to
provide for a pleasing distribution of land—as it did after the expiration of the Pre-Emption Act—the settlers made their own law. "As
the time approaches when there is to be a large sale of public lands at
this place," wrote the editor of the Chicago *Democrat,*

and as there will doubtless be many here who are unacquainted with the
situation of settlers on the tracts of land and with the local customs of this
western country, we feel it our duty to allude to this subject at this time.
Custom, as well as the acts of the General Government, has sanctioned the

40. For an illustration, see Ben: Perley Poore, *Perley's Reminiscences of Sixty Years in
the National Metropolis,* 2 vols. (Philadelphia: Hubbard Bros., 1886), 1: 155.
41. Leonard White, *The Jeffersonians: A Study in Administrative History, 1801–1829*
(New York: Macmillan Co., 1951), pp. 443–54.
42. *American State Papers: Public Lands,* 8 vols. (Washington: Gales & Seaton, 1832–
1861), 7: 194–95.

locations of settlements on the unsurveyed public lands, and the Government has encouraged the settlers in such lands, by granting them a pre-emption right to a sufficiency for a small farm. Many of the settlers on the tract now offered . . . came to the West and made their locations under the implied pledge of the Government by its past acts: that they should have a preference and a right to purchase the lots on which they located, when the same came to market, and at a minimum price. Government was then morally bound to provide for these settlers, and have [*sic*] been guilty of bringing these lands to market without making such a provision. "Public opinion is stronger than law," it has been said, and we trust it may prove so in this case, and that the strangers who come among us, and especially our own citizens, will not attempt to commit so gross an act of injustice as to interfere with the purchase of the quarter section, on which improvements have been made by the actual settler. We trust for the peace and quietness of our town that these local customs, to which long usage has given the force of law . . . will not be outraged at the coming sales.[43]

The squatters meant business. Any newcomer who was brash enough to buy one of their claims could expect a visit from the dispossessed settler and a group of his friends. They would attempt to persuade the claim jumper to sign a warranty conveying the disputed land to the squatter. The persuasion completed, a justice of the peace, who usually happened to drop in at about that time, would acknowledge the new deed.[44] Occasionally, the squatters might arrange the auction itself so that such visits were unnecessary. The illegal settlers in a neighborhood could form a claim association, which would register the claim of each member. When the time came for a land auction, the officers of the organization, carrying a list of the tracts claimed by its members, would step up onto the platform with the government's auctioneer, while the squatters stood in a compact semicircle on the ground below. The auction was generally quick and, except for the perfunctory call of the auctioneer, very quiet.[45]

Back in Washington, Commissioner Hayward simply capitulated to the law-defying forces of the frontier. The squatters, he wrote,

naturally desire to adapt such means as are in their power, to prevent the tract occupied from being appropriated by another—This results in the establishment of certain rules of etiquette among them, whereby it is made a point of honor not to bid against each other for their respective improvements—When a large

43. Chicago *Democrat*, 4 June 1835, quoted in Benjamin H. Hibbard, *A History of the Public Land Policies* (New York: Peter Smith, 1939), p. 201.

44. Hibbard, *A History of the Public Land Policies*, pp. 205–6.

45. Ibid., pp. 205–6; see also Benjamin F. Shambaugh, ed., *Constitution and Records of the Claims Association of Johnson County, Iowa* (Iowa City: State Historical Society of Iowa, 1894).

population stands thus affected it is futile to attempt to counteract such combinations. . . ."[46]

Hayward was probably right. One could not insure obedience to the law by producing more laws. These new regulations would be turned aside just as the old ones had been—by "mutual support and open menace," as Commissioner Brown put it. When the public interest collided with neighborhood sentiment, there was little that government officials could do to avoid capitulating to the wishes of the community. In fact, they were dependent on those wishes.

A decrease in the regulatory power of major social institutions had made it desirable for the government to develop alternative mechanisms of social control. To this end, the federal establishment had begun to exploit the forces that operated within local communities. Public administrators like Amos Kendall were willing to offer public resources in return for the use of these community energies, and others, like Elijah Hayward and Ethan Brown, gave the local community an informal place in the structure of their agencies. The practice was a risky one. It was not that neighborhood institutions were necessarily corrupt, but their perception of virtue and vice was often uncertain—as vague as the Jacksonian creed itself. Townsmen sometimes seemed willing to erase their communities' moral blemishes by committing crimes themselves. Mississippi gamblers were lynched; unscrupulous land speculators were threatened with violence.[47] Frequently, the neighborhood moral code did not "move in so limited a circle" as the one that prevailed in Washington. The frontier standards were often incompatible with those of the capital's administrative elite, and such disjointedness was understandable. Institutions which had once functioned to produce moral uniformity had become seriously weakened. The nation's morality was determined less and less by institutions that transcended community attachment. It was generated at a variety of points scattered across the nation.

46. Hayward to McLane, 15 May 1833, General Land Office, lbk. 4 (n.s.), pp. 103–4. Commissioner Brown took a somewhat different view, but he seems to have been no more successful in opposing community sentiments. In a report to Congress, he suggested some legal safeguard against the tricks of the squatters. "The interest of the Treasury seems to demand a guard against force as well as fraud. I allude to that system of terror that threatens the competitor for the purchase of public land with the vengeance of the settler with whose usurpation he may interfere. In some quarters, the state of things has become formidable; probably finding its origins . . . in the pre-emption laws, whose repeated enactment have led the settlers to the erroneous persuasion that they have acquired rights not given by the law. Be this as it may, experience has shown, that by mutual support and open menace, they have deterred others from bidding against them at the public sales . . ." (*American State Papers: Public Lands*, 8: 442–44).

47. *Niles Weekly Register*, 8 August 1835, 22 August 1835.

It cannot be said that the federal establishment, a national institution, was pulled to pieces by the parochialism of local communities. For if national institutions had become more subject to local influences, it was also true that localities were more exposed to the influence of national institutions and elites. Amos Kendall's overtures to the frontier journalists and his proposal for a western express mail service represented steps toward the creation of a communications system that would link local communities with national centers of power. And federal administrators were not the only ones who made such attempts to reach into American towns and villages. Their efforts ran parallel to those of the political parties, which had begun to extend their organizational structures from the state legislatures into election districts and townships.[48] In fact, the community-oriented activities of the political party and the federal establishment were not merely parallel; they were closely interrelated. The patronage of the federal administrative agencies, after all, was one of the chief resources used in the construction of locally based party organizations. And the same local newspapers to which Amos Kendall extended the assistance of his department provided a means for maintaining the cohesiveness of a party organization.

The Jacksonian era in administration reflected not merely the decline of established institutions but the emergence of new ones, and a key element in the new order was communications. Its importance was evident in the kinds of people that President Jackson chose as his personal advisers, most of whom were journalists. The emergence of "communications" as a profession was reflected in the career of Amos Kendall himself—frontier editor, Jacksonian propagandist, reformer of the postal system, and after his retirement from public service, an associate of Samuel F. B. Morse in the telegraph business.

48. See Richard P. McCormick, *The Second American Party System: Party Formation in the Jacksonian Era* (Chapel Hill: University of North Carolina Press, 1966), pp. 95, 172, 253, 324.

CONCLUSION

When the sun came up on 15 December 1836, the Post Office was in ruins. Just after 3 A.M., a wisp of smoke had floated from a basement window near the building's east end. Twenty minutes later, Amos Kendall raced around the corner from his home on Seventh Street, dashed into his office, and gathered up some valuable documents. He emerged from the building just in time to see a column of flames erupt through the wooden floor and the windows of a local mail room. By dawn, it was over. A thick band of soot traced the passage of the fire across the Post Office's Grecian facade, and at the east end of the building, the sunlight shone directly on the earthen basement floor. To the west, empty, soot-fringed windows marked the places where John McLean, William Barry, Abraham and Phineas Bradley, and others had once managed the "veins and arteries" of the body politic.[1]

Amos Kendall and his clerks packed up what they could salvage and abandoned their E Street building for offices in a Fourteenth Street hotel. Others were moving as well. The small cluster of executive departments which had once surrounded the White House was temporarily broken up and scattered. The Land Office took over the old French Embassy on H Street. The rest of the Treasury Department's personnel awaited the completion of a fine new stone building on G Street, and the State Department had already moved to larger quarters on G Street. The departments had undergone some internal rearrangements, too. Clerks who had once worked in remote corners

1. *Niles Weekly Register,* 17 December 1836; U.S., Congress, House of Representatives, *Committee Reports*, House Report 134, 24 Cong. 2 sess. (1837).

of government buildings now labored under the direct supervision of department heads and bureau chiefs, and when the clerks themselves were not transferred to new offices, their duties often were. Not since the British invasion of 1814 had public documents and officers been moved about so much. From all the bustle, from the half-finished and half-destroyed government buildings, a newcomer to Washington might well have judged that the British had just launched a second attack—or that eight years of Jacksonian rule had left the executive branch in a shambles.

The noise and confusion which rattled the old federal establishment in 1836 were painful signs that the republic was losing its youth. The first generation of American administrators had grown old, and the time had come for many of them to transfer their responsibilities to younger and less experienced men. A portion of the bureaucratic bustle was the understandable consequence of this transfer, for the replacement of old gentlemen like the Bradley brothers often required a substantial renovation of the government's organizational arrangements. At many places in the executive branch, the aged administrators had themselves shaped administrative structure. Often they had not done so consciously; they had simply adapted bureaucratic arrangements to their own preferences, personalities, and talents. In many respects, the administrative edifice depended upon their presence. They had made it; they understood it, and it responded only to their personal touch.

It was necessary to set apart the conduct of public business from the elderly men who had been responsible for it. The mysteries of public management could not be allowed to go into retirement with the administrative master craftsmen. Their duties had to be rendered "so plain and simple" that apprentice administrators might readily understand and perform them. By itself, however, the passing of the administrative founding fathers need not have imposed any substantial alterations upon the executive branch. Duties might have been simplified so that they could be handled by administrative novices. As the newcomers gained experience, they, like their predecessors, might adapt the administrative system to their own tastes and temperaments. In the end, the federal establishment might have returned to its original form—an inexplicit form based upon the personal characteristics of administrators.

In the early years of Old Hickory's tenure, Jacksonian administration gave every indication that it would run this course. Jackson and his men at first aimed to return the government to its "original simplicity," a simplicity, perhaps, that would enable a collection of inexperienced executives to assume the responsibilities of public management. But the Jacksonian simplification did not depart from the tradition of personal organization, unless it was by an overenthusiastic enforcement of traditional administrative principles. The first reorganization plans that Jackson presented to Congress were fashioned after the old Hamiltonian model. His proposals for renovating the Navy Department and the attorney general's office reflected a new emphasis on unity of command and a renewed reliance on the agency chief's good character and "regard for reputation."

There were perhaps some other developments in the early period of Jacksonian administration which, while they did not themselves mark a break with the tradition of personal organization, nevertheless suggested the possibility that such a change might occur. In particular, the practice of rotation in office promised to bring a new crop of public executives into the federal establishment with every change of administration. The process by which administrators gradually shaped their offices to fit their own personalities would thereby be disrupted; thus, the spoils system might some day contribute to the impersonality of federal administration. It would create an opportunity "to organize the executive department as a rationalized complex of offices, ordered by function, and defined by rules and regulations, so as to be free in so far as possible from irregular custom and individual personalities."[2] At first, the Jackson men did little to exploit this opportunity for bureaucratic organization. But occasionally, even in the early days of their regime, they revealed a vague inclination to conduct public business through explicit rules and regulations. The tendency was evident in Amos Kendall's code of conduct for the clerks in the fourth auditor's office and in similar codes devised by Jacksonian executives in other agencies.[3]

In these attempts to formalize the standards of clerical behavior, hostile observers glimpsed something forbidding for the future of the federal establishment. The Adams-Clay press saw the federal civil servant converted into a "mechanical automaton." But such premonitions of bureaucracy should not obscure the fact that the Jacksonians remained staunchly loyal to the tradition of personal organization. They were using formal rules and regulations, not to define the functions of offices or to specify administrative procedures, but

2. Lynn Marshall, "The Strange Stillbirth of the Whig Party," *American Historical Review* 72 (January 1967): 445.
3. See above, pp. 77–78.

to promulgate standards of civil service morality. Being explicit about these standards may have represented a new attitude, but the standards themselves were a sign of continuing confidence in the old belief that good administration rested on good character. The theory of rotation in office reflected a similar conviction. Administrative change was to be achieved, not by tinkering with the structures of administrative agencies, but by replacing the administrators. Good men made good administration.

The Jacksonians came to Washington bent on reform, but they conceived of their initial reforms as attempts to restore an old order, not to create a new one. As there was something self-contradictory in the notion of retrieving the past through reform, so there was self-contradiction in many of the administrative measures that were shaped by this notion. The Navy Department and the attorney general's office were to be returned to a traditional mode of administration—but by the untraditional means of administrative reorganization. Drawing up an explicit code of ethics for civil servants might reflect the government's continuing reliance on the "good character" of its employees, but such collections of formal rules might also reduce the government's dependence on individual character by making the administrative process more impersonal. Finally, there was the spoils system. Because it would bring frequent changes in government personnel, it might liberate administrative organization from its dependence on individual personalities. But as an instrument of reform, it was founded on the assumption that the administrative order was to be defined by individual personalities. To change administrative organizations, one must change the men who worked in them.

The initial reforms of the Jackson men did not lead inexorably to a bureaucratic mode of administration. Their significance for the nature of the federal establishment was ambiguous. While they sometimes hinted at a new style in federal administration, they could also be regarded as an attempt to reinforce the tradition of personal organization. Indeed, the Jackson men themselves seem to have treated these reforms more as restorations than as innovations. Yet these restorers of administrative tradition eventually brought about a major transformation of the federal establishment. If they did not originally set out to produce this alteration, and if their initial reforms did not compel them to pursue the path of innovation, then what was it that led them to abandon the tradition which they had at first attempted to reinforce?

They were not, as we have seen, men whose social stations differed from those of Federalist or Jeffersonian administrators. It is difficult, therefore, to attribute the Jacksonian innovations to the unique class origins of the Jackson men. Old Hickory's administrators did, however, subscribe to a distinctive political creed, but it was a vague set of beliefs and not likely to exert a powerful influence upon the handling of specific administrative problems. The ideology of Jacksonian Democracy was more an expression of discontent than a prescription for action, but it did reflect the social conditions to which the Jackson men were sensitive. Again and again, Jacksonian orators and journalists called the attention of the faithful to the alleged moral depravity of their society.

The loose morality which so annoyed the Jackson men came in the wake of marked social change. The legal profession and the business community—two institutions closely tied to the federal establishment—had expanded. An influx of newcomers to commerce and the law made these institutions less cohesive than they had been a generation earlier. Moreover, with the settlement of frontier lands, the legal profession and the business community had begun to stretch toward the West. The disjointedness caused by an increase in the number of entrepreneurs and attorneys was thus aggravated by the new geographic dispersion of these men of affairs. The result was a decline in the ability of the legal profession and the business community to regulate the conduct of their members. Businessmen and lawyers had more opportunities to stray from the moral standards which had traditionally governed the behavior of men of their respective professions.

These changes in institutional authority and individual conduct helped to undermine the very administrative tradition that the Jacksonians had at first attempted to revive—the tradition of personal organization. It was a tradition that owed little to administrative abstraction. Administrative organizations reflected the qualities of character and temperament of their members. Those few abstract principles which did govern the handling of public business tended to accentuate this humane aspect of the federal establishment. The Hamiltonian emphasis upon unity of command and individual responsibility contributed to that personal attachment which the head of an office or a bureau felt for his agency and its affairs. Such attachments constituted the principal reliance of the pre-Jacksonian public service.

But these connections continued to be worthy of reliance only as long as certain social conditions prevailed. The nature of these attachments and of the civil service itself depended upon the characters of administrators, and the trustworthiness of these connections depended upon good character. Hence, it was essential that society provide the civil service with reliable, competent, and reasonably honest men. Those institutions which supplied the federal establishment with manpower were, in effect, responsible for the quality of the public service. As long as the legal profession and the business community were vigorous enough to establish and enforce appropriate standards of conduct, the executive branch might continue to enjoy the service of relatively dependable men. When the regulatory authority of these institutions began to decline, the behavior of administrators also deteriorated. Because personal organizations depended so heavily upon good character for success, they were also especially vulnerable to the inroads of bad character.

When the Jacksonians took control of the executive branch, they were already sensitive to a growing element of apparent unreliability in the behavior of Americans. Within the federal establishment, they countered the private vices of civil servants with the strict rule of republican virtue and a reinforcement of personal administration. But the sad experience of a few years in office seems to have demonstrated to the Jackson men the infeasibility of their original course. They found that a professed devotion to the party of republican virtue gave no assurance of an administrator's good character. It was no longer safe to place public trust in private, personal virtue, in feelings of personal responsibility for the successful conduct of public business. Many public servants seemed unconcerned that the "infamy of a bad action" might blemish their reputations, and they played fast and loose with public funds or the privileges of office.

It cannot be said that the Jacksonian generation had repudiated uprightness and honesty, but their perception of traditional moral standards appears to have become clouded. They were no longer so able to translate moral sentiments into reliable behavior. In part, the problem may have been that principles of conduct had become estranged from their social roots. The sudden upsurge in the publication of etiquette manuals during the late 1820s was a trifling but also a revealing sign of the new order. Gentlemanly habits, once the province of gentlemen alone, were now to be transmitted without the agency of the gentlemen or their gentlemanly society. It was not that old standards had been discarded, but simply that they had broken loose from their old institutional moorings. As a result, they also became detached from the established centers of social power. Institutionalized power had once given teeth to standards of traditional morality, but traditional standards of conduct did not receive the same strong backing when they floated free from their institutional foundations.

The administrative proposals of the Jackson men were responses to these conditions. Old Hickory's administrators began to erect a formal bureaucratic structure which was designed to produce mechanical adherence to some of the old standards of decency. By means of the new administrative apparatus, the Jacksonian planners sought to free the federal establishment from its dependence on the established social institutions that molded men's characters and conduct. Public servants could no longer be relied upon to have a delicate regard for their reputations, and institutions like the legal profession and the business community were no longer so tight-knit that they could follow up the "infamy of a bad action" with real punishments. The Jackson men supplanted good character and the informal processes of institutional socialization and regulation with a formal administrative system.

The operation of this machinery was impersonal; it fed on bookkeeping entries and was not sustained by the personalities of men. Indeed, it was designed to counteract the unreliability of individual personalities. Administrative duties were no longer distributed informally, according to the "adaptation of the individual to the service to be performed." The functions of an office were now to be defined explicitly, independent of the officeholder's character and capabilities. This formal division of administrative labor was not merely a means to secure efficiency. Perhaps the chief purpose of functional, bureaucratic specialization was to curb the waywardness of individual civil servants. Thoughtfully imposed limitations on the range of duties performed by an administrator might not eliminate the impulse to corruption, but they could restrict the opportunities to pursue that impulse.

The elaborate accounting systems devised for the Post Office Department and the General Land Office were even more obviously intended to counter the personal frailties of civil servants with an impersonal check. In addition, they seem to have changed the nature of the relationship between superiors and subordinates. Agency executives engaged less and less in the direct, personal supervision of their employees. Instead, the chief of the organization surrounded himself with accountants and bookkeepers—an embryonic "executive staff"—who exercised no independent authority in the administrative hierarchy, but whose function was to supply the chief with a steady flow of information about the performance of his agency. Federal executives began to supervise their subordinates from a distance, through impersonal information systems. Not only had the structures of federal agencies been rendered more impersonal by the formal specification of official duties, but the relationships between agency personnel had also become somewhat more impersonal.

Administrative agencies had acquired an existence that was independent of the particular people who worked in them. In a sense, the new configuration of the federal establishment corresponded to the shape of the society in which it did business. In the society, old moral values still commanded loyalty, but they were no longer firmly rooted in established social institutions. Within the civil service, standards of conduct had become similarly disembodied. They had been detached from human beings, relying for their enforcement on mechanical administrative systems.

During the Jacksonian era, writes Leonard White, "the basic forces that played upon the public business and affected its conduct were three: magnitude, facility of communication, and democracy."[4] White's assessment, of course, embraces a much longer span of years than that covered by the present study, and some of the forces whose operation he perceived had hardly begun to function by the close of Old Hickory's second administration. The railroad entrepreneurs, for example, had barely started to extend iron rails across the countryside, and it would be several years before Samuel F. B. Morse would inquire what God had wrought. The revolution in communications had scarcely begun.

The impact of democracy on the federal establishment was perhaps more substantial than the effect of communications technology. But, in White's view, even the "rising spirit of democracy" had only a limited influence on the conduct of public business. Democracy, he says, imposed changes on the executive branch from without, and the consequences of these changes were primarily external, altering relationships between the federal establishment and other political

4. Leonard White, *The Jacksonians: A Study in Administrative History,* 1829–1861 (New York: Macmillan Co., 1954), p. 530.

institutions. The spoils system rendered the public service more vulnerable to political pressure, which was applied by means of the newly crystallized party organizations. But the democratic spirit of Jacksonism left the interior of the executive branch essentially unaltered, for it "did not require organizational changes in the public service. It simply took possession of the system through the instrumentality of the political party. . . ." There was, says White, no break in the administrative system itself.[5]

Such changes as there were in the internal structure of the executive branch represented extensions or elaborations of this system:

> The structure of the executive departments in 1860 was much more complex than in 1800; they were not merely larger, they had patterns of organization consistent with original principles but substantially more complex and highly developed. The difference may be stated, with some exaggeration, by asserting that in 1800 a department consisted of the Secretary, clerks, and a field establishment, while in 1860 a department consisted of a Secretary, a group of bureaus handling the mass of routine business usually without the intervention or even the knowledge of the Secretary, and a field service that, in the larger establishments, exceeded in size the parent departments of an earlier day.[6]

These changes White attributes to the expanded "magnitude" of the federal enterprise—the need to relieve executive officers of the growing mass of administrative trivia, the need to promote specialization so that a great volume of business might be handled expeditiously, and the need to manage a federal field establishment that stretched across an ever greater expanse of territory.[7]

The problems of scale undoubtedly played a significant role in stimulating the innovations of Jacksonian administrators. We know, for example, that executives like Elijah Hayward and William Barry were sensitive to the enormous growth in the volume of business conducted by their agencies. Some of their first, tentative efforts at administrative change seem to have been responses to this growth. Moreover, it is quite likely that the later and more dramatic changes in Jacksonian administration might have taken a different direction had it not been for the expansion of the federal establishment. Rather than resort to the impersonal devices of bureaucratic administration, the Jackson men might have developed a more traditional response to the problem of regulating administrative behavior.

Bigness alone, however, does not provide a sufficient explanation for the structural changes that occurred within the Jacksonian execu-

5. Ibid., pp. 552–53.
6. Ibid., p. 533.
7. Ibid., p. 539.

tive branch. In the first place, it does not account for the Jacksonian preoccupation with the policing of administrative behavior. Controlling the conduct of subordinates is only one of several problems that may arise as a consequence of organizational growth. If mere bigness were the sole concern of the Jacksonian administrators, they might just as easily have concentrated on other difficulties associated with organizational scale—problems of coordination, administrative expedition, cost effectiveness, or public finance. Yet the problem that came to dominate the attention of the Jacksonian executives was a particular manifestation of bigness, not bigness in general. To guarantee the good behavior of civil servants seems to have been their leading concern.

That this became the chief problem of Jacksonian administration is attributable not simply to the growth of the federal establishment but to the fact that this growth was occurring along with other changes in American society. The principal change, insofar as the affairs of the executive branch were concerned, was a deterioration in the regulatory authority and the internal discipline of major social institutions—including those institutions that supplied the federal civil service with the great bulk of its manpower. The occurrence of such broad institutional changes may help to account for the fact that administrative renovation in the Jacksonian federal establishment was not confined to those agencies that were experiencing substantial growth but also occurred in executive departments that were relatively stable in size. In any case, it is clear that something besides mere expansion in scale must have played a significant part in the emergence of bureaucratic administration.[8]

Historical variations in the scale of administrative operations remain a powerful source of organizational change and probably offer the most attractive way of explaining it. Size, after all, is a universal characteristic of administrative enterprises. Every organization in every historical era must have some scale, and scale is rarely stable. Its variability helps to make it an unavoidable factor in the explanation of administrative change. But it is a factor which acquires special importance in a particular view of administration and administrative development.

The concept of scale is politically and historically neutral. Administrative magnitude may respond to prosperity or depression, revolution or reaction, but bigness itself is the same under communism or

8. See chap 3 above, n 21.

monarchy, the same in modern Indonesia as in ancient Greece. Organizational scale therefore provides a useful common denominator for the analysis of administrative enterprises in diverse cultures and historical periods. It lends itself to a view of administration as a generalized art or science, an exercise of neutral competence that transcends the particularities of time and place—"something in part at least independent from constitutional structure and adaptable from an undemocratic to a democratic environment."[9]

The conception of administration as a unified, universal process, essentially the same wherever it occurs, is one that Leonard White and many other students of the subject have shared.[10] Some of them have also recognized that administrative bigness is one of the prerequisites for a generalized craft of administration. "Management" emerges as a distinct field of endeavor in large-scale bureaucratic organizations.[11] The growth of organizational scale therefore plays an important part in Leonard White's administrative histories, whose central theme is the gradual development of this generalized managerial art under Federalists, Jeffersonians, Jacksonians, and Republicans. He traces the emergence of public administration in the United States as a distinct sphere of competence, at least partly independent of the vagaries of politics. Yet, as White himself seems to recognize, one of the most significant features of public administration in the United States is the extent to which it has failed to achieve this independent status.[12] Americans have been less willing than Europeans to grant their administrative officials a position of neutrality in the political system; they have been less persuaded that the process of administration itself is distinct from the political process.

To the Jacksonians and the "spirit of Jacksonian democracy" has gone much of the credit or blame for this condition. It was the Jacksonian spoils system, after all, that interrupted the development of a career civil service by uprooting the small group of professional managers that had established itself within the federal government. And it was the Jacksonians who permitted their party to forage for patronage within the federal establishment. The executive branch became an auxiliary of the party organization, and the "art of administration" was absorbed by the art of politics.

9. White, *The Jacksonians*, p. 553.
10. Leonard White, *Introduction to the Study of Public Administration*, 4th ed. (New York: Macmillan Co., 1955), pp. 1–3.
11. Luther Gulick and Lyndall Urwick, eds., *Papers on the Science of Administration* (New York: Institute of Public Administration, 1937), p. 3.
12. White, *Introduction to the Study of Administration*, p. 8.

Yet while the Jacksonians were destroying the incipient independence of the administrative art, they were creating a kind of organizational structure that might be well suited to the practice of this art. They had taken major steps toward the depersonalization of the administrative process; in several agencies, they had created the rudiments of an executive staff; they had introduced functional specialization at a number of points in the executive branch; and they had done much to rationalize the relationships between superiors and subordinates. These earmarks of bureaucratic administration might normally be expected to accompany the appearance of the professional administrator and the emergence of an independent "science of administration." In the case of the Jacksonians, however, they marked the beginning of a movement in the opposite direction. It was a curious state of affairs—but certainly no more curious than the fact that the presumed representatives of frontier rusticity had become the agents of governmental bureaucratization.

It is possible to make too much of these apparent inconsistencies in Jacksonian administration. The Jacksonians, after all, were not so rustic as they sometimes pretended to be, and their partiality to bureaucratic administration stopped short of the creation of a career civil service. Furthermore, their practice of spoilsmanship also had its limits. In filling some offices, even the Jacksonians deferred to professional competence. Nevertheless, the relationship between spoilsmanship and bureaucracy, between frontier populism and administrative impersonality, is not so self-evident that it can go without an explanation.

Bureaucratization was the Jacksonian response to a decline in the authority of institutions which provided manpower and support for the executive branch. In effect, the new bureaucratic machinery was a substitute for those social institutions which had once molded and regulated the conduct of civil servants and would-be civil servants. The Jacksonians replaced the informal processes of institutional regulation with a formal administrative system. It was an impersonal system, depending for its effectiveness, not on the character of its administrators, but on the accuracy of its bookkeeping.

But ledgers alone could not provide the federal establishment with the sustenance it needed. The executive branch had more strenuous tasks to perform than the simple policing of routine business, which itself sometimes required more than any accounting system could provide. Some information about the conduct of field administrators could be supplied only by their neighbors—local newspaper editors, congressmen, politicians. Moreover, the abstract administrative systems devised by the Jackson men possessed no independent strength, and they could hardly be expected to survive for very long without it. If the old standards of decency that they embodied were to continue to be effective, those standards would have to be invested with power. But the institutions which had once supplied this enforcement power could no longer be relied upon to do so. The Jackson men met this deficiency by recruiting new sources of energy for the executive branch from the scattered enclaves of community power. The direction of the Jacksonian effort was evident in Old Hickory's handling of the crisis triggered by the incendiary abolitionist tracts. It was also evident in Amos Kendall's benevolence toward the frontier editors. But perhaps the most important manifestation of the Jacksonian attempt to provide political support for the administrative machinery of the executive branch was the effort to harness the federal establishment to the political party organization.

Civil service reformers would later charge that the Jacksonians, through the spoils system, had made public administration the slave of party politics. The conduct of public business, it was argued, had been subordinated to the conduct of party business, and public agencies had been used, not to serve the public, but to provide places of rest and rehabilitation for the party's troops. The spoils system seemed to have forced the federal establishment into a lopsided partnership with the political parties, in which the parties enjoyed the benefits of patronage and public agencies bore the resulting costs of corruption and inefficiency. The partnership, however, may not have been so lopsided as the reformers thought it to be. There were ways in which the conduct of public business might benefit from the spoils system.

In a society whose major institutions had lost the power to enforce internal discipline, deference to institutionalized authority had become a scarce commodity. The federal government, like other institutions, suffered the indignity of defiance. Often, civil servants seemed indifferent to their public responsibilities. Frontier squatters rudely shouldered aside the law of the land and substituted their own will. The loyalty of other western settlers, who held land under grants from the French or Spanish governments, was doubtful. In the more genteel Southeast, defiance of government authority went by the name of "nullification." But the scholarly constitutional arguments of southern gentlemen could not conceal the fact that the threat of armed force was as immediate here as it was in the mob actions of frontier settlers. Federal administrative agencies, whose duty it was to carry out the law, stood in the government's front lines, facing defiant citizens. The ability of the lone civil servant to secure the compliance of the public could not be taken for granted. But there were ways of strengthening that ability.

It was not altogether unreasonable to suppose that a man who could command the votes of his fellow citizens might also be able to command their obedience to federal law. The popularity of the party politician, as well as his organizational resources, might contribute something to the efficacy, if not the efficiency, of the administrative process. At the same time that Jackson's system of rotation in office was providing spoils for political party organizations, therefore, it might also augment the popular support and authority of the federal establishment. Jackson was not the first president to use such means for invigorating the executive branch. In appointing federal administrators, George Washington had looked for men "who had been esteemed and honored by their neighbors." For Washington, the acid test of esteem and honor was a man's ability to get his neighbors to elect him to a public office.[13] Such men could supplement the formal authority of administrative office with their own personal authority. In some ways, therefore, Jackson's rotation policy was related to Washington's appointment policy. And the policy was, in fact, much older than Washington. In sixteenth-century England, Queen Elizabeth had selected as her justices of the peace men who already occupied social positions from which they could command the deference of their neighbors. The socially prominent justices "placed at the disposal of the crown a system of social relations in which they were already superiors, independently of their official tenure."[14]

In Jacksonian America, however, the network of social relations that gave some men authority over others had become seriously weakened, and in some regions of the country such networks hardly existed at all. But at the same time, the political party was beginning

13. Carl Russell Fish, *The Civil Service and the Patronage* (New York: Longmans, Green & Co., 1905), p. 9.
14. Vernon Dibble, "The Organization of Traditional Authority: English County Government, 1558–1640," in James G. March, ed., *Handbook of Organization* (Chicago: Rand McNally, 1965), pp. 884–85.

to provide a measure of the organization that was lacking in the social order. The emergent party organizations were reaching beyond the established social notables to cultivate the good will of citizens in their own towns and villages. And so it was to the party organization that Jackson turned in order to find new administrators for the federal government.

Jacksonian spoilsmanship was not necessarily inconsistent with Jacksonian bureaucratic administration. Both were responses to problems of public order which had become prominent at that time. Old Hickory's administrators resorted to bureaucratic methods in order to compensate for a decline in the disciplinary power of social institutions and a concurrent decline in the disciplinary power of the executive branch. Impersonal administrative systems were devices for strengthening the government's authority over its own civil servants. Appointing party politicians to public office was a way of reinforcing the authority that these civil servants enjoyed with respect to the public. It is true that the spoils system may not have been congenial to the efficient delivery of public services. But efficiency was not the only end of the administrative process in Jacksonian government. Administrators were also guardians of the government's legitimacy. They were expected to "win the good will and affections of the people for the government" or to "possess such traits of character as [were] calculated to gain the esteem and confidence of the people." The civil servant, through the "faithful, prompt, and polite" performance of his duties, might make himself "beloved in the circle which surrounds him . . . and the popularity which he gathers round him, [might be] shared by the administration under which he acts." [15] Since civil servants could no longer be relied upon to act faithfully, promptly, and politely of their own accord, the Jacksonians took new measures to control their behavior. These bureaucratic innovations were introduced not simply for the sake of economy and efficiency within the executive branch but also with an eye to the increasingly uncertain "affections" of the people for their government.

The loyalties of the people may not have been the only concern of the Jackson men. The moral character of the citizens also seems to have caused them considerable worry, and administrative agencies

15. *American State Papers: Public Lands,* 8 vols. (Washington: Gales & Seaton, 1832–61), 7: 193; William Claggett to Andrew Jackson, 24 November 1829, Department of State, Letters of Application and Recommendation during the Administration of Andrew Jackson, National Archives, Washington; *Niles Weekly Register,* 29 October 1836.

had a role to play in restoring republican virtue to American society. The Jacksonians seem to have held the belief that the character of the nation's civil servants might help to shape the character of its people. This belief, as Herbert Storing points out, was not new. George Washington had sought out honored and esteemed men to fill government offices because he was concerned not only "with getting the work of government done but also with distributing the patronage of government in such a way as to set the public stamp of approval on certain human qualities."[16] Jackson undoubtedly had different qualities in mind than Washington did, but his effort to expel from the public service those who considered office "as a species of property and government as a means of promoting individual interests" was at least partly motivated by a concern for the moral character of the civil service and the face that it showed to the public. The same intentions were clearly evident in Old Hickory's attempt to police the behavior of civil servants so that "the government may be relieved from the imputation of acts, and the sanctioning of acts, so injurious to the morals of the country. . . ."[17]

The Jacksonians believed that the actions of the government could have a direct effect on the morals of the nation. The operations of the United States Bank, they argued, had seriously compromised the honesty and diligence of the nation. A liberal internal improvements policy could inflame petty jealousies, give encouragement to "personal ambition and self-aggrandizement," and "sap the foundations of public virtue."[18] What the government did and what it stood for could have much to do with what the people were like. It was essential, therefore, that the government and its officials do nothing that might lead the citizens toward vice. Controlling the vicious impulses of civil servants through bureaucratic regulations could of course contribute much to the moral uprightness of the citizens.

Nearly half a century after the Jacksonians had done their work, those who attempted to undo some of the Jacksonian reforms still looked to the civil service primarily as a source of moral virtue in American society. "[I]n my opinion," said Carl Schurz,

the question whether the Departments at Washington are managed well or badly, is, in proportion to the whole problem an insignificant question after all. Neither

16. Herbert J. Storing, "Political Parties and Bureaucracy," in Robert A Goldwin, ed., *Political Parties, U.S.A.* (Chicago: Rand McNally, 1964), p. 155.

17. Jackson to Kendall, 21 May 1835, Andrew Jackson and Amos Kendall Correspondence, Library of Congress, Manuscript Division, Washington.

18. James D. Richardson, ed., *A Compilation of the Messages and Papers of the Presidents,* 10 vols. (Washington: Government Printing Office, 1899), 2: 440.

does the question whether our civil service is as efficient as it ought to be, cover the whole ground. The most important point to my mind is, how can we remove that element of demoralization which the now prevailing mode of distributing office has introduced into the body-politic.[19]

The Jacksonians may have failed to foresee the damaging consequences of their spoils system, but they perceived, perhaps more clearly than the civil service reformers of a later time, that the implementation of public policy could never be merely "neutral" and that the manner in which public services were delivered to the public might be a matter of some moment for the values and loyalties of citizens.

19. Frederic Bancroft, ed., *Speeches, Correspondence, and Political Papers of Carl Schurz,* 6 vols. (New York: G. P. Putnam's Sons, 1913), 2: 123.

BIBLIOGRAPHY

MANUSCRIPT SOURCES

Andrew Jackson and Amos Kendall Correspondence. Library of Congress, Manuscript Division. Washington.

Baltimore and Ohio Railroad Company, Office of the Corporation Secretary. Minute Books C–D, 1835–36. Baltimore.

Department of State, Letters of Application and Recommendation during the Administration of Andrew Jackson. National Archives. Washington.

_____, Letters of Application and Recommendation during the Administration of James Monroe. National Archives. Washington.

_____, Letters of Application and Recommendation during the Administration of John Quincy Adams. National Archives. Washington.

General Land Office, Miscellaneous Letters Sent, Letterbooks O.S. 16 and N.S. 4–7. National Archives, Washington.

Levi Woodbury Papers. Library of Congress, Manuscript Division. Washington.

Martin Van Buren Papers. Library of Congress, Manuscript Division. Washington.

Post Office Department, Letterbooks of the Postmaster General, Letterbooks A–D. National Archives. Washington.

PUBLIC DOCUMENTS

American State Papers: Post Office. Washington: Gales & Seaton, 1834.

American State Papers: Public Lands. 8 vols. Washington: Gales & Seaton, 1832–61.

Amos Kendall, Postmaster General. *The Organization of the Post Office Department*. Washington, 1835.

James D. Richardson, ed. *A Compilation of the Messages and Papers of the Presidents*. 10 vols. Washington: Government Printing Office, 1899.

Register of Debates in Congress. 14 vols. Washington: Gales & Seaton, 1825–37.

U.S. Congress. House of Representatives. *Committee Reports* (1828–37).

U.S. Congress. House of Representatives. *Executive Documents* (1822–37).

U.S. Congress. Senate. *Committee Reports* (1828–34).

U.S. Congress. Senate. *Executive Documents* (1827–37).

U.S. Congress. Senate. *Journal of the Executive Proceedings of the Senate* (1829–37).

U.S. *Statutes at Large,* vol. 5.

BOOKS

Adams, John Quincy. *The Diary of John Quincy Adams, 1794–1845: American Political, Social, and Intellectual Life from Washington to Polk.* Edited by Allan Nevins. New York: Longmans, Green & Co., 1928.

——. *Memoirs of John Quincy Adams, Composing Portions of His Diary from 1795 to 1848.* Edited by Charles Francis Adams. 12 vols. Philadelphia: J. B. Lippincott & Co., 1876.

Albion, Robert Greenhalgh. *The Rise of New York Port, 1815–1860.* New York: Charles Scribner's Sons, 1939.

Ambler, Charles H. *The Life and Diary of John Floyd.* Richmond: Richmond Press, 1918.

Amory, Cleveland. *The Proper Bostonians.* New York: E. P. Dutton, 1947.

Aronson, Sidney H. *Status and Kinship in the Higher Civil Service.* Cambridge: Harvard University Press, 1964.

Asbury, Herbert. *The Great Illusion.* Garden City, N.Y.: Doubleday & Co., 1950.

Bancroft, Frederic, ed. *Speeches, Correspondence, and Political Papers of Carl Schurz.* 6 vols. New York: G. P. Putnam's Sons, 1913.

Bassett, John Spencer, ed. *Correspondence of Andrew Jackson.* 7 vols. Washington: Carnegie Institution of Washington, 1926–35.

Beard, Miriam. *A History of Business.* Ann Arbor: University of Michigan Paperbacks, 1962.

Benson, Lee. *The Concept of Jacksonian Democracy: New York as a Test Case.* Princeton: Princeton University Press, 1961.

Benton, Thomas Hart. *Thirty Years' View.* 2 vols. New York: D. Appleton & Co., 1854.

Boudinot, Elias. *Journey to Boston in 1809.* Edited by Milton Halsey Thomas. Princeton: Princeton University Library, 1955.

Bowers, Claude. *Party Battles of the Jackson Period.* New York: Houghton Mifflin Co., 1922.

Brubacher, John S., and Rudy, Willis. *Higher Education in Transition.* New York: Harper Bros., 1958.

Burgess, John. *The Middle Period, 1817–1858.* New York: Charles Scribner's Sons, 1897.

Caldwell, Lynton K. *The Administrative Theories of Hamilton and Jefferson.* Chicago: University of Chicago Press, 1944.

Caton, John. *Early Bench and Bar of Illinois.* Chicago: Chicago Legal News Co., 1893.

Chevalier, Michel. *Society, Manners, and Politics in the United States.* Boston: Weeks, Jordan, & Co., 1839.

Chroust, Anton-Hermann. *The Rise of the Legal Profession in America.* 2 vols. Norman: University of Oklahoma Press, 1965.

Clark, Victor S. *History of Manufactures in the United States.* New York: McGraw-Hill, 1929.

Crozier, Michel. *The Bureaucratic Phenomenon.* Chicago: University of Chicago Press, 1964.

Degler, Carl N. *Out of Our Past.* New York: Harper & Row, 1959.

Diamond, Sigmund. *The Reputation of the American Businessman.* Cambridge: Harvard University Press, 1955.

East, Robert A. *Business Enterprises of the American Revolutionary Era.* New York: Columbia University Press, 1938.

Elkins, Stanley. *Slavery.* New York: Universal Library, 1963.

Elliot, Jonathan, ed. *Debates in the Several State Conventions on the Adoption of the Federal Constitution.* 2d ed. 5 vols. Washington: Taylor & Maury, 1845–54.

Fish, Carl Russell. *The Civil Service and the Patronage.* New York: Longmans, Green & Co., 1905.

Flint, Timothy. *Recollections of the Last Ten Years.* Boston: Cummings, Hilliard & Company, 1826.

Foote, Henry S. *The Bench and Bar of the South and Southwest.* St. Louis: Soule, Thomas, & Wentworth, 1876.

Fowler, Dorothy G. *The Cabinet Politician.* New York: Columbia University Press, 1943.

Gerth, Hans, and C. Wright Mills, eds. *From Max Weber: Essays in Sociology.* New York: Oxford University Press, 1958.

Goldwin, Robert A., ed. *Political Parties, U.S.A.* Chicago: Rand McNally, 1964.

Grund, Francis J. *Aristocracy in America.* 2 vols. London: R. Bentley, 1839.

Gulick, Luther, and Urwick, Lyndall, eds. *Papers on the Science of Administration.* New York: Institute of Public Administration, 1937.

Hamilton, James A. *Reminiscences of James A. Hamilton.* New York: C. Scribner & Co., 1869.

Hammond, Bray. *Banks and Politics in America.* Princeton: Princeton University Press, 1959.

Haney, Louis H. *Business Organization and Combination.* 3d ed. New York: Macmillan Co., 1934.

Hibbard, Benjamin H. *A History of the Public Land Policies.* New York: Peter Smith, 1939.

Hofstadter, Richard. *The American Political Tradition.* New York: Vintage Books, 1954.

Holbrook, James. *Ten Years among the Mail Bags.* Philadelphia: H. Cowperthwaite & Co., 1855.

Holland, William M. *The Life and Political Opinions of Martin Van Buren.* Hartford, Conn.: Belknap & Hammerslea, 1835.

Hone, Philip. *The Diary of Philip Hone.* Edited by Bayard Tuckerman. 2 vols. New York: Dodd, Mead, & Co., 1889.

Johnson, Gerald W. *American Heroes and Hero Worship.* New York: Harper Bros., 1943.

Kendall, Amos. *Autobiography of Amos Kendall.* Edited by William Stickney. Boston: Lee & Shepard, 1872.

Linder, Usher F. *Reminiscences of the Early Bench and Bar of Illinois.* Chicago: Chicago Legal News Co., 1879.

Livermore, Shaw. *The Twilight of Federalism: The Disintegration of the Federalist Party, 1815–1830.* Princeton: Princeton University Press, 1962.

Lyle, Maria Catharine Nourse, comp. *James Nourse and His Descendents.* Lexington, Ky.: Transylvania Printing Co., 1897.

McCormick, Richard P. *The Second American Party System: Party Formation in the Jacksonian Era.* Chapel Hill: University of North Carolina Press, 1966.

March, James G., ed. *Handbook of Organization.* Chicago: Rand McNally, 1965.

Martineau, Harriet. *Retrospect of Western Travels.* 3 vols. London: Saunders & Otley, 1838.

Marx, Fritz Morstein. *The Administrative State.* Chicago: University of Chicago Press, 1957.

Matthews, Donald R. *The Social Backgrounds of Political Decision Makers.* Garden City, N.Y.: Doubleday & Co., 1954.

Mayo, Robert. *Political Sketches of Eight Years in Washington.* Baltimore: Fielding Lucas, 1839.

———. *The Treasury Department and Its Various Fiscal Bureaus, Their Origin, Organization, and Practical Operations.* Washington: William Q. Force, 1847.

Meyers, Marvin. *The Jacksonian Persuasion: Politics and Belief.* Stanford: Stanford University Press, 1957.

Miller, Douglas T. *The Birth of Modern America.* New York: Pegasus, 1970.

———. *Jacksonian Aristocracy: Class and Democracy in New York.* New York: Oxford University Press, 1967.

Nichols, Thomas Low, *Forty Years of American Life, 1821–1861.* New York: Stackpole Sons, 1937.

Ostrogorski, Moise. *Democracy and the Organization of Political Parties.* Edited by Seymour M. Lipset. 2 vols. New York: Vintage Books, 1964.

Parrington, Vernon L. *Main Currents in American Thought.* 3 vols. New York: Harvest Books, 1954.

Parton, James. *The Life of Andrew Jackson.* 3 vols. New York: Mason Bros., 1860.

Pessen, Edward. *Jacksonian America: Society, Personality, and Politics.* Homewood, Ill.: Dorsey Press, 1969.

Poore, Ben: Perley. *Perley's Reminiscences of Sixty Years in the National Metropolis.* 2 vols. Philadelphia: Hubbard Bros., 1886.

———. *The Political and Congressional Directory.* Boston: Houghton, Osgood, & Co., 1878.

Riegal, Robert. *Young America.* Norman: University of Oklahoma Press, 1949.

Robbins, Roy M. *Our Landed Heritage: The Public Domain, 1776–1930.* Gloucester, Mass.: Peter Smith, 1960.

Rohrbough, Malcolm J. *The Land Office Business: The Settlement and Administration of American Public Lands, 1789–1837.* New York: Oxford University Press, 1971.

Rossiter, Clinton, ed. *The Federalist Papers.* New York: New American Library, 1961.

Rozwenc, Edwin C., ed. *Ideology and Power in the Age of Jackson.* New York: Anchor Books, 1964.

Schlesinger, Arthur M., Jr. *The Age of Jackson.* Boston: Little, Brown & Co., 1945.

Schlesinger, Arthur M., Sr. *Learning How to Behave.* New York: Macmillan Co., 1946.

Schmeckebier, Laurence. *The Customs Service.* Baltimore: Johns Hopkins Press, 1924.

Shambaugh, Benjamin F., ed. *Constitution and Records of the Claims Association of Johnson County, Iowa.* Iowa City: State Historical Society of Iowa, 1894.

Short, Lloyd M. *The Development of National Administrative Organization in the United States.* Baltimore: Johns Hopkins Press, 1923.

Sumner, William Graham. *Andrew Jackson as a Public Man.* Boston: Houghton Mifflin Co., 1883.

Thompson, Slason. *When Railroads Were Young.* New York, 1926.

Tocqueville, Alexis de. *Democracy in America.* Translated by Henry Reeve. 2 vols. New York: Vintage Books, 1964.

Tucker, George. *Progress of the United States in Population and Wealth in Fifty Years as Exhibited by the Decennial Census.* New York: Press of Hunt's Merchants' Magazine, 1843.

Turner, Frederick Jackson. *The Frontier in American History.* New York: Henry Holt & Co., 1920.

Tyler, Alice Felt. *Freedom's Ferment.* New York: Harper & Row, 1962.

Van Buren, Martin. *The Autobiography of Martin Van Buren.* Edited by John C. Fitzpatrick. Vol. 2 of the *Annual Report of the American Historical Association, 1918.* Washington: Government Printing Office, 1920.

Van Riper, Paul P. *History of the United States Civil Service.* Evanston, Ill.: Row, Peterson, & Company, 1958.

Wade, Richard C. *The Urban Frontier: The Rise of Western Cities, 1790–1830.* Cambridge: Harvard University Press, 1959.

Waldo, Dwight. *The Administrative State.* New York: Ronald Press, 1948.

Walker, Tom L. *History of the Lexington Post Office, 1794 to 1901.* Lexington, Ky., 1901.

Ward, John. *Andrew Jackson: Symbol for an Age.* New York: Oxford University Press, 1955.

Warren, Charles. *History of the American Bar.* Boston: Little, Brown & Co., 1911.

Weber, Max. *The Theory of Social and Economic Organization.* Translated and edited by A. M. Henderson and Talcott Parsons. Glencoe, Ill.: Free Press, 1964.

Webster, Daniel. *The Letters of Daniel Webster, from Documents Owned Principally by the New Hampshire Historical Society.* Edited by Claude H. Van Tyne. New York: McClure, Phillips, & Co., 1902.

Weisenburger, Francis P. *The Life of John McLean: A Politician of the United States Supreme Court.* Columbus: Ohio State University Press, 1937.

Wellington, Raynor G. *The Political and Sectional Influence of the Public Lands.* Cambridge, Mass.: Riverside Press, 1914.

White, Leonard. *Introduction to the Study of Public Administration.* 4th ed. New York: Macmillan Co., 1955.

———. *The Jacksonians: A Study in Administrative History, 1829–1861*. New York: Macmillan Co., 1954.

———. *The Jeffersonians: A Study in Administrative History, 1801–1829*. New York: Macmillan Co., 1951.

Willard, Joseph. Address to the Members of the Bar of Worcester County, Massachusetts. Lancaster, Mass.: Carter, Andrews, & Co., 1830.

Wiltse, Charles. *John C. Calhoun*. 1st ed. 3 vols. Indianapolis: Bobbs-Merrill, 1944–51.

Wise, Henry A. *Seven Decades of the Union*. Philadelphia: J. B. Lippincott & Co., 1881.

ARTICLES AND PERIODICALS

"Amos Kendall." *The United States Magazine and Democratic Review* 1 (March 1838): 403–12.

Bretz, Julian P. "Some Aspects of Postal Extension into the West." *Annual Report of the American Historical Association, 1909*, vol. 2. Washington: Government Printing Office, 1911.

English, William Francis. "The Pioneer Lawyer and Jurist in Missouri," *The University of Missouri Studies* 21, no. 2 (1947).

Eriksson, Erik M. "The Federal Civil Service under President Jackson," *Mississippi Valley Historical Review* 13 (March 1927): 517–40.

———. "President Jackson's Propaganda Agencies," *Pacific Historical Review* 6, no. 1 (1937): 47–57.

Goodman, Paul. "Ethics and Enterprise: The Values of the Boston Elite, 1800–1860," *American Quarterly* 18 (Fall 1966): 437–51.

Gregory, Frances W. "The Office of President in the American Textile Industry," *Bulletin of the Business Historical Society* 26 (September 1952): 122–34.

Hammond, Bray. "Public Policy and National Banks," *Journal of Economic History* 6 (May 1946: 79–86.

Main, Jackson Turner. "Trends in Wealth Concentration before 1860," *Journal of Economic History* 31 (June 1971): 445–47.

Marshall, Lynn. "The Strange Stillbirth of the Whig Party," *American Historical Review* 72 (January 1967): 445–68.

The National Calendar (Washington), vol. 6 (1828) and vol. 9 (1831).

National Intelligencer (Washington), 1828–1830.

Niles Weekly Register (Baltimore), 1828–1837.

Pessen, Edward. "The Egalitarian Myth and the American Social Reality: Wealth, Nobility, and Equality in the 'Era of the Common Man,'" *American Historical Review* 76 (October 1971): 989–1034.

Soltow, Lee. "Economic Inequality in the United States in the Period from 1790 to 1860," *Journal of Economic History* 31 (December 1971): 822–39.

Somit, Albert. "Andrew Jackson as an Administrative Reformer," *Tennessee Historical Quarterly* 13 (September 1954): 204–23.

Stevens, Harry R. "Bank Enterprisers in a Western Town," *Business History Review* 29 (June 1955): 139–56.

Topham, Washington. "The Benning-McGuire House, E Street and Neighborhood," *Records of the Columbia Historical Society* 33 (1932): 82–131.
United States Telegraph (Washington), 1828–1831.

OTHER SOURCES

Aronson, Sidney H. "Status and Kinship in the Higher Civil Service: The
Administrations of John Adams, Thomas Jefferson, and Andrew Jackson."
Ph.D. dissertation, Columbia University, Department of Sociology, 1961.
Somit, Albert. "The Political and Administrative Ideas of Andrew Jackson."
Ph.D. dissertation, University of Chicago, Department of Political Science,
1947.

INDEX

kinship relations among, 99 n; political
activities of, 146; social status of, 7–8,
12–14, 16–17, 46, 162
Claiborne, John, 85
Clark, James, 97
Clay, Henry, 117
Columbus People's Press, 153
Congressional Caucus, 2, 32
Congress of the United States: appropriations by, for General Land Office clerks,
116–17, 121; and arrearages in General
Land Office, 119, 125; committees of,
93–94, 123, 125, 137–38; and General Land Office reorganization, 125–
26; investigation of Post Office Department by, 93–96, 104, 115; and Post
Office Department reorganization, 108;
and Treasury Department reorganization,
137–38
Crawfordsville, Ind., land office in, 86, 89,
123, 154
Cumberland, Md., 97

Dallas, Alexander, 88–89
Decatur, John, 17
Democratic party, 22–23
Duane, William, 67–68
Dunstable, Mass., 74

Eaton, John H., 58–59, 62
Edwards, Justin, 44 n
Elizabeth City, N.C., 88
Elkins, Stanley, 32
Ewing, Thomas, 93
Ewing, William, 17
Executive staff: in General Land Office,
130–31, 164–65; in Post Office Depart-
ment, 135–36, 164–65

Federalist party, 22–23
Ficklin, Joseph, 83
Fish, Carl Russell, 56
Flint, Timothy, 39
Flood, Thomas, 84
Floyd, John, 59–60
Foot, Samuel, 117
Frankfort, Ky., 74
Franklin, Benjamin, 24
Friends, Joseph, 17

Gardner, Charles K., 113
General Land Office, 63, 136; and administrative corruption, 84–87, 123, 125,

129–30; and district land officers,
65–66, 83–87, 102, 122–23, 129–30;
inspection system of, 88–92; and local
communities, 152–56; recorder of, 127;
reorganization of, 3, 10, 115–26,
133–36, 164; and squatters, attitude
toward, 151–56
Gilbert, Charles C., 84, 89
Gouge, William, 43–44
Gouverneur, Samuel, 149–50
Graham, George, 89–90, 103, 118–22, 129
Granger, Gideon, 100
Green Bay, Wis., 98
Green, Duff, 58, 78
Green, Willis, 17

Hagerstown, Md., 95
Hagner, Peter, 63
Hamilton, Alexander, 52–53
Hamilton, James A., 58, 81
Hammond, Bray, 2, 19–20, 23
Harris, W. P., 85, 92
Hawkins, Littlebury, 86
Hayward, Elijah, 86, 102, 166; and General
Land Office inspection system, 90–91;
and reorganization of General Land
Office, 115–26, 133–35; response to
corruption by, 84, 92, 129, 154; and
squatters, attitude toward, 155
Helena, Ark., 86
Hill, Isaac, 59, 61, 76
Hobbie, Selah R., 114
Hoffman, M. W., 141, 144
Hofstadter, Richard, 20, 23
Holbrook, James, 83
Hone, Philip, 74, 150, 152

Impersonality, in administrative agencies:
and administrative supervision, 136;
functions of, 136, 164–65; in Kitchen
Cabinet, 57, 66; as result of
reorganization, 4, 133; and spoils
system, 56, 160–61
Indianapolis, Ind., 17, 123
Ingham, Samuel D., 61
Internal improvements, 24, 173

Jackson, Andrew, 1, 11, 50, 99, 147; and
abolitionist tracts, 150–51, 170;
administrative appointments of, 75, 105;
and attorney generalship, 69; cabinet of,
61, 66–68; and Kitchen Cabinet, 57–58,
60, 62; as military administrator, 51;

THE JOHNS HOPKINS UNIVERSITY PRESS

This book was composed in Baskerville text and Baskerville display type by
The Composing Room, from a design by James S. Johnston. It was printed on
60-lb. Warren 1854 paper and bound in Holliston Roxite vellum by
Universal Lithographers, Inc.

Library of Congress Cataloging in Publication Data

Crenson, Matthew A   1943-
  The Federal machine.

  Bibliography: p.
  Includes index.
  1. United States—Executive departments—History.
2. United States—Politics and government—1829-1837.
3. United States—Social conditions—To 1865.
I. Title.
JK686.C74   353'.0009'034   74-6818
ISBN 0-8018-1586-X